THE FACE OF WATER

THE FACE OF WATER

*A Translator on
Beauty and Meaning
in the Bible*

SARAH RUDEN

Pantheon Books, New York

All rights reserved. Published in the United States by Pantheon Books,
a division of Penguin Random House LLC, New York,
and distributed in Canada by Random House of Canada,
a division of Penguin Random House Canada Limited, Toronto.

Pantheon Books and colophon are registered trademarks of
Penguin Random House LLC.

"After Reading the Journals of George Fox" originally appeared in
National Review 62, no. 23 (December 20, 2010).

Library of Congress Cataloging-in-Publication Data
Name: Ruden, Sarah, author.
Title: The face of water : a translator on beauty and meaning in the Bible /
Sarah Ruden.
Description: First Edition. New York : Pantheon Books, 2017. Includes
bibliographical references and index.
Identifiers: LCCN 2016014872 (print). LCCN 2016025767 (ebook).
ISBN 9780307908568 (hardcover : alk. paper). ISBN 9780307908575 (ebook).
Subjects: LCSH: Bible—Criticism, interpretation, etc. Bible—Translating.
Bible English—Versions—Authorized.
Classification: LCC BS511.3 .R83 2017 (print). LCC BS511.3 (ebook).
DDC 220.5/209—dc23 LC record available at lccn.loc.gov/2016014872

www.pantheonbooks.com

Jacket image: DEA Picture Library / Getty Images
Jacket design by Oliver Munday

Printed in the United States of America
First Edition
2   4   6   8   9   7   5   3   1

This book is dedicated to its editor, Vicky Wilson,
and to its agent, Will Lippincott

After Reading the Journals of George Fox

They told me, "We're quite busy here."
I told him, "Stay away from me."
I lay awake. I watched the wind
Unwind the branches of a tree.

I passed exams, unpacked and packed,
Ordered and cancelled. Time went by
Like a foreign-language broadcast. Then
I saw a river in the sky.

Clear as the air but bright as ice,
It let the sun through to the wheat,
It rippled like a flare of song,
It pounded like a runner's feet.

Down here, a form rocked in the surf,
A sidewalk stain was dirty red.
I saw the miracle reversed,
And what had been alive was dead;

And yet the flood of light above
Only swelled stronger, like a storm
Of joy, a conquest of delight,
A dream there was no waking from.

Contents

PART THREE
An Account of the Fuller Facts

Acknowledgments

Where do I even start? I owe heartfelt thanks to Wesleyan and Brown Universities for the visiting research appointments that brought scholarly help, advice, and companionship while I worked on this book. I am grateful to Dennis Clarke, Anna Beth Keim, John Olsen, Daniel Wade, and Leslie Williams—I'm just alphabetizing here—for their readings of portions of the draft manuscript.

I profess a huge debt to Yale Divinity School and three teachers of Hebrew there: Joel Baden, John Collins, and Victoria Hoffer—again, I'm alphabetizing; Vicki took the brunt of introducing a middle-aged student, vain of her (long-past) linguistic prowess, to this difficult language. And what would I have done had not Joel and Harry Attridge—it was under Harry's and Paul Stuehrenberg's aegis that I came to Yale in the first place—guided and encouraged me? Before any of this, Nechama Sataty of the University of Pennsylvania taught me beginning Modern Hebrew.

My indebtedness to my husband, Tom Conroy, is beyond any hope of description. But let me point out anyway that without him, I'm only about 10 percent of myself, so that this book is really more his than mine.

Preface

Opening the Tome

I'm probably supposed to start with the story of some inspirational encounter with the Bible, or some rebellious discovery about it, which sent me self-consciously down a life-changing road of learning or unlearning.

Sorry, not this time. You want a moment of inspiration? I am six or seven, and walking on the freshly mown lawn in my backyard, off the highway in Ohio. I am imagining how wonderful a pair of new Keds sneakers would be—and then there are all the other purchases I crave: bright, in fresh packaging, nothing homemade, mended with epoxy, or handed down. I have just been watching Saturday morning cartoons, and a commercial for Keds—showing children running and jumping in colorful footwear—has propelled me outdoors, humming the jingle, in the sheer ecstasy of hope for a lifetime of consumerism.

About the Bible, I felt nothing more than about the bowl of rubber fruit in the parlor at Christ United Methodist Church in the town of Portage, after the weekly worship service and Sunday School. If you were particularly bored, waiting for the adults to shut up about local politics and crop prices and take you home, you might pull a synthetic grape off its stem and try to turn it inside out. You could never quite do that, or tear the thing either, but the sheer foreign toughness of the material was more interesting than nothing. I had an hour-a-day TV limit at home, so sometimes I read the Bible in the same spirit as kept me fiddling with the grape.

To the eye, the book typically offers a pebbly black vinyl cover (like nothing on a book you'd yearn to open up and explore), a gold-colored inset title ("The Holy Bible," which to a lot of people says, "I think I'm too holy for you to touch"), and a withered-looking ribbon bookmark attached at the spine (as if it would be a big problem to lose your place in the ordinary way, and stray from the prescribed devotional verses).

What's more, if you're unfamiliar with the Bible and open it at random, you may be put right off, as when you venture into the higher digits of cable TV and narrow your eyes at *Extreme Mutt Makeovers* or *Dirty Dirndls: Hitler's Secret Porn Stash* or whatever. Given the Bible's content by proportions, you're likely to land on a long genealogy or the recited failures of one kingship after another, or a strong-lunged praise-song or lament or sermon or set of regulations. Hefty commentaries and minute footnotes, both commonly full of modern religious doctrine, hardly enliven the text, which may seem as uniquely dull as its encasement. The Bible is in a rut; it seems to need professional help.

But how do *I* dare try to expound the book? I'm the opposite of a cleric or theologian or philosopher: I'm a Quaker, which means I'm admonished to speak my own mind plainly and briefly if I feel an undeniable need, but otherwise to search quietly for the Light—in whatever form It happens to take—in other people. Many Quakers (though not myself) stop short of calling themselves "religious." How can I have the gall to pronounce on the character of Scripture, in the original languages or not?

What's more, I have no formal qualifications whatsoever as a Biblical scholar—not one degree, not even a single course credit, let alone peer-reviewed publications in scholarly journals, or a teaching post. I can only read the Bible in Hebrew and Greek and give my impressions—all the while remembering that old stricture: "Using a language doesn't make you an expert on it, any more than spending money makes you an economist."

But here's the thing. A few years ago, I stumbled onto Paul of Tarsus's letters as the subject of a book and began to research Biblical Greek. I experienced then—the biggest surprise of my life—that I could really be of use. The experience grew more convincing at Yale Divinity School, where I received generous instruction in Hebrew. The Bible, I recognized, was a book that profoundly mattered, more even than ancient pagan literature (in which I do have qualifications). For all of us, it is near at hand in modern culture, though

wildly far off in its origins, and we all to some degree define ourselves in relation to it, whether we mean to or not. I developed an
ambition that found steady encouragement among clergy, studious
laypeople, and people with no extensive background in the Bible
but a desire to learn more. I would read in the original languages
some of the best-known passages of the Bible and describe what I
saw and heard there.

So here I am now, trying to make the book less a thing of paper
and glue and ink and petrochemicals, and more a living thing.

Introduction

Okay, the Bible—What About It?

In the original Hebrew of 2 Samuel, chapter 12, David's words about his dead baby in verse 23 mean, "I shall go to him, but he shall not return to me."* But that meaning in English is *very* rough. When I first heard the Hebrew words, they struck me as one of the most moving pieces of phrasing there could be.

They had better be that, for the experience they have to describe. Most of us can't imagine a beloved life simply gone, annihilated, nowhere, so we concentrate on asking, "Where?" "In memory," "In descendants," "In achievements," are common answers, but the loss of a newborn baby doesn't leave any such solid comforts. The parents' main memory itself will usually be of watching the child die. Moreover, "I will see my child in the afterlife" must be a rather numb self-assurance, because to get there, the parent must cross through life dutifully without the child, though missing him every moment. This is why, I reckon, at the news of the tragedy a few verses earlier, David has suddenly stopped fasting and lying in the dirt as well as beseeching God for his son's life. He now turns to getting on with things in a hollowed-out world, because what else can he do?

The Hebrew conveys much better than the English translation the poignancy of David's resignation. In typical proportion, there are only seven Hebrew words to the twelve of the English "I shall go to him, but he shall not return to me." Also typically, in the Hebrew

---

*The King James Version, because of its beauty and familiarity, is here and everywhere my default source for existing Bible translation to adduce.

there is no physically distinct "but" or "although" or anything like that, only the all-purpose word usually rendered as "and." One general impression I have from Hebrew's stark poverty of conjunctions is that statements about the world do not go into writerly columns (showing the same or contrasting qualities, situations, opinions, etc.), tidied up ahead of time by human rationality; instead, things are presented as simply being the way they are, and from the earliest times, *readers* needed to sort them out.

But less typically for Hebrew, the subject pronouns in David's statement are expressed in separate words, and not just for the first verb, actually a participle (translatable in English as "going," or better, "walking"), which needs that pronoun because on its own it doesn't contain sufficient information about the subject. (As normally, the Hebrew participle has no "helping verb" with it: on the page, this isn't "am going" but merely "going"—therefore the "I" idea is lacking in the verbal construct.) No, there's a subject pronoun also for the finite verb ("will return"), which by itself in Hebrew plainly indicates the masculine third person, "he"—the child. This overexplicit pairing suggests emphasis. "*I* will go to him, but *he* will not return to me." The two very different beings, the powerful, sinning adult and the helpless, innocent baby; the living man who can still speak in the first person, and think, plan, and act, and the third-person child who has passed beyond even his quite limited—and, to others, unknowable—physical consciousness: these two persons are aligned yet set apart from each other in this extra way, by pronouns. This would be very hard, if not impossible, to show in English.

Almost unavoidably as well, in splitting differences with such an alien and complicated verbal system (see Chapter 1), the English version has a flattened-out rendering of the tenses: "I *shall go* to him, but he *shall not return* to me." In the original, the first clause contains (as already noted) a participle; it is literally, "I [am] walking to him." Hebrew favors the participle for habitual or continuous action. David may be picturing himself in a lifelong trudge toward his lost child, not just transported to him after his own death. Somewhat similarly, the child's *in*action in not returning is expressed in the imperfect form of the verb. This form can be used for the future (and is often translated that way), but more important is continuity. This is the form of "Thou shalt," as in, "Thou shalt love the Lord thy God [*always*]." The child is gone from earth with a more absolute finality than any simple verb in English can express. A fuller sense might be "He will *never* return to me." But in a way, the active continuity of the participle comes to the rescue: the father *will* keep moving toward the child. He will never lose the will to see him again.

Mightily impressed with the Hebrew writer's insight and craftsmanship (though I was only half-conscious of its details; I needed Professor Joel's help later to know exactly what I had been looking at), I wrote the following:

King David Refuses to Mourn His Son
2 Samuel 12:20–23

I'm dressed. The sky is stone, my path a sea.
I'm going to him, he won't return to me.

I eat. The shattering waves have calmed the sea.
I'm going to him, he won't return to me.

I worship, sowing grain across the sea.
I'm going to him, he won't return to me.

Thus I became a translator of the Bible, sort of, and in doing that found myself reckoning more urgently than ever before with a critical circumstance of ancient literature: form and content are inseparable, and equally important. These languages were not like modern globalized ones, serving mainly to convey information in explicit and interchangeable forms—but with a dimension called "style" for artistic uses on the side. Instead, the original Bible was, like all of ancient rhetoric and poetry, primarily a set of live performances, and *what* they meant was tightly bound up in *the way* they meant it.

Here's a modern analogy. If a male comedian wearing a tutu and a hat with plastic fruit on it repeats a presidential speech word for word, his meaning is pretty much the opposite of what the president meant. I'm not kidding you: this degree of difference can prevail when the Bible is translated without attention to its original forms, particularly those that *in*form its striking and moving expressiveness—that is, its beauty. Almost literally, if we can't dance to it, we don't understand it. That's true of all ancient literature, but for the Bible, on which so much of our society was built, the implications are far more important.

The Bible's beauty helps explain the astonishing amount of influence this set of texts gained in itself, in defiance of hard and even disastrous circumstances. It had to be something people were genuinely attached to—not distasteful or stern or dull writing they resignedly learned and obeyed; and not decrees they regarded as trivially or oppressively superstitious but went along with for pragmatic reasons. It had to be *their* book; it had to win their assent by every means available.

It is sometimes argued that the Bible isn't all that special, because it contains so many elements of ancient Middle Eastern and Mediterranean lore. Sumerian legend, for example, which is dizzyingly old, yields a story of a child, who is destined for greatness, saved as an infant when his mother places him in a rush basket and launches him on a river. The child is called Sargon, not Moses, but you see my point. Also, Sumerian law can show great concern for the poor and unprotected, such as widows and orphans—as the Bible does.

But in spite of the vast material power of some regimes that generated such literature, the Bible is its cherished, unitary monument. The Bible emerged in tiny, frequently overrun Palestine, on the western side of the so-called Fertile Crescent and between two regions with immense resources for irrigation, Egypt with its Nile River, and Mesopotamia, the "Land Between the Rivers," the Tigris and Euphrates (flowing from—according to the modern map—Turkey and Syria and through Iraq).

Widespread and highly organized irrigation in these places increased agricultural productivity; the ability to give or withhold water invested some rulers with godlike status; and giant building projects and distant military expeditions were among the enterprises that significant agricultural surpluses enabled. Compared to such neighbors as the Egyptians, the Israelites didn't have the material resources with which to defend themselves effectively, let alone to stretch an empire over any significant part of the known world.

Though a couple of the Twelve Tribes of Israel* were associated with the sea, adventurous voyaging and international coastal raiding and trading were also not characteristic of Israelites—too bad for them, as these were alternate routes to concentrated riches and imperial power. Phoenicians, dominating seafaring to the north (and eventually as far off as Spain), and other sea peoples, chiefly the Philistines crowding up on the coastline to the south, ensured that, for most practical purposes, Israel didn't *have* a coastline.

But scholars actually can't point to hegemony of the "Israelites" *anywhere* at any early date. In their remote heredity, they are hard to distinguish from other Canaanite peoples such as the Moabites, from whom the Bible is at pains to set them apart. But in this the Bible itself falters: Ruth, for example, the virtuous ancestress of King David, is a Moabite married to two Israelite men in succession, her personal life apparently driven more by famine and flourishing fields in different regions than by anything as abstract as her husbands' or her own ancestry. Common sense sides with this depiction of sanctioned, sometimes migratory intermarriage rather than with the prohibitions—shown as almost primordial—on "whoring after" foreign women and foreign gods alike. These ethnic groupings in general appear from archaeology to have had a small-scale economy based on farming and herding, and social organization around villages and extended families, and there is no way to tell Israelite (whatever that meant) pottery shards and dwelling foundations from non-Israelite ones.

Nor were the early Israelites in any way strong enough to vindicate a unique religion. The sharp distinctions in belief and practice came much later, and the Bible itself preserves a lot of evidence for this. The text, for example, to some extent endorses teraphim, or household cult images. Early bans on the worship of foreign deities—particularly bull statues, and Baals or "Lords"†—to the limited degree that they can be considered factual, evidently had a quite pragmatic function: worshipping someone else's local god(s)

---

*The twelve were said to be the descendants of Reuben, Simeon, Levi, Judah, Dan, Naphtali, Gad, Asher, Issachar, Zebulun, Joseph, and Benjamin. These are the sons of Jacob, also called Israel.
†The Hebrew word *Adonai* also means "Lord" (originally "my Lord"), and with slight grammatical changes can apply to human beings as well as to the one God.

signaled subordination; the establishment of one's own cult was supposed to bestow mastery of the land.

The people of the Bible apparently had a hard time getting control of anything, as is reflected in the fraught struggles for survival and prosperity in their stories. If the group did not originate in Mesopotamia and migrate to Palestine (an area that owes its name and the clearest designations of its boundaries first to the Greeks and later to the Roman imperial administration) with their tents and herds, as their progenitor Abraham is said to have done, and if Abraham's descendants did not migrate from Egypt to the Promised Land of Canaan (more or less Palestine, but variously demarcated over the centuries), they nevertheless defined themselves in part through these episodes and still do.

The obscurity of the Israelites can be downright comical. The first evidence of outsiders noticing them as a distinct entity comes only late in the Bronze Age, at the end of the thirteenth century B.C.E., and only because the pharaoh Merneptah lists them in an inscription, among other peoples he has wiped out. (Obviously, he exaggerates—he cannot have wiped them out altogether.) From around 1000 B.C.E., the reigns of David and Solomon are supposed to have represented the height of Israel's power, but there's no extant corroboration by foreign contemporaries that the kingdom existed at all. Archaeology confirms that it did, but if it flourished (perhaps on a locally impressive scale), that was probably only because this was now a dark age, and empires (or shrinking or former empires) all around were struggling with their own problems.

How, then, did the Jews come to establish the greatest, most enduring book on earth? The best answer seems to be that their weakness eventually found a paradoxical strength. In the late eighth and early seventh centuries B.C.E., and then in the late seventh century, during and after an era of narrowly survived Assyrian incursions, two kings in Jerusalem,* Hezekiah and Josiah, are said to have instituted important reforms, including banning the worship of foreign gods in the Temple, establishing exclusive and centralized worship of the God Yahweh there, and rediscovering Scrip-

---

*The capital of the southern kingdom of Judah. Confusingly—to us, anyway—the northern kingdom, from which Judah had, according to the Bible, split some generations before, was called Israel; its capital was Samaria. In time, however, the whole of Jewish territory, with its capital in Jerusalem, came to be called Israel.

ture and decreeing it to be binding law. The thoroughgoing idea in these policies (or in a half-legendary take on such policies) seems to have been that whatever had gone wrong for the nation was God's punishment for disobedience and unfaithfulness, and that faithfulness would ensure God's mercy. Starting in this age, too, the most familiar prophets arose, historically plausible figures like Isaiah with their cries against injustice and godlessness *within* Israelite society, and their calls to repentance and a return to God. Biblical writings attributed to them are an indispensable concomitant to Biblical law.

The roots of Hebrew Scripture are thus quite sturdy and deep; they clung to reforms that seemed essential and in fact existential. The later main compilation and editing of the Hebrew Bible were of a piece with this process.

Even for that period, the chronology is not all secure, but it's clear that an important impetus for developing a national consciousness through literature was the Babylonian Exile, which occurred in several waves in the very late seventh and the early sixth centuries B.C.E. and was relaxed from 538 B.C.E., allowing a critical scholarly group to start returning. The Babylonian conquerors had concentrated on removing the elite, and it was to these that the Persian king Cyrus the Great, who ruled after toppling the Babylonian Empire, looked to rejuvenate and stabilize their homeland with the help of their precious scrolls. He also sponsored a replacement for Solomon's Temple, which the Babylonians had destroyed in 586 B.C.E. The Second Temple was completed around 517 B.C.E.—a nation-building exercise similar to constructing a literary edifice.

When a substantial part of the retrieval, transcription, amalgamation, editing, and new composition of this Scripture was completed, the documents were ceremonially read out loud to the assembled people, and instruction in their meaning was provided at the same time. The Bible shows as the leader of these reforms a scribe called Ezra, also a Persian protégé; he was probably active in the mid-fifth century B.C.E.

The new Temple, Jerusalem's new walls, and compiled and edited Scripture were impressive not only because they marked national survival; they also came into being with the help of a massive alien power, the Persian Empire. For the Jews, it had to have been a time to climactically pursue the questions "Who were we, and who are we, and what are we supposed to be, and why?" and "Who is this God who can rouse a foreign conqueror to restore us to ourselves?"

But the whole era of the Assyrian, Babylonian, and Persian ascendancies would have been ripe for the idea to flower that God was a transcendently powerful and loving redeemer, who would grant a life worth living to beings who by rights should be beneath his notice, and even to those who had been troublesome to him. The primary meaning of the word for "redemption" in Hebrew, as well as in Greek and Latin, is quite concrete: it's about buying a person back from captivity or slavery or some other distress (also, in Hebrew, vindicating him in a critical way). From the sheer number of slaves in the ancient world (along with land, they were the main rewards of successful military campaigns, and their labor underlay many imperial economies), it can be inferred what a far-fetched, forlorn hope redemption was in most cases.

In the context of history, therefore, the special significance of a whole redeemed people becomes plain. In fact, the Jews harked back to a much earlier time and explained both their unique identity and their close relationship with God by citing their escape from slavery in Egypt and their arrival at and acquisition of the land of Canaan as an independent nation (events for which archaeologists are still looking for corroborating evidence) as God's greatest gifts from his side of the covenant, or bond, with them.

It wasn't a huge step from the idea of redemption to that of resurrection: God could give the whole land, the whole people, a new life. In particular, Ezekiel's vision, in chapter 37 of the Biblical book named for him, of the dry bones of his nation "rising up" and "standing straight up" corresponds to the image in both the Greek and the Latin Scriptural words for resurrection—getting to one's feet after the prostration of death—and certainly fed into the New Testament imagery of individual resurrection.

However, during the period after Alexander the Great's death (323 B.C.E.), when the Greek dynasties of his generals' heirs dominated the Middle East, any notion that the Jewish people were holy in themselves, and ipso facto entitled to autonomy and prosperity, must have taken a heavy blow. In the mid-second century B.C.E., the Maccabean rebellion vindicated the ritual Judaism the Greeks had defiled and repressed under the rule of Antiochus IV, but the Jewish regime then established for around the next hundred years proved violent, corrupt, and power-hungry.

The rebels against the Romans in the mid-first century C.E. brought even worse on their people: the destruction of the Second Temple (technically the Third Temple, Herod the Great's magnificent renovation), massacre, and enslavement, as well as large-scale dispersal. ("Diaspora" means "scattering.") A harshly repressed rebellion of the early second century was the end of the line. Jews thereafter tended to place their hope in personal piety and lawfulness according to the Scriptures, and in the mere preservation of their scattered communities. They did not lose the idea that they were special, but it was a specialness that demanded submission to God's very special demands and restrictions on them.

The Hebrew Bible is therefore a highly unusual outgrowth of nationalism, if the word "nationalism" even applies. The typical emblematic literature of a nation, from Homer to Vergil's *Aeneid* to "The Battle Hymn of the Republic" and beyond, says, "We conquer and rule because of special divine favor." The Hebrew Bible says, "God's favor punishes and teaches us; it is only through his mercy and justice that we survive, and we survive to testify to this."

The Bible therefore tends toward a characterization of deity that was absolutely unique in the ancient world, and his favored identity was Yahweh.* In remote history, there seems to have been nothing more special about this deity than about the Israelites. The Bible preserves relics of mundane characteristics (familiar to any student of ancient culture at large) attributed to him that were eventually of little or no importance. He was associated with storms, like a typical sky god. The term "Lord of Hosts" (meaning "commander of armies") suggests his role as a war god. He was sometimes envisioned, like Jupiter or Zeus, as a king of all the other gods. Like many anthropomorphic gods—particularly the tricksters—he would intervene in human affairs in ways that flaunted humanlike quirks; in certain Bible stories, there is no good explanation for his actions except *personality* in a bad sense.

---

*The names "Israelite" and "Hebrew" became outdated early on, and ancient versions of "Jewish"—words related to the word "Yahweh"—became the common and permanent designation of this group.

But later the Jewish concept of the divine was developed in a very special way by means of this god. Wherever the name Yahweh comes from, it is dramatized in Scripture as coming from the verb "to be" or "to become." In Exodus 3:13–14, when asked for his name, God declares to Moses, "I AM THAT I AM," which would make this divinity about his own sheer presence or existence. This does not fit neatly into Jerusalem Temple practice, which differed from much of Scripture in depicting the deity almost as a very powerful person in his mansion, receiving costly gifts from his visitors and dispensing vital favors to them through his trusty servants, much as a pagan god surrounded by priests was thought to do.

The obvious contradictions concerning what and where God *was* were a painful source of internal Jewish controversy around the Temple and its rituals, controversies that spread broadly into issues of social inequality and the handling of foreign rule. Over time, at least, Hebrew Scripture—sometimes in explicit defiance of what went on at the Temple—was held to depict a God who *was* everywhere, and not only lovingly accessible to bare pleas of human need but actively reaching out to the perplexed, the lost, the defiant, the helpless, and the hopeless; teaching and guiding selflessly, so that even terrible human wrongdoing could turn into meaningful redemption. This is why the stories of Jacob and of Joseph, for example, are still retold in all three great "religions of the Book": Judaism, Christianity, and Islam.

But even the Bible's ritual instructions allowed, at least in the long run, humane mediation and liberty within community. The official remedy for a husband's jealous suspicion (absent any evidence) was to haul his wife to the altar, pay the priest to feed her what must originally have been a poison, and see whether her guilt showed in a disabling seizure that rendered her a general outcast (Numbers 5:11–31). Thing is, those verses, in themselves, are not in charge. Jewish religious scholars have paid intricate, loving attention to them, to the effect that for many centuries they have not had to be implemented literally but still yield guidance, instruction, and inspiration. Christians ignore the passage and choose others to help them think about and structure marriage. But in either religion, Scripture has, over time and on balance, *not* been placed in the position of a tyrant but rather at the service of ideas about a just and protecting God.

Paradoxically, however, Yahweh is also about mystery: his existence is utterly self-sufficient, so that only the circular wording of "I AM THAT I AM" can represent it. He is above normal questions such as "Who?" or "What?" So thick is the veil around the Jewish concept of God that the Jews eventually ceased to speak aloud the name as it appeared in their Scriptures. Written Hebrew for a long period consisted of consonants alone, and Yahweh's name was written with four of these, YHWH (that's the standard English transliteration, anyway); later, this word was "pointed," or had the now-conventional marks for vowels added to it, but this was done as if the word were *Adonai* (which I transliterate, when emphasizing sound, as *ahdōnai*), the word for "Lord," a more mundane appellation. The written vowels remind the reader to say "*Adonai*"—and the Look of Liquid Nitrogen from the teacher tends to prevent more than one disrespectful mistake. (The prescribed reverent spelling in English is "G-d." "*HaShem,*" or "The Name," serves for simply speaking, as opposed to reading, about God in traditional Jewish practice.) Somewhat similarly, Christian Scripture—the earliest extant versions of which are in Greek—developed a system of *nomina sacra,* or "sacred names," abbreviations of the most important words such as "God," "Jesus," and "cross."

But what was in the Hebrew Bible as a whole, as it turned out? The Torah (Hebrew for "Teaching") or Pentateuch (Greek for "Five Books") comes first (though much of it was written or placed in its final form relatively late) in both Jewish and Christian Bibles: Genesis, Exodus, Leviticus, Numbers, Deuteronomy. These narrate the creation of the world, the early history of mankind, the lives of the patriarchs and matriarchs and their initial descendants, the enslavement in Egypt, the deliverance to and conquest of the Promised Land, and the establishment of the law; the second through the fifth of these books lay out a considerable number of rules, from the very general to the details of farming, dressing, and so on.

It is in the Torah, thick with competing versions of both folklore and charter-like material (and of passages that function as both at once), that a "source critic" can have the liveliest time positing how the Hebrew part of the Bible came together. According to the most prevalent account of the process, late scribes fused documents from four main sources (or groups of sources). There is the Jahwist (J), a term based on the word "Yahweh," which this source favors;

and the Elohist (E), leaning toward *Elohim* (*"Elōheem"*), technically "Gods" (though it clearly was understood as singular during the scribal period); then there is the Deuteronomist (D), since the Book of Deuteronomy (Greek for "Second Law") represents a separate tradition from the law as laid out in Exodus, Leviticus, and Numbers; and the Priestly source (P), certain priests of the Babylonian Exile. I'm not going to go into the specific arguments in my book, as they're not essential to my exposition, but I thought I should mention source criticism as especially good authority for the fact, which I rely on everywhere, that the Bible is a highly *synthetic* work. Aaron, for example, pops in and out of the Moses story in Exodus like a commercial for his purported descendants, the Jewish high priests. Even when in the Bible there is a single, undoubted historical author, as for roughly half of the New Testament letters traditionally ascribed to Paul, scribes in subsequent generations have often had their way with the text. I'll get back to synthetic composition later.

After the Torah but in different places in Jewish and Christian Bibles are other books. A Hebrew acronym designates the whole of the Hebrew Bible: the Tanakh, formed from the first letters of the Hebrew words for the Torah, the Prophets, and the Writings. The Jewish tradition is broad in its classification of prophetic books and includes in this list Joshua, Judges, First and Second Samuel, and First and Second Kings. These books give accounts of the "Former Prophets," who do not match the mainly preaching, declaiming character of the "Latter Prophets": Isaiah, Jeremiah, Ezekiel, and the twelve Minor Prophets, each of whom has an eponymous book of his own.

The Writings are even more complicated, comprising "wisdom books" (Job, Ecclesiastes, and Proverbs), poetry (Psalms, Lamentations, and the Song of Songs or Song of Solomon), and history (First and Second Chronicles, Ezra and Nehemiah, and Ruth, Esther, and Daniel).

I'm not alone in calling the traditional Tanakh divisions and subdivisions rather arbitrary-looking. "History" would seem to be a natural fourth main category, comprising those Former Prophets (Joshua and company) and Writings (Ezra and company) that are mainly narrative and purport to show past events that are public or of public importance (unlike the story of Job, nowadays often called "novelistic"). First and Second Chronicles, part of the Writings, actually reiterate much of the history found in the Former Prophets. But—right, right, "history" was a very slowly developing concept; and placing fact here and legend, speculation, prescription, worship, and all the rest somewhere else obviously isn't in line with a Scriptural mind-set.

The Apocrypha, or "Hidden-Away" portions of the Old Testament, comprise still other books, the Greek of whose extant forms marks them as later compositions, revisions, or translations. They must come from the Hellenistic period starting in the late fourth century B.C.E., after the conquests of Alexander the Great had established Greek rulers and a Greek public culture throughout the Middle East. The Septuagint ("Seventy [Interpreters]," a title that commemorates the translators), which is a Greek translation of the Hebrew Bible begun sometime in the third century B.C.E. and authorized for use by Greek-speaking Jews for several centuries that followed, features a number of Apocrypha, but they were then dropped from the Jewish Scriptures, during a process that for both Jewish and Christian Scripture is called canonization and results in an official, prescribed selection of writings.

The Apocrypha are mainly additions to and elaborations of Hebrew Scriptures (for example, the Apocryphal Esther adds verses to the Hebrew Book of Esther, and the Wisdom of Solomon echoes wisdom books such as Proverbs), but the Books of Maccabees, occasioned by the success of the second-century B.C.E. Jewish rebellion against the Greek ruler Antiochus, are obviously brand-new and historically informative. Some books, such as Tobit, a romantic adventure tale of pious Jews in the aftermath of Assyrian conquest, show the influence of Greek literary forms. Catholic and Orthodox Christian Bibles included Apocryphal books in the Old Testament, but early Protestant Bibles segregated and then dropped them.

The Christian books of the Bible, or the New Testament, continued the Old Testament's striking assertion of spiritual strength in material weakness, though now the assertion took a different direction. These books are all in Greek and were probably written between about 50 and 150 C.E. They contain first Matthew, Mark, Luke, and John, the Gospels (from an Old English word for "good news") or favored accounts of Jesus's life, teachings, death, and resurrection. The Gospels' narration continues in the Acts of the Apostles, about the early spread of the new faith. After Acts comes a number of Epistles, a fancy term for letters, concerned mainly with worship, metaphysics, and social prescription. The Book of Revelation is placed last in the New Testament and is about the end of the world and the Second Coming of Christ. (All this is, however, only the *physical* arrangement of the New Testament; the probable dates of the texts' composition are not reflected in their order.)

The full, canonical New Testament was more or less established, with a roster of books that has endured until today, from the fifth century C.E. for both the Eastern Orthodox and the Catholic (Western) Church. The only truly strange-looking and persistently controversial inclusion was Revelation. This book's wildly colorful, dramatic scenes overshadow all other mentions and descriptions of the world's end in the rest of the New Testament.

The background to the new, Christian writings was the flattened-out world of the Roman Empire, with almost steady and almost universal peace achieved at the expense of local assertiveness. Unrest would periodically threaten at the barbarian periphery, in places like Britain and Germany and Scythia (an area beyond the Black Sea), and Rome would send expeditions to intimidate or crush those populations. But in general, the Roman sphere of influence grew impressively with little resistance. Many peoples around the Mediterranean had been caught up in Rome's roughly hundred years of civil wars (ending in 31 B.C.E.); the experience had not been much fun. Now, with help and encouragement from Rome, they made the most of peace. They adopted or expanded Roman-style public works and monuments; traditional Roman institutions, including the cult of Greco-Roman gods (though the Romans had no interest in getting rid of local cults that wouldn't cause trouble); and emperor-worship that indispensably symbolized the end of political independence.

But in Palestine, not so much. Jewish client kings, military occupation, brutal crackdowns on insurgencies and suspected nascent insurgencies, co-opting of the clergy, and even the granting of extraordinary privileges (such as a tax exemption for the Jerusalem Temple, and a draft exemption for Jewish men)—none of it worked, and in 70 C.E. the Romans did everything they could to ensure that the Jews as a nation, though not as a religion, disappeared.

Even vis-à-vis the Jews, and even when they *were* Jews—as at first they all were—early followers of Jesus found themselves in a position of extreme weakness. On the evidence, the most influential disciples and apostles would have been glad to remain within the Jewish sphere, but they would not give up their conviction that Jesus, a shamefully crucified troublemaker, had risen from the dead and so must be the Messiah ("Anointed One"), the savior sanctified by God. The doctrine, of which the first evidence lies in the Jewish Paul of Tarsus's letters, that this miracle vouchsafed eternal life for all believers, both Jews and non-Jews, made enemies of the Jewish hierarchy, particularly because all the immemorial ritual and moral identifiers of Jews—most important, circumcision and the dietary and sexual laws—were now supposed to be of no essential value, or even inimical if they got in the way of pagans' converting to the worship of Christ (the Greek translation of "Messiah").

The proto-Christians' novel beliefs were of a piece with their very awkward place in history. The New Testament is in large part occupied with setting these beliefs out—with an appropriately heavy use of negation, irony, and paradox. Those belonging to "The Way" (better: "The Road," suggesting the precarious journeying and sojourning of Jesus and those proselytizing in his name) did not depend on God's helping them on earth, reunifying and empowering them in exchange for good behavior. This was the Jewish outlook (which by force devolved into the mere plea that God would preserve his people from annihilation). Followers of Christ placed their hopes firmly in the afterlife, which they were liable to assert was going to start right now, after the end of the world. Parts of the Gospels and Epistles make powerful demands on conduct as part of the religious life, but in the middle of the New Testament stand the six or seven authentic letters of Paul, insisting that humankind is saved by faith. He does not come down on the faith side of an either-or, faith vs. works argument (which can be the modern impression), but he does hold that faith is primary, and that good works are necessarily fused into faith.

The New Testament, therefore, is—even more than the Old—deeply unliterary in an important sense both ancient and modern: it doesn't celebrate either a group's or a human individual's talents or achievements as such, or in fact any ultimate quality or significance in the material world; indeed, the New Testament fights hard to get beyond anything like those. This otherworldliness, however, proved powerful: anyone, clearly, could become and remain a Christian—nothing in life was in the way. Of course, anybody could also persecute a Christian, who wasn't even supposed to object to this but to welcome it as a chance for the ultimate testimony of transcendent faith, dying under torture.

Compilation and canonization were how the Biblical texts came together into their present form, and these processes helped make the Bible such an extraordinary book. But first I need to warn about the term "compiled," and I wish there were a better term. Forget about pages "piled together," or a single bound book. (That's what you would think the Latin-derived word originally meant; ah, no: it meant "plundered" or "plagiarized.") For a long period, the vehicle was papyrus scrolls ("Bible" comes from the word for papyrus), which kept the basic unit of writing to the length of what we might call a long chapter, such as the Book of Genesis, and must have encouraged a notion of "books" as separate, and relatively inter-changeable and disposable, particularly because scrolls are bulky and awkward to store and transport, and because papyrus doesn't last long except in a virtually rainless climate, which most of Palestine and the whole of Asia Minor and Europe didn't have. Leaders, scholars, and scribes—as well as ordinary readers—had to think of material constraints and make quite conscious choices of what to keep, copy, and recopy. Only in late antiquity did there arise the modern form of book, the rectangular bound codex that might hold as much writing as fifty or so scrolls could and came to preserve that writing on a type of leather, which is what vellum is. Rigid, ornate covers, and pages with colorful decorative letters and pictures, known as illuminating, emphasized the value of the content. This was an ideal presentation of the longer canonical Bible, the Christian one.

On the whole, the development of the Bible seems to have been more about popular favor than institutional authority: people knew what they liked and discarded what they didn't, on criteria not too hard to project backward from our own tastes. It was not until the early first millennium C.E. that the Jewish Scriptures were enshrined in what could be called a canon, and by that time vast numbers of Jewish documents had fallen by the wayside. The Dead Sea Scrolls (stashed in caves during antiquity and rediscovered in the twentieth century) include not only the Book of Isaiah but many works never cited elsewhere, among them a copper treasure map, for cryin' out

loud. Eminently learned persons tried to get me interested in the
Dead Sea Scrolls, but in my humble opinion most of the writing
unattested elsewhere is pretty boring.

On the Christian side, before the several important steps in canonization that took place in late antiquity, the Gnostic Gospels supported an exclusive, secretive religion; "Gnostic" means (roughly)
"based on [true] knowledge," and the groups seem to me to have
been significantly more cultlike than modern Christianity's ances-
tors were. It therefore doesn't surprise me that Gnostic writings
didn't survive a ban; in my (admittedly not universal) opinion,
they wouldn't have survived the most extravagant publicity, simply
because then everybody would have known what they said. I'm supposed to ooh and aah over the Gnostic Gospels and deplore their
"censorship." I don't.

Moreover, hardly all of the books that did enter the canon entered
easily, under what we could imagine as the beaming eyes of officious
pedants. The Old Testament Book of Ecclesiastes or Kohelet (something like "Preacher") is pretty nihilistic, the Song of Songs quite
erotic, and in Job, God has all the benevolence of a psychologist
experimenting on animals. But these are really ravishing works, and
I would have fast-talked them into acceptance as vigorously as their
advocates apparently did. The Book of Revelation, the most poetic
part of the New Testament, slipped in despite its author's, um, lack
of perspective (or raving lunacy), and despite a distinct shortage of
passages likely to inculcate practical virtues in youth. The more you
look at what's known and logically inferred about the process, the
less solid appear the old (and new) stories of canonical inquisition
for the sake of official self-interest.

Absolutely, the Scriptures have been developed in quite messy
ways. The Old Testament compilers could be heavy-handed in their
emphasis on ritual and bloodline; factionalism operates in these passages (and others), no question. And as for the New Testament, don't
get me started on anti-Semitism and Neoplatonism—as a Classicist,
I can just picture carpetbagging orator-philosophers as they huff-
ily realized that this new and increasingly influential movement,
with leaders mostly from outside the Greco-Roman mainstream,
and with many illiterate and semiliterate followers, eschewed pagan
intellectualism. How dare they? We'll fix that, won't we?

But no book has experienced such a long, aerobic winnowing of its claims to be revealed truth, and to be truth revealed in the proper forms. I'm a Quaker, experienced in communal authority's mediation of individual revelation, and this adds to the appeal the Bible has for me over religious writings flowing directly from one person's vision and substantially unprocessed afterward. Every Quaker is welcome to put something out there, and nothing is judged "right" or "wrong," but most contributions are forgotten, and hardly any end up in *Faith and Practice,* our book of selected testimonies. Worldly power plays a part in the choices, as it does in all canonization—the Quaker with money or position or just more time to spend with the organization gets a bigger say—but bad choices always tell in time, if only in that people will neglect flaky editions of *Faith and Practice* or even leave the Quakers, punishments we endured in abundance over the late twentieth century, when New Age spirituality and other trendiness came in virtually unopposed.

For these reasons, I see absolutely no conflict between acknowledging that the production of Scripture is a fallible (if not pathetic) human process, and believing that, over time, Scripture reveals God's will. Abraham Lincoln held that God works through history, no matter how tragic, and I believe that God works through speaking, listening, reading, and writing, no matter how faulty. I have a special esteem for the Bible in part because God has had the longest time to work on it: to allow various documents and collections to come and go, to funnel the survivors to populous conferences for final vetting, and—in the great fullness of time—to release the texts to a common readership.

This readership, moreover, over the centuries continues to enshrine only the passages it really loves. A very incomplete knowledge of or interest in the Bible isn't blameworthy even on the part of people who profess themselves dedicated to the book: they are exercising a sort of popular editorship, usually one affirmed by a beloved heritage and reaffirmed by their own thought and experience. They live the Bible in part by putting uncongenial segments of the canon aside—which means that the real, active canon is the unofficial, still-changing one. It was with this in mind that I chose passages to describe in this book of my own. They're not just of historical and theological importance; they also get from quarters both religious and nonreligious that almost erotic individual assent to great words, as well as a certain homey embrace in communal memory.

When, given all this, I consider the role of Bible translators, I'm pulled wildly in different directions. Of course I understand the indispensability of Bible translation, not only in allowing the book to be widely available and to continue its own popularizing development, but also in perpetuating its usefulness for political evolution. For the Jews (as well as for the pagan Greeks and Romans), having the law at hand in written form in the first place, for the whole populace to consult and to be subject to, promoted accountability, helping send public life down a more liberal path. Later, the Aramaic paraphrases, known as the Targum, ensured that the Hebrew text, though archaic, didn't become deeply arcane, and meaningfully accessible only to elite scholars. In a similar way, for Renaissance Christians, finally having the Bible, their own most important law, in vernacular languages enabled challenges to authority whose results we're still enjoying today. That societies pulled the translation along with them, so to speak, making sure it reflected their own current concerns more and the concerns of the texts' long-gone originators less, should be surprising to nobody and is blameworthy only in the eyes of perfectionist prigs. Nor, being a translator myself, am I inclined to join the pretentious whining about the aesthetic inferiority of translations to original texts. Yes, newer versions in alien languages aren't as lovely. And humanity is fallen, and the U.S. Congress is self-serving.

Moreover, Biblical translation, since it's considered so important, has been comparatively careful, comparatively dependent on outstanding talent and long study. Jerome, who produced the authoritative Latin Bible (the Vulgate) in the late fourth and early fifth centuries C.E., actually moved to Jerusalem to improve his knowledge of Hebrew. Martin Luther's Bible, published in the early sixteenth century, is called vital to the establishment of German as a literary language. Around the same time, William Tyndale risked—and lost—his life in the cause of popularizing Scripture, and his English translations are the basis for the best of earthy beauty in the King James Version (1611).

This and other Bibles have depended on the work of committees, but the old slurs on the integrity and efficiency of such groups are not valid here. King James's translators were tasked not just with making everything correct and proper, but also with reconciling whatever theological differences they could between Puritans and the Church of England. Famously, "faith, hope, charity" instead of "faith, hope, love" (1 Corinthians 13:13) is a concession to the Anglo-Catholic emphasis on earthly good works as opposed to pure faith. "Love" is more accurate (as well as more beautiful, in my view), but I admire the spirit of compromise (especially when I think of the later seventeenth century's religious wars, which that spirit was trying to prevent). Similarly, the twentieth-century New Revised Standard Version represents a constant stretch among different religious and nonreligious sensibilities as well as differing scholarly opinions. The more you know about the process, the less paranoia about censorious clergy messing with the Bible survives.

Still, to me as a *reader* of ancient literature, most of what I see in English Bibles is loss: the loss of sound, the loss of literary imagery, the loss of emotion, and—inevitably, because these texts were performances deeply integrated into the lives of the authors and early readers and listeners—the loss of thought and experience. A deep irony is that reverence—fear of God, deference to the religious community, reluctance to impose personal judgment on a sacred text—has the effect, over time, of flattening out the inspiring expressiveness of the original: not only the physical beauty but the actual meanings, as—I have to insist—the two aren't separate.

In the book that follows, I will use description, analogy, speculation, and experiment in attempts to convey something of what's lost. I may provoke a great deal of disagreement, but that's fine. If I merely bring a fuller and more nuanced discussion of the Bible into the public sphere, where it belongs, I will have made a bigger contribution than, a few years ago, I imagined possible.

PART ONE

IMPOSSIBILITIES ILLUSTRATED

The Character of the Languages and Texts

Legos, Not Rocks: Grammar

David and Bathsheba (2 Samuel 11–12:7)
The Lord's Prayer (Matthew 6:9–13 and Luke 11:2–4)

Imagine that you're at a moving and meaningful rock concert—say, Paul Simon with Ladysmith Black Mambazo playing Sun City, South Africa, during apartheid. You happen to send the only surviving record of the event, and only through text messaging (and yes, I know this didn't exist in the 1980s), and only to a monolingual English speaker in White Plains, New York, who is an obsessive collector of American Girl dolls. Having gamely transmitted the abbreviated first lines of "Nkosi Sikelel' iAfrika" ("God Bless Africa"), you get back to singing and swaying.

We don't get a much better record of what Psalm 137, for example, was like in its early incarnations. Here is the King James Version:

1   By the rivers of Babylon, there we sat down, yea, we wept, when we remembered Zion.

2   We hanged our harps upon the willows in the midst thereof.

3   For there they that carried us away captive required of us a song; and they that wasted us required of us mirth, saying, Sing us one of the songs of Zion.

4   How shall we sing the Lord's song in a strange land?

5   If I forget thee, O Jerusalem, let my right hand forget her cunning.

6   If I do not remember thee, let my tongue cleave to the roof of my mouth; if I prefer not Jerusalem above my chief joy.

7   Remember, O Lord, the children of Edom in the day

of Jerusalem; who said, Rase it, rase it, even to the foundation thereof.

8   O daughter of Babylon, who art to be destroyed; happy shall he be, that rewardeth thee as thou hast served us.

9   Happy shall he be, that taketh and dasheth thy little ones against the stones.

What is this scene of lamenting and cherishing and threatening? It is so vivid and so specific that I'm convinced it was based on direct experience. It does appear that some of the Jewish elite of the Babylonian Exile lived near Mesopotamian canals. But why exactly would you hang harps on willow trees? And why the change to a vengeful mood in verse 7? And what to make of the horrifying verse 9? Was this originally two or even three poems?

Much of this puzzlement naturally comes from the present harrowing shortage of the data that were available to early performers and their audiences. In their oldest written form, the Hebrew words represented by the English "By the rivers of Babylon" would have consisted of ten consonant letters (written and read from right to left) and nothing else. Original written Greek—in a dialect of which, Koinē ("Common"), the whole of the New Testament was written—is *so* much more decipherable: it has vowels! Early Hebrew writing didn't. But in both languages a short, handy phonetic alphabet, adapted from that of the Phoenicians, probably served for centuries as little more (at least in the realm of literature) than performance notes in a stubbornly oral culture.

A standard example of the gap between ancient performance and the texts and translations in their evolved forms is fifth-century B.C.E. Classical Athenian tragedy and comedy—for which we have no original stage directions. But at least we know something about that staging from other sources, such as vase painting. How much deeper is the mystery around early Hebrew literature. Was a Psalm "of Ascents," for instance, one repeated while climbing up to the Temple or other place of worship, or perhaps one sung as the smoke of a sacrifice "ascended" to heaven? And though Psalms were, it's clear, performed musically, what *kind* of music was it? And what did New Testament hymns in Greek sound like? Were they chanted or sung? In harmony, or perhaps in rounds? If I declared—according to my strong inclination as a translator—that the first written texts (as far as these can be reconstructed) are *it,* my logical and proper main interest here, how would I get closer to what *that* actually *was*—that is, how it was experienced?

Does a translator just fill things in? In the case of ordinary ancient literature, it's an unashamed yes. When I translated Aristophanes's *Lysistrata,* a Classical Greek comedy that imagines all the wives in Greece going on a sexual strike until a war ends, I counted on jokes occurring at fairly regular intervals, even though modern scholarly commentators couldn't find all of them. Every turn in the action, every windup in dialogue, and everything unexplainable otherwise was probably a hoot to the original audience—and where there was nothing verbally funny, stage business must have filled in, so that even bland words were funny when paired with, say, slapstick, the imitation of some public figure's voice, or just a strategic pause.

A Classics translator is readily forgiven if, to restore an arguably essential quality of the work (humor, in this case), she goes beyond analogy (the analogous modern joke is very common and very much accepted in secular translating, since humor dates—more like dies—so easily) and invents rather than leaves semantic blanks. When the protagonist Lysistrata proposes that the women withhold sex from their husbands, two wives respond with one line each. The lines are similar and contain an identical clause (usually translated as "but let the war go on"), yet I changed the second line into something much different:

CALONICE: No, I don't think so. Let the war go on.
MYRRHINE: Me? Not a chance in hell, so screw the war.

This kind of reconstruction allows an ancient play to keep doing the basic thing it was created to do: hold a theatrical audience's attention. Reconstruction can also allow an ancient poem to stay poetic, ancient law to maintain its tone of authority, and ancient rhetoric to show how it played on the passions and compunctions of crowds and juries.

A translator of the Bible can just try to get away with reconstruction. She had better, in fact, concentrate on the palpable intricacies of the languages and see what insights they yield. Those small marks in a modern, scholarly text (in Hebrew, a word can look like a cartoon character being beaten up) teach most usefully about grammar. Grammar is not just (obviously) for deciphering the text—that is, for setting more or less acceptable words of a modern language beside the original words; but also for observing how those original words act, how they express more than their bare lexical projections into the year Now: how they put on a show.

Ancient Hebrew and Greek are inflected, not phrasal languages, a fact that makes a momentous difference in their literatures. If in English I want to express (for instance) the concept that one thing belongs to another, I usually have to string out separate words in a fixed order—say, "a house belonging to a man," "the house of this man," or "a man's house." It's relatively rare in English for individual words themselves to change much as their meanings change, in such a way that different meanings can branch out of a single word. An example is the principal parts of the verbs "lay" and "lie": I lay the book down (present-tense meaning), I laid the book down (simple past), I have laid the book down (present perfect); I lie down (present), I lay down (simple past), I have lain down (present perfect). The reason it's so hard to keep these forms straight is that we're not used to expressing ourselves that way. But intricate phrasing is easy for native English speakers; one of my professors reported that his two-year-old daughter had spontaneously come out with, "What did you bring that book I didn't want to be read to out of up for?"—with that bizarre series of prepositions and an adverb ("up"), no problem for the likes of us, but liable to drive a foreign student of English around the bend.

In either Hebrew or Greek, the words in that sentence would be much fewer, with concepts like "I want" and "what for" and "to be read to" and "bring up" expressed by single words, each containing substantial meaning and often through their structure entailing close relationships with other words. In an English sentence, in contrast, words tend to develop their meanings and their relationships through their order. "What . . . for" in "What did you bring that book I didn't want to be read to out of up for?" can't mean "why" unless the words are where they are (or maybe right beside each other at the start, but that would be awkward and not standard).

In Hebrew and Greek, word order is—on semantic if not stylistic grounds—much more flexible: the subject pronoun "you" is expressed through a finite verb's form,* so wherever you put that verb, the subject of the little girl's sentence, "you," won't be mixed up with the direct object of the verb, "book." Both "you" and "book" in English become gibberish if they're moved at all. In Greek, that noun actually has a special form to show that it's a direct object, so heck, put it anywhere you want.

Hebrew has a nifty device called a construct chain for binding words together without the benefit of an "of" word; the words do have to stand side by side (showing that the first item belongs to the second), but beyond that their forms are usually just altered a little. "The hand of Yahweh" (traditionally translated as "the hand of the Lord") is two words in Hebrew. But, hey, "of a person having been set free" can be one word in Greek; Hebrew does that kind of thing, too, just not as often.

I call such handy, highly cohesive units Legos, and I compare them to the rocks of English, which won't stay on top of each other unless you place them just right. In these ancient languages, you didn't have a great variety of words to choose from (see my next chapter, on vocabularies), as in an old-fashioned Lego set there are only a few kinds of bricks. But you sure could *combine* words more freely, to create structures of great size, diversity, and nuance. Custom—especially in literary languages—might dictate acceptable word deployment or even strings of specific words, which are called syntax and formulae, respectively; but those were powerful tools more than straitjackets. You could make a small change, fit an eight-pronged red brick in where two four-pronged blue bricks were expected, and it would be striking. Furthermore, most of these are inflected words, or bricks you can individually alter—say, by turning a four-point green one into a two-point white one. Nothing is in the way of creating very expressive and impressive edifices.

Standard narrative Hebrew word order is finite verb, subject, objects and/or other elements. But see how interestingly that expectation, and the variations possible, are used in a famous story in the Second Book of Samuel. First, the King James:

---

*A finite verb ("is," "has gamboled," "will splatter," "Look!") must have a subject, if only the impersonal "it" or the unexpressed "you"; in contrast, an infinitive or participle (to be, gamboling, besplattered) is effectively a noun or an adjective: no finite verb, no subject necessary.

11:1   And it came to pass, after the year was expired, at the time when kings go forth to battle, that David sent Joab, and his servants with him, and all Israel; and they destroyed the children of Ammon, and besieged Rabbah. But David tarried still at Jerusalem.

2   And it came to pass in an eveningtide, that David arose from off his bed, and walked upon the roof of the king's house: and from the roof he saw a woman washing herself; and the woman was very beautiful to look upon.

3   And David sent and enquired after the woman. And one said, Is not this Bathsheba, the daughter of Eliam, the wife of Uriah the Hittite?

4   And David sent messengers, and took her; and she came in unto him, and he lay with her; for she was purified from her uncleanness: and she returned unto her house.

5   And the woman conceived, and sent and told David, and said, I am with child.

6   And David sent to Joab, saying, Send me Uriah the Hittite. And Joab sent Uriah to David.

7   And when Uriah was come unto him, David demanded of him how Joab did, and how the people did, and how the war prospered.

8   And David said to Uriah, Go down to thy house, and wash thy feet. And Uriah departed out of the king's house, and there followed him a mess of meat from the king.

9   But Uriah slept at the door of the king's house with all the servants of his lord, and went not down to his house.

10   And when they had told David, saying, Uriah went not down unto his house, David said unto Uriah, Camest thou not from thy journey? why then didst thou not go down unto thine house?

11   And Uriah said unto David, The ark, and Israel, and Judah, abide in tents; and my lord Joab, and the servants of my lord, are encamped in the open fields; shall I then go into mine house, to eat and to drink, and to lie with my wife? as thou livest, and as thy soul liveth, I will not do this thing.

12   And David said to Uriah, Tarry here to day also, and to morrow I will let thee depart. So Uriah abode in Jerusalem that day, and the morrow.

13 And when David had called him, he did eat and drink before him; and he made him drunk: and at even he went out to lie on his bed with the servants of his lord, but went not down to his house.

14 And it came to pass in the morning, that David wrote a letter to Joab, and sent it by the hand of Uriah.

15 And he wrote in the letter, saying, Set ye Uriah in the forefront of the hottest battle, and retire ye from him, that he may be smitten, and die.

16 And it came to pass, when Joab observed the city, that he assigned Uriah unto a place where he knew that valiant men were.

17 And the men of the city went out, and fought with Joab: and there fell some of the people of the servants of David; and Uriah the Hittite died also.

18 Then Joab sent and told David all the things concerning the war;

19 And charged the messenger, saying, When thou hast made an end of telling the matters of the war unto the king,

20 And if so be that the king's wrath arise, and he say unto thee, Wherefore approached ye so nigh unto the city when ye did fight? knew ye not that they would shoot from the wall?

21 Who smote Abimelech the son of Jerubbesheth? Did not a woman cast a piece of a millstone upon him from the wall, that he died in Thebez? why went ye nigh the wall? then say thou, Thy servant Uriah the Hittite is dead also.

22 So the messenger went, and came and shewed David all that Joab had sent him for.

23 And the messenger said unto David, Surely the men prevailed against us, and came out unto us into the field, and we were upon them even unto the entering of the gate.

24 And the shooters shot from off the wall upon thy servants; and some of the king's servants be dead, and thy servant Uriah the Hittite is dead also.

25 Then David said unto the messenger, Thus shalt thou say unto Joab, Let not this thing displease thee, for the sword devoureth one as well as another: make thy battle more strong against the city, and overthrow it: and encourage thou him.

26   And when the wife of Uriah heard that Uriah her husband was dead, she mourned for her husband.

27   And when the mourning was past, David sent and fetched her to his house, and she became his wife, and bare him a son. But the thing that David had done displeased the Lord.

12:1   And the Lord sent Nathan unto David. And he came unto him, and said unto him, There were two men in one city; the one rich, and the other poor.

2   The rich man had exceeding many flocks and herds:

3   But the poor man had nothing, save one little ewe lamb, which he had bought and nourished up: and it grew up together with him, and with his children; it did eat of his own meat, and drank of his own cup, and lay in his bosom, and was unto him as a daughter.

4   And there came a traveller unto the rich man, and he spared to take of his own flock and of his own herd, to dress for the wayfaring man that was come unto him; but took the poor man's lamb, and dressed it for the man that was come to him.

5   And David's anger was greatly kindled against the man; and he said to Nathan, As the Lord liveth, the man that hath done this thing shall surely die:

6   And he shall restore the lamb fourfold, because he did this thing, and because he had no pity.

7   And Nathan said to David, Thou art the man.

Certain words and phrases, and certain patterns of syntax, are repeated relentlessly in Hebrew Scripture. One thing to consider, however, in speculating about their effects, is that their flawless pedigrees as individual units could have made their artistic use in new and revised compositions both inviting and unassailable, and could have soothed and intrigued audiences at the same time. If you wanted to do something interesting, you could do it *with* the usual pieces, just by deploying them somewhat differently—and how could someone reject or forbid that out of hand? More likely, you got points both for employing the traditional material and for adapting it. The Legos are a family gift, an approved educational and recreational resource. They may come with a construction design—say, the "Mountain House"—including a picture on the front of the box and instructions inside. But are the children going to keep docilely building the "Mountain House"? My friends and I soon had different structures in mind to house Thicky, Patheta, Puppydog the Clydesdale, and the Raunchy Rats of Sicktown. And our parents and other children were entertained, not disapproving.

Look, in the King James Version of the David and Bathsheba story, at 2 Samuel 11:1, 2, 14, and 16: in these verses, respectively, David stays home from war; David is strolling on his roof one evening and sees Bathsheba bathing; David sends Uriah back to the front carrying orders to Joab the field commander to deploy Uriah in the most dangerous spot; Joab carries out the orders. Each verse begins with a clause dully familiar to many readers in English translation, "And it came to pass." Once in a Hebrew class I was auditing, a Protestant student translated the Hebrew by merely quoting that English clause, and the Jewish professor snapped, "That's not what the Hebrew says; that's just what's on the tape of the Bible running in your head twenty-four hours a day." It was a moment I still cherish.

Technically, the Hebrew clause (more like a mini-clause) is a "vav consecutive" or "vav conversive" constructed out of the verb for "to be" or "to become" or "to happen" and the one-letter word for "and," vav (which happens to be, on its own, visually, a straight vertical line). In a vav consecutive, vav is glommed right onto the front of a certain form of verb (well, visually, onto the back, as we're reading right to left) and changes that verb's quasi tense or aspect (or something). Don't close this book and turn on a PBS documentary about ferrets: what I'm about to tell you is way more interesting.

In this particular vav conversive, the two reconstructed syllables mean, "Something new arose," or "Then" or "Now" or "Next" or "And get this"*—the variety of ways to translate resulting in part from the special character of Hebrew verbs. These don't have a strict relation to linear time, and they don't through their forms alone express any opinion on whether anything actually does, can, or should happen. (The "moods" in other languages take care of this: most familiar are the indicative ["It is . . ."] and the subjunctive ["If it were . . ."].) There is no progress or positivism here; we're in the

*In Part Two, I use this clause to show a variety of criteria for applying practical considerations to translation choices (pp. 119–22).

realm of circular human inadequacy and bafflement and cyclical divine mercy. Hebrew verbs do express whether action is "perfect" or "imperfect," but that means, respectively, finished/simple or ongoing, so that the "perfect" can refer to either the past or present, and the "imperfect" to the past, present, or future, and can even express an effective command, often translated as "Thou shalt . . ."

The vav conversive is a common way of expressing the perfect, oddly by adding the "and" word to a verb in what looks like the imperfect form (but isn't). The special vav conversive "and-it-was" (or "and now at *this other* moment") apparently marks the passage of time, introduces a new scene or a turn in the action, or just establishes that these events are in the past—all quite convenient, when there are no true tenses to throw around.

All this is why the English translation "And it came to pass" is so deeply inappropriate. It feels like a train, chugging (coming) into the present and then chugging off (passing) into the future, with a slow momentum and maybe even on long tracks of inevitability, but in any case without any sense that, if not for what happens in this instant, everything would be different. There's not a shred of the proper drama in "And it came to pass."

What's more, the plodding sound of this clause does nothing to reflect the Hebrew, *vai-hee,* which reminds me of the yip as you trip and fall: the noise of no return. But that's not right: though it may designate no return, it's just a brief, simple vav conversive, marking a moment not as noticeable to the people in the stories.

But from the authors' and readers' point of view, as a formulaic element, quite ordinary (something people wrote and heard again and again and again) and at the same time deeply significant (as part of a vast, ancient literary tradition, bound up with the culture's most important ideas), *vai-hee* was a critical element in storytelling. By merely deploying it somewhat differently, you could effect your own subtle but authoritative interpretation of hinge events.

One unusual thing about *vai-hee*'s deployment in the David and Bathsheba passage is that it occurs twice in quick succession for setups of action early on (how David came to be entangled with Bathsheba), and twice likewise toward the middle (how David and Joab got rid of Bathsheba's husband, Uriah)—but not later. The expression does tend to mark a new episode or a change of scene or viewpoint, but clearly not mechanically, at every start or change.

In this story, at least, the shifts are where the most trouble starts, when David or someone else could have held back the wrecking ball. David could have gone to war in the first place; failing that, he could have turned his back on the beautiful nude woman; failing that, he could have let Uriah live, inconvenient as that would have been; Joab, finally, could have stood up to David, quietly ignored the instructions he knew were murderous, or figured something else out—he clearly doesn't lack brains. The transition *vai-hee* fills a variety of functions in Hebrew Bible narrative, but one thing it does here is mark points of decision. But at the same time—look at what it means, and its "perfect" aspect—it reproaches speculation and second-guessing like mine. The reader or listener may smugly think, "I would have done something different," but *vai-hee* says, "Yeah, but who cares?" This *did happen,* it's over and can't be replanned and improved; just contemplate it and don't meddle in it.

But *vai-hee* is just an edge of the story, so to speak. The artistry in the structure is pervasive. In the Hebrew, the first two verses of the story (for example) are slyly but instructively laid out. To recap: the first verse, in the King James, goes, "And it came to pass, after the year was expired, at the time when kings go forth to battle, that David sent Joab, and his servants with him, and all Israel; and they destroyed the children of Ammon, and besieged Rabbah. But David tarried still at Jerusalem."

In the original language, after the initial *vai-hee,* with its finite verb, we get a rather stately seasonal setup (literally "at-[the]-return [of] the-year") and read what people typically do then ("at-[the]-time/season [of the] to-go-out [of] the-kings"). Only then do we read, via another finite verb, what David has done himself to instigate such activity—he has dispatched a military force—and what those he has dispatched are doing, namely warfare of two sorts (finite verbs for destroying and besieging). After that, David is shown doing diddly-squat, just sitting there (not a finite verb, but a participle, and most literally translatable as "sitting"); that's going to be the problem. In this story, then, the first sentence* reads, "And-it-

---

*"Sentence" is a term of mere convenience, based on European notions of rounded out or "periodic" syntax; in construing the Bible, the notion of a "sentence" is also based on the Renaissance division of the text into numbered "verses" according to scholarly judgment of where each natural pause came. But admittedly, "sentences" and "verses" are very convenient for discussing the Bible.

was/happened at-[the]-return [of] the-year at-[the]-time/season [of] the] to-go-out [of] the-kings and-sent David Joab and-servants-his with-him and-all [of] Israel and-they-destroyed [the] sons [of] Ammon and-they-besieged Rabbah, and-David [was] sitting/staying in-Jerusalem."

To show how subtle yet relentless a bad impression of David can rise from such compositional nuances, I need to point out what's not in the Hebrew, and by extension what the nuances on their own are conveying. The rather officious syntactical props that any English translator has to add in a formal rendering do not even exist in Hebrew. Vav or (basically) "and" is the all-purpose conjunction, and it appears everywhere in Hebrew Scripture; linguists, philologists, and translators interpret it—and represent it in modern languages—as seems best to them in each instance. (The King James: "*And* it came to pass, after the year was expired, at the time when kings go forth to battle, *that* David sent Joab, *and* his servants with him, *and* all Israel; *and* they destroyed the children of Ammon, *and* besieged Rabbah. *But* David tarried still at Jerusalem.")

Really: among many other absences, Hebrew hasn't got an ordinary "but" or an "although," distinct in itself, that could be used to comment more explicitly, to us anyway, on the king's staying home, notwithstanding that this is the season for royal military campaigning, and notwithstanding that he himself has sent out a full force, and that such and such are the force's activities. The narrative just records the conventional actions in the conventional manner and leaves David "sitting" at the end, a nonaction emphasized by the static tenor of the participle. But in the Hebrew there's no need for a finger-pointing authorial "however": David, according to the way the representation of him is arranged syntactically, *is* the judgment on himself. The three vavs attached to active verbs and then a vav attached to the word "David" lead the reader rhythmically along and then bring her up short.

There's another stumble already at verse 2. The King James goes, "And it came to pass in an eveningtide, that David arose from off his bed, and walked upon the roof of the king's house: and from the roof he saw a woman washing herself; and the woman was very beautiful to look upon."

Vai-hee: then something else ominous happened. "And-it-was/ happened at-[the]-time/season [of] the-evening and-got-up David from-on bed-his and-he-strolled on [the] roof [of the] house [of] the-king and-he-saw [a] woman bathing from-on the-roof and-the-woman [was] beautiful/good to-see very." Notice, first of all, the shorter, then the longer, construct chain ([of] expression): the text lingers over the idle time, and even more over the empty place where he's puttering around—much as the verb for that puttering is a special, longer form of the verb for "walk."*

Then, within the verse, look at the shift from the king's roof to "[the] roof," as if this had no home under it worth mentioning, no location even in relation to David's line of sight, no "across the way" or suchlike; as if it had no significance except in what is going on there visibly right now. Next, there is the shift from simply seeing the woman to seeing her beauty so as to appreciate it fully. "Woman" is repeated as notice grows into definite interest. The second instance of the word for seeing—that word is repeated, too—is enclosed by the words "beautiful/good" and "very," so that the sequence of thought is "Good—now that I really see her—extremely good."

But the big news is how alike yet how different the first two verses are. I'll repeat both literal translations here, with their main elements set out vertically for easier comparison:

and-it-was/happened
at-[the]-return [of] the-year
at-[the]-time/season [of the] to-go-out [of] the-kings
and-sent David Joab and-servants-his with-him and-all [of]
    Israel
and-they-destroyed [the] sons [of] Ammon
and-they-besieged Rabbah
and-David [was] sitting/staying in-Jerusalem.

and-it-was/happened
at-[the]-time/season [of] the-evening
and-got-up David from-on bed-his
and-he-strolled on [the] roof [of the] house [of] the-king
and-he-saw

*There are separate verbal forms for actions that are repetitive, or perhaps even frustrating or pointless, as well as for clearer categories like intensive, causative, passive, and reflexive.

[a] woman bathing from-on the-roof
and-the-woman [was] beautiful/good to-see very.

Both verses start with "and it was/happened," and three more vav consecutives follow, then a participle linked to the noun for a major actor. In the second verse, however, the phrasing then lingers along with David's eye, and the woman's prolonged designation as beautiful hangs tantalizingly at the end of the sentence.

But an even sharper contrast is in the meanings of parallel and formally quite similar verbs across verses 1 and 2. In verse 2, David restlessly gets up from bed instead of waging war as other kings do. Instead of leading the campaign he has set in motion, he walks back and forth. Much unlike his officers and men occupied with destroying and besieging, he sees a woman—and this is the last finite verb. At this point, as in verse 1, everything goes still, or nearly so. The woman's lingering participial "bathing," with its formal sameness to David's "sitting" or "staying" at home, may represent an eerie *comparison:* both these people indulge themselves. (A full-body cleansing was quite a luxury.) They fritter away the time.

This story as a whole is a marvelous illustration of the Hebrew Bible's typical narrative panache as an inflected language. I won't go verse by verse through a number of the tightly woven patterns— I could, but it would take two hundred pages in itself. Instead, I'll just point out a few more characteristic and very effective features.

The stark centrality of verbs—and in Hebrew they suck in subject and direct-object and possessive pronouns, as well as containing a lot of other information—keeps heavy emphasis on the deployment of power. Leaders, especially, do what they want; moment by moment, they choose. Hebrew Bible narratives about them tend even to be free from notions of inborn character or immutable fate or rhetorical weighing of alternatives, as in Classical literature.

English (or even Greek or Latin) cannot really depict, as Hebrew does, the full horror of David deciding and doing, indistinguishably. For one thing, Hebrew can much more thoroughly elide the presence and the activities of the king's subordinates. Granted, the English of the King James in verse 3 ("And David sent and enquired after the woman. And one said, Is not this Bathsheba, the daughter of Eliam, the wife of Uriah the Hittite?") is accurate in showing that David does not send or ask a person or persons but just "sends" and "enquires," as if giving orders to a sort of disembodied servitude around him. But English, significantly, doesn't allow a truly literal translation of the way David is answered: "And-he-said, 'Is-not this [woman] . . . ?' " In the King James English, there is "one [person]"—separate pronoun—doing the saying. In the Hebrew, a separate pronoun is not there. Though information about the speaker (a single one, male) is indeed encased in "and-he-said," Hebrew allows for less strong a sense of the person-ness, if you will, of the person answering David.

As the subordinates are (and are to remain) so shadowy, this response is quite ironic. It is a tentatively, questioningly worded one but contains quite detailed identification about the woman: her name, whose daughter she is, and whose wife, and the ethnicity of her husband. *She's* certainly someone, isn't she? The sentence points up something quite creepy about the story: everyone around David and Bathsheba knows everything, at every stage. That's a cost of being able to open your mouth and cause things to happen.

Moreover, as the story soon shows—especially after verse 17, when Joab subtly but insolently challenges what David has done—this is anything but a totalitarian state, in which far-reaching control of subordinates can protect a leader from their views. David may treat them as objects and use them for evil, but this will only make things worse for him in the long run. We are, significantly, only in the second generation of the kingship here. According to 1 Samuel, chapter 8, the people have begged for a king and been warned by a credible religious leader that they won't like monarchy once they get a taste of it. They became acquainted, through their first king, Saul, with a common hazard of despotism, that the despot may become paranoid. Now the second king, David, is threatening to fulfill Samuel's specific prediction, that a king will exploit the people for his own ends—including appropriating women—and that they won't be able to do anything about it.

But from a Scriptural perspective—and from an actual historical one, as far back as it's possible to see—this is not the basic character of the nation. A political leader (or a religious one, or a combination of both), no matter how powerful, was never the ultimate authority, never regarded as a god-king. In Scripture, in fact, any great wrongdoing that his great power leads him into will result in a punishment packed with drama and ironic edification. Traditional Hebrew narrative downplays the eyes that see and the minds that predict what is coming but doesn't allow the reader to forget they're there. All this makes their vindication in the end more impressive. God has not neglected them, any more than he has neglected wrongdoing.

Here, that spring is wound very tightly. Not only does *vai-hee* show up again at the beginning of 2 Samuel 11:14 and 16, the two most blameworthy turns in the action, but the employment of another extremely common vav consecutive, *vai-yōmer*, "and he said" (already heard in David's exchange with the servant), helps create strong tensions.

Like *vai-hee*, *vai-yōmer* ("and-he-said") normally heads up a clause; unlike *vai-hee*, of course, it is often closely followed by the explicit subject of the verb: "And-said Speaker A . . . , and-said Speaker B . . ." is the typical form of dialogue, creating far different emphases than dialogue in English literature tends to. In Hebrew, the act of speaking and the identity of the speaker (if named) usually take precedence as information.

The medium is very much the message here. It suggests what linguists and anthropologists say about "speech acts," that very special category of performance such as oaths. A speech act, in itself, creates consequences. ("I take thee, Mary, to be my lawful wedded wife.") It is as a rule far more momentous than questioning, commenting, narrating, or describing. ("Said Simple Simon to the pie man, 'What have you got there?'—'Pies, you twit.'")

Therefore, a great difference in ethical tone is inherent between the Hebrew, which goes essentially, "Now there was speaking; So-and-So was doing it," and modern literary lines of dialogue, some standing alone without even a verb of speaking, most others with verbs of speaking and speech attributions only in the middle or at the end, and some with verbs of speaking that suggest that the important thing is the speaker's mood or personality. ("'It has been my experience that folks who have no vices have very few virtues,' Abraham Lincoln quipped.")

For modern dialogue that really drives home the implications of the sheer act of speaking, we have to look, tellingly, to theater and film among our own literary art forms—vehicles of performance, in which a set of subordinate components (lighting, physical background, costume, music, dance, facial expressions, etc., very roughly analogous to the intricate arrangements of words we can still see in the Hebrew text) sets off the two central components, speaking and acting, in such a way as to squeeze the most oomph out of that primal source of hope and horror: people speak and act.

Such drama is plentiful in the story of David and Bathsheba. In verse 7, David's questioning of Uriah, as a pretext for summoning him, sounds quite a bit more idiotic in Hebrew than in an English translation ("And when Uriah was come unto him, David demanded of him how Joab did, and how the people did, and how the war prospered"). First, after a mini-buildup of "and-inquired David" (with an initial vav consecutive similar to *vai-yōmer*), the king's actual questions are, literally, about the *shalōm* of Joab and the *shalōm* of the people and the *shalōm* of the army. We are used to the translation "peace" for *shalōm,* and that can sometimes work in Classical Hebrew (not here, of course, concerning the activities of a military expedition). But more commonly, the word means "welfare," "wholeness," or something like that, and an ordinary courteous inquiry goes (sort of), "Does So-and-So have *shalōm?*" Uriah must wonder why he was summoned for such a bland interrogation, which in fact points up, through its dense, singsong repetition as represented in the original language, the waste of everyone's time.

Worse, Uriah is a subordinate commander and a foreigner. He can't figure out why it's he who's been brought all this distance to be so softly but lingeringly drilled. What's going on? The text contains nothing of his reply and doesn't need to: we can intuit a reply that it is broad, cautious, content-free. The Hebrew text allows Uriah a dignified silence instead of putting an equally inane speech into his mouth: "And-said Uriah, 'Welfare [is] with-Joab. . . .'"

Nor, in verse 8 ("And David said to Uriah, Go down to thy house, and wash thy feet . . ."), is he shown assenting or not when David tries to jolly him toward spending the night at home—starting this speech with the first of several formulaic *vai-yōmer*s written around their interaction. "To wash the feet" is a Hebrew euphemism for having sex. "Go back to your house and have a nice time with your wife" is the effective command. I was brought here in order to *have sex with my wife?* Uriah must ask himself. What *is* this? A test of my loyalty and commitment? Perhaps not voicing his intentions at all, so as to avoid open defiance, he leaves the palace only to rough it all night in the servants' quarters or the guardhouse (verse 9)—letting members of the king's household keep an eye on him.

In verse 10, the disembodied voices of subordinates again report to David, and this time, when the king delivers his challenge to Uriah after *vai-yōmer*—the rhythmic stateliness of this dialogue framing is starting to look, in comparison to the dialogue's content, kind of farcical—Uriah replies in kind, with the same lead-in (verse 11); but the author includes a pointed "to David" (who else would Uriah be talking to?) and a long, passionate speech to cut through David's palaver: "The ark, and Israel, and Judah, abide in tents; and my lord Joab, and the servants of my lord, are encamped in the open fields; shall I then go into mine house, to eat and to drink, and to lie with my wife? As thou liveth, and as thy soul liveth, I will not do this thing."

The Hebrew of Uriah's speech is a striking contrast to ordinary narrative diction, in which this story has been set up and is to continue, as David administrates himself further and further into trouble. Instead of a clause opening with a finite verb followed by its subject, Uriah uses three grand nouns and a participle ("[are] sitting/staying") for what these entities are doing—and it's the same verb that's used, in a participial form there as well, for David at the end of verse 1; but what a contrast with David's lingering in Jerusalem. Next, it's the very deferentially named Joab and the officers or men (or both), who, in syntactic parallel to the Ark, Israel, and Judah, "[are] camping" on the open plain. When we finally get a finite verb, it's for the unthinkable thing Uriah *won't* do under these circumstances: go home—the way he *won't* act to upset this honorable stasis. The outburst so far goes literally like this: "The-Ark and-Israel and-Judah [are] sitting/staying in-the-tents/sheds and lord-my Joab and-[the]-servants [of] lord-my on [the] face [of] the-field [are] camping and-I will-go to house-my to-eat and-to-drink and-to-lie with my-wife . . . ?" Uriah, notably, brushes aside euphemism and names the act as it was named when David did it with the same woman (verse 4).

At the end of verse 11, Uriah swears an oath, not on his own life and soul but on that of his adopted king. Usually a destructive outcome of an oath, in the event of nonperformance, is for the speaker; but Uriah, with ironic foreshadowing, in effect calls down disaster on his ruler, not himself. Speaking of speech acts, an oath is the ultimate one; and in this case, as if we needed a reminder of the closeness of words and action as depicted in Hebrew, Uriah literally winds up with, "if I-do this thing/word/action." It's the same term, and the one used in "The word of the Lord came" to a patriarch or prophet. "Word" can point to momentous intentionality and responsibility. It is David's "word/action" in commandeering Bathsheba and killing her husband that God disapproves of (verse 27).

In verse 12, David's *vai-yōmer* answer to Uriah's speech is feeble: an order to stay another day; and he tries to soften up this dedicated man with food and drink. Uriah is again shown as wordless, only carrying the words of his own doom back to his commander in a sealed letter (verse 14). More creepy verbal sparring occurs when the messenger returns with news of his death—this time with both parties understanding exactly what has happened, and each knowing that the other knows (verses 22–25). When Nathan shows up in the next chapter with his own verbal snare, telling the story of a powerful man who murders a weak one in order to slaughter and consume his cherished pet instead of an animal out of his own abundant herds, David bursts out in smug, unthinking anger, swearing by God that the man must die because he did "this thing/word" (12:6). Like David, the fictional man doesn't need to do the dirty work himself, but can use words to make other people do it. In the Bible, the only being who can't go wrong in speaking and causing things to happen is God.

David is to endure the slow death of his and Bathsheba's child, and then he must face the violent and humiliating loss of his kingdom, including the appropriation of his own concubines by his son, Absalom (2 Samuel 16:21–22), who is reacting to his sister Tamar's rape—which was known to David but went unpunished by him, because the rapist was his eldest son. Absalom promises justice and equality under his own rule (15:4).

It's critical to register what this passage may have been at its historical core: an ugly court scandal. The early kingdom was, and either part of the divided kingdom continued to be, an autocracy (though, as I've noted, not a god-kingship), with autocrats inevitably behaving badly and subjects typically having little recourse but to remember. It's hardly surprising that the rage in the mind(s) behind this composition is expressed with stealth. But this is a strong stealth, built up in a very careful pattern, which plays an indispensable role in the story's becoming far more than gossip or a trivial homily. This occurs through the tight fusing of manner and matter, style and substance, story and message.

*

In all the special intricacies that a highly inflected language allows, New Testament Greek is like ancient Hebrew, only more so—or, at any rate, because the depth to which a language can be read depends on the evidence available, scholars can *tell* more about the stunts Greek pulls. The Greek of the New Testament has a vast context in surviving pagan literature and the known social history of the Greco-Roman world, so it's clear how hard there the producers of formal language worked, and how demanding the consumers were.

Particularly important was rhetoric, the art of speaking and writing, which was vital to the conduct of public life. Rhetoric was the basis for all prose literature, even what we might consider private and analytical, such as history. Herodotus, "the first historian," read out loud from his work in public in Athens in the fifth century B.C.E.; it was a performance, whose charms we can intuit from the surviving text. In ancient Classical literature, there was no hard distinction between poetic and rhetorical devices. Many of us learned in school that simile, metaphor, and personification—that somewhat cartoonish trio—are "poetic" devices. Well, they weren't alien even to Greek and Roman scientific prose; and the poetry is crammed with rhetorical phenomena that have classifications suggesting rare butterflies, like "antimetabole."

Granted, it's a good question exactly how much pagan literary sentiment and practice penetrated the New Testament, which was of course about much more than individual literary skill exuberantly flaunted and passionately vetted. But Koinē Greek *was* the same basic language as that of Sophocles. It had a similar propensity for dance-ability, for exuberant rhythms that suited public recitation.

What's more, in early Christianity the Greek language arrived full circle back at a state somewhat like the one it evinces in the early "Homeric" hymns, which are full of the formulaic language and religious preoccupations that go so well together. In the New Testament also there is a compositional tension between, on the one hand, inherently cautious conservatism in telling of the unseen, and

in melding together traditional material from multiple sources;*
and, on the other hand, impetuous efforts to create a dramatically
appealing work that could defeat the ranks of competition (much
of it saying more or less the same things) and become a beloved,
official, authoritative text. And it's my strong feeling, as both a poet
and a student of literature, that in Homer, the Old Testament, and
the New Testament, the simultaneous cohesion and flexibility of an
inflected language gave the means to manipulate even traditional,
formulaic phrasing—especially through word order—to produce
resounding effects.

Here is an instance of Greek-speaking early Christians' turning a
short piece of cryptography into a poem, through the arrangement
of formulaic language alone.

A plausible legend says that the outline of a fish stood for Christianity and could be drawn in the dust for covert mutual identification during persecutions, because the Greek word for "fish" is an
anagram of the Greek words for "Jesus Christ Son of God Savior."
So far, so much like a movie that Charlton Heston stars in. But if
he knew of the exquisite expressiveness of the anagram, Charlton
would lift his lip and draw down his eyebrows in that inimitable
way, staring with his teeth as if at the ultimate pagan decadence.

If the anagram is read out loud—*Yeisūs Christos theh-ū hwios
sōteir*—a powerful rhythm emerges. Only a moderate number of Greek nouns accent the final syllable, yet every one of the
two-syllable words here is so accented. It's a chant. And there's an
interlocking pattern of *ū* and *os* sounds in four of those accented
syllables, and a matching *ei* vowel sound at the beginning and end
syllables of the whole phrase.

But, you may object, there wasn't much room to move in designating Jesus—these are just his most important epithets, presented
in a mandatory-looking way. Ah, but Greek, as a highly inflected
language, had the malleability to make the formulaic powerfully
witty through word order alone. In this case, there appears to be a
poetically theological sneak-attack.

First comes the word "Jesus." This was one of the most com-

---

*I say this even of Paul of Tarsus, who, though he was a true original author, came
late to the apostolic scene and had to deal with many things that had been said if
not written already about the new religious movement—and of course he drew on
Jewish Scripture, primarily that of the Septuagint Greek translation.

mon names in Palestine, a region stereotyped for its foreign oddity. Early on, ancient Europeans probably perceived "Jesus" somewhat as Americans used to perceive "José" or "Pierre": as a cliché label for an outsider. To Palestinian Jews, however, who were numerous among early followers of Jesus, his name was more like "Bob" or "John"—which might help explain the violent controversy that raged once Jesus's followers tried to establish themselves within Judaism and recruit other Jews. Imagine being asked to come follow "Bob" on the "Road"—and he doesn't even have a full name. To believers, he would not have been "Jesus the Son of Joseph," because, well, get this—

Now the anagram starts to swell in its claims: he's Jesus/Pierre/ Bob the Anointed: he has had ceremonial oil poured over his head, as King David had. He has been anointed by God, and God is the next word, but that single word is in the genitive form, signifying "of God," and the next word is "son"—here's your patronymic! The words aren't in themselves an outrage: "son of God" was an established Jewish honorific. But as such it *wasn't* meant literally, that's for darn tootin'. That's, however, the way the Christians meant it—and they didn't mean it in the Greco-Roman sense either, designating a half-divine hero, the offspring—mortal himself—of a philandering Olympian by a mortal woman. They meant that the sole, all-powerful God had a son, human but also divine like himself, as divine as a son of two homo sapiens would be mortal, yet here's what he did with him, the last word of the anagram.

Jesus is the savior. By dying in the flesh, he delivered humankind from death, which is—as both Jews and pagans faced with this statement might have noticed—more than his father himself was supposed to have done for humankind by any means. Oh, you crazy Greek speakers! The buildup is like a slow explosion, from the ordinary name of a crucified criminal to the hope of the universe. It is five short words of total defiance—and, as usual, you can dance to it.

Imagine what Biblical Greek could do in an important passage several verses long, such as the Lord's Prayer. The commonly used version, in Matthew 6:9–13, is a particularly good example of the expressive power of an inflected language.

But first, some background. The "harmony of the Gospels" is a major issue in New Testament studies: the four stories of Jesus's life and teachings—the Books of Matthew, Mark, Luke, and John—have a number of parallel passages but are almost nowhere identical, which naturally undercuts them all as documentary history. But because the news of the resurrection changed everything, starting a millennia-long scramble to explain why Jesus was more than history, more than another wandering preacher and healer or political leader, Christians prefer passages of the Gospels that are (however inauthentically) elaborated, as long as that elaboration serves to explain more. This is why the Matthew Lord's Prayer has been preferred over the Lord's Prayer in Luke 11:2–4. We like passages that make more sense of events and bind that sense together with fuller word patterns, so that we not only tell ourselves why but can more easily remember, recite, sing, and be comforted by that why.

Science and religion are not so very far apart in this respect. A bare, isolated fact is pretty useless; such a fact in an intrusive, alarming form (a hurricane, a sharp drop in genetic diversity in a region, or the disappearance of a corpse from its sealed tomb) demands an explanation, and the explanation is likely to be more formal, more patterned, more intricate the more important it is. Your peer-reviewed, published research *will* include a Methods section, so that everyone can see how you set up the experiment or observation. Your traditional prayer *will,* among other things, invoke the deity quite specifically, and according to a well-established formula, so that there is no confusion. For the same reason, you will clearly indicate when the prayer is over and you return to mundane life.

Here are the Matthew and Luke Lord's Prayers (in that order) in the King James translation.* In Part Three, the full literal translation in English and the full phonetic transliteration of the Greek are set out in short lines, like poetry, because the Greek editions set them out this way.

Check out how much more prayer appears in the King James Version of *both* passages, reflecting how many Greek words were added onto the texts even after they diverged into two quite distinct versions of what Jesus said. This made for very "corrupt" bases for

---

*It's important to note, however, that the last clause ("For thine is the kingdom . . .") of Matthew 6:13 is absent in Catholic Bibles; this is one place where the Protestant and Catholic Scriptures are significantly different.

early English translation; and since some corruptions became part of the liturgy, later translators have naturally been shy about "correcting" them. But now we all have the cleaned-up Nestle-Aland Greek New Testament to work with, and I have used it alone for my own experimental literary translation, shown in Part Two.

But I'm going to concentrate here on how much fuller, in the most plausible version of the original text, the Matthew prayer (which is, again, the first of the two King James passages below) is than the Luke one. These differences came about because the prayer as prescribed by Jesus flowered and seeded itself, so to speak.

Matthew 6:9–13

9 . . . Our Father which art in heaven, Hallowed be thy name.

10 Thy kingdom come, Thy will be done in earth, as it is in heaven.

11 Give us this day our daily bread.

12 And forgive us our debts, as we forgive our debtors.

13 And lead us not into temptation, but deliver us from evil: For thine is the kingdom, and the power, and the glory for ever. Amen.

Luke 11:2–4

2 . . . Our Father which art in heaven, Hallowed be thy name. Thy kingdom come. Thy will be done, as in heaven, so in earth.

3 Give us day by day our daily bread.

4 And forgive us our sins; for we also forgive every one that is indebted to us. And lead us not into temptation; but deliver us from evil.

In Matthew 6:7–8, Jesus says, as a prelude to assigning the prayer in that Gospel, "But when ye pray, use not vain repetitions, as the heathen do: for they think that they shall be heard for their much speaking. Be not ye therefore like unto them: for your Father knoweth what things ye have need of, before ye ask him." Is Jesus's special disapproval directed at cosmopolitan, Hellenized Jews who prayed to their own Jewish God in Greek, a language that, besides coming from a pagan (= "heathen") culture, was highly developed for literary display and competition?* This might well bother a Jewish reformer from the local backwater of Galilee; Hellenizing influences weren't absent there, but they would have stood out more sharply than elsewhere. Consider also that Jesus has shown himself concerned that prayer be humble and private, not a self-aggrandizing public production (6:5–6).

All this suggests certain looming paradoxes in these two Lord's Prayers. Both are written in Greek, of course, not Jesus's own Semitic language, Aramaic (closely related to Hebrew). Moreover, following Jesus's strictures in Matthew, we get the version of the Lord's Prayer that reflects them less than does the shorter, simpler Lord's Prayer in Luke, which is also shown as a response to the request to be taught how to pray, but is set out without any comments as to the proper manner or form of prayer. But on the pretty solid principle that New Testament passages tended to be added onto over time, rather than stripped down, it's the more elaborate, repetitious, formulaic Matthew Lord's Prayer that's less authentic than the Luke Lord's Prayer—which itself appeared in many manuscripts in longer renditions that the modern scholarly text shows.

In the most plausible Greek version of the Luke Lord's Prayer, nothing is said (for example) of "the sky" or "skies" or "heaven" at all, let alone twice, ring-compositionally, at the beginning and end of the prayer's first verse ("Our Father which art in heaven, Hallowed be thy name. Thy kingdom come. Thy will be done, as in heaven, so in earth.") The posited original Matthew Lord's Prayer, for its part, is missing the whole crescendo of praise at the end in verse 13 of the King James translation, "For thine is the kingdom, and the power, and the glory for ever. Amen."

Am I outraged? Am I saying, "Tsk, tsk"? Hardly. In fact, I'm risking the fury of other Christians by writing that, well, preferring brief, simple prayers in the confidence that God already knew what was needed and would certainly provide it was easier for Jesus than for ordinary believers, wasn't it? To my mind, a significant boon of his words' coming to us through a long Scriptural tradition, and in another language from near the start, is the greater allowance

---

*In fact, the Psalms as quoted in Greek in the New Testament look to me almost like the lyrics of Broadway musicals: they are sometimes bunched into stanzas with an overt, jingly structure.

for Christians to quietly act on a sense of their own more extensive needs. They need, in this case, a prayer to teach their children
that can get quickly beyond questions such as " 'Father?' Whose
father? Mine? You? Aren't you my father? If I have another father,
why haven't I ever seen him? Where is he?" They need a prayer that
doesn't end with an image of torture (that's more or less what "temptation," or "testing," in "And lead us not into temptation" would
imply here) but instead rounds itself out in reassurance that, as precarious as things are now, what is permanent is the majestic power
of the creator they've invoked at the beginning. While people are at
it, of course, they will form these changes in patterns more powerful
than the earlier Greek prayer showed, probably *way* more powerful than the Aramaic words of Jesus, with his stress on brevity and
humility.

This is evident in the most obscure details. In the Matthew prayer
in Greek, there are tiny words in the middle of each of the first four
lines (verses 9 and 10):* *hŏ, tŏ, hei, tŏ.* Those are just the definite
article, for "the," in all three genders, in clauses that go, literally,

Matthew 6:9–10
9 father of-us, *the* [one] in the skies/heavens   (1)
   let-be-made-holy *the* name of-you   (2)
10 let-come *the* kingdom of-you   (3)
   let-come-into-being *the* wanting of-you   (4)
   as in [the] sky/heaven also/even on land/earth   (5)

The article occurs in the order masculine, neuter, feminine, neuter. The middle of a clause tends to be a place of less emphasis than
the beginning or the end, but even here, repetition with variation is
at play. In the more authentic-looking Luke prayer, there is patterning with the article, but it is less fancy patterning.

In Matthew, the second through fourth lines each begin with a
similar-sounding jussive verb ("let such and such happen"—expressed
in one word), and each ends with a noun and the pronoun for

---

*I am going by the Greek layout—and I follow it throughout my literal translation
and transliteration in Part Three—not the much later verse numbers, shown everywhere in my book on the left, as is conventional.

"of-you"—weighing the first part of the prayer strongly in favor of God, who is "of-us" only in the second word of the first line.*

Earlier in chapter 6 of Matthew, as I've noted, Jesus has warned against religious hypocrisy, which to him means praying in public as well as displays of charity. Instead, he commands, shut yourself up in your room and pray in secret (verse 6). But Jesus was a Jew, and Judaism was a communal religion—so in fact were the main pagan religions of the wider Roman Empire; only the edgy "mystery" religions were primarily about a special, individual relationship with divinity. It's significant in the Lord's Prayer, and stressed more in the Matthew one with all its repetitions of us-ness, that the sincere worshipper, though she's supposed to be completely alone or even furtive, does not in a single line pray for herself as an individual, but always for the entire community.

The deployment of the pronoun for "we" is very expressive in the prayer's second half—and again, particularly in the Matthew version. Here is the literal English:

11 the loaf/bread *of-us* the [one] coming-on give *to-us* today (1)
12 and let-go *to-us* the debts *of-us* (2)
      as also/even *we* [have?] let-go to-the debtors *of-us* (3)
13 and do-not [please] into-bring *us* into testing (4)
      but save *us* from the evil [one] (5)

For the Greeks, "we," "us," "to us," and "of us" were a single word, *heim-*, which varied only in its ending—hence there is a much more extensive repetition of sounds than we see in the English. The plea of the prayer's first line, that the addressee is the father "of us," is picked up later in a frantic stress on the idea of "we," God's people. The word occurs eight times in five short clauses as the speaker pleads for the collective gift of food, for the collective forgiveness of sins (in exchange for collectively forgiving each other), and for the collective exemption from what the King James calls "temptation." But the emotion does not get in the way of careful patterning. Note,

*Classical Greek prefers possessive *adjectives* such as "your" and "our"; New Testament Greek's possessive *pronouns* are stronger both in their longer vowel sounds and in their position after nouns, which is often at the emphatic end of a phrase, clause, or sentence.

in the literal translation, the parallel positions of "we" words: three times they are the third word in a clause, twice (in the same form) the final word.

The word *kai*—"and" or "also" or "even"—plays a meaningful role itself. In Matthew, "*kai* on earth" (from verse 10, literally "as in [the] sky/heaven also/even on land/earth") brings the prayer down to human concerns, the humble, urgent needs of humankind in contrast to God's distance, holiness, and power. The King James has the courtly overwriting "in earth, as it is in heaven," but if the emotional weight is to fall (as often) at the end of a line, the translation should be something like "actually on earth."

Other clauses beginning with *kai,* occurring two and then again four lines later (the King James: "And forgive . . . ," "And lead us not") are pretty clunky Greek, even in the colloquial "Common" dialect of the New Testament. This sounds like a child's nervous or hopeful petition ("Oh, and bless Aunt Grace, and also bless Fluffo—and can we go on the roller coaster at the fair on Saturday?"). Between these two lines, the phrase *hōs kai heimeis ahfeikamen* . . . (King James: "as we forgive . . ."—again, the *kai* idea is left out) comes in, for humans acting in obedient imitation of God's mercy: as heaven and earth form a harmonious contrast emphasized by *kai* (verse 10), so do mortals and the deity. The possible "even" meaning for *kai* might be a special source of plaintiveness in both lines. God is present and powerful "even" down here on earth. "Even" we can strive to behave as God does, forgiving all wrongs.

There was never any solid justification for the translation "daily bread" (Matthew 6:11 and Luke 11:3: literally "the loaf/bread of-us the [one] coming-on give to-us . . ."), as the only material thing the faithful ask for. The adjective (perhaps) means "coming on" and could refer to either tomorrow's food or to rations, but in any case the pairing of the word in Matthew with "today" and in Luke with "day by day" in the same lines suggests anxiety—the speaker wants to know that the food will be here on schedule. Moreover, this isn't properly "bread," but "the loaf." Many inhabitants of the Roman Empire would have pictured a regulation loaf from the public dole or household rations. The word as a collective singular for "bread," however, often occurred in such expressions as "eating the bread of slavery"—the usual sense being that this was essential, *very* basic food.

Fittingly, the syntax suddenly changes here in Matthew 6:11 (as in Luke 11:3), in the plea for bread. Instead of a quite abstract and impersonal verb coming first, the noun for "bread" does. Again, the verse goes, "the loaf/bread of-us the [one] coming-on give to-us . . ." The attention fixes on that loaf. The verb "give" follows its direct object, the long phrase "the loaf/bread of-us the [one] coming-on" in both Matthew and Luke; both Gospels then add a redundant-looking "to us" after "give": the loaf "is ours," but not really, unless God acts. Here, also, the verbal form switches from the more circumspect jussive ("Let such and such happen") of previous lines, and becomes a straight imperative ("Do this"). Though it's not the same tense of the imperative in both versions, in both the meaning is stark: Give us our food, God.

The "debts" to be forgiven by God and between human beings in Matthew (verse 12: literally, "and let-go to-us the debts of-us / as also/even we [have?] let-go to-the debtors of-us"; compare verse 4 in Luke) are usually taken as a metaphor for sins (and are often translated as "trespasses"), but I think the actual debt crisis at the time the prayer arose is worth considering. To those just getting by—or not getting by—in ancient Palestine, debt meant they could be thrown off their land, or kept on it as struggling (and probably soon re-indebted) tenants once the lender seized the plot, or maybe forced to give up their children or themselves as slaves to settle the account. In several components, this verse echoes the previous one, the plea for bread, which is about survival. There is a plain imperative verb, and a "to us" and an "of us" (though in the Greek the order is different): God is to "let-go to-us" (= separate us from) these terrible entities that are (alas) "of-us" (we could almost read, "fastened to us").

"As we forgive" isn't in an ordinary present tense, the way it's translated. This is an aorist; as to time, it normally refers to the simple past, but can also be used to indicate a generally occurring event. In either case, we could understand a special force in the condition that we forgive. Only once we've forgiven, and not before, can we expect forgiveness; or we must forgive as a rule. Moreover, there's *kai heimeis* to consider, probably "even we"; the King James takes no account of the *kai* and reads simply "as we forgive." (In Luke, *kai gar owtoi* is more like "as in fact [we] ourselves.")

In any event, in the Greek there is a weight on the human duty that's invisible or even distorted in English translations. "Do this, as we do it" sounds almost like an attempt to stipulate an equal exchange with God. The Greek words, in contrast, seem to contain all the wild drama of basic Christian theology, expressed by John Newton (the coauthor of the hymn "Amazing Grace") as "I remember two things: that I am a great sinner, and that Christ is a great Saviour."

The first line in Matthew 6:13 (the last of Luke 11:4) is mistranslated with true abandon as "And lead us not into temptation." In this context, there are only two plausible sets of images for *peirasmon,* the Greek word for "temptation" or testing: hardships that test character and commitment, and judicial or administrative investigation, which could include torture. (The basic verbal idea of the *peir-* root is "to see what someone/something is made of"—sacrilegiously in the case of a divinity, aggressively in the case of another person.) I favor the latter set of images as more plausibly grounded in the urgent concerns of New Testament readers.

Only Roman citizens, with their high status, were immune from inquisitorial abuse and extreme punishments. When Christians, a mainly lower-class and servile group, systematically refused to sacrifice to an image of the Roman emperor as a god, routine enforcement of norms could turn into elaborate persecutions. Christians were tortured sadistically, often in public, in efforts to make them recant their beliefs and conform, and to name other Christians. This must be what they begged in this prayer to be spared—no longer begging with the imperative of command, but with the subjunctive of a respectful request. Please God, do not bring us into testing. Given the Greek verb "into-bring," with the supplementary, repetitive preposition "into" coming after it, there may be an actual suggestion of the torture chamber door or the archway into the amphitheater: you are led through it to unspeakable agony. But in any case this is very certainly not a plea to be spared enticements to forbidden self-indulgence, the prevailing modern meaning.

If Christianity offered the ultimate comfort, eternal life in exchange for faith alone, it also offered the ultimate precipice. There was no sure providence on earth, no guarantee of favor for the righteous, but rather extra suffering and danger, and perhaps a shameful, excruciating death like Jesus's own. In Matthew, chapter 6, in the famous "lilies of the field" passage, Jesus assures his followers that God will provide the necessities of life for them—or more precisely, he protests that worrying will not help: in the logical course of things, given their lofty position in creation, they can expect to do at least as well as wild birds and flowering weeds (verses 25–30). But here in the Lord's Prayer, they are taught to *ask* for survival rations, for the "loaf" making its painful way toward them. Forgiveness of sins is a promise, but a dauntingly contingent one. And they can ask to be spared a terrible death, but Jesus himself asked his father (Mark 14:36, Luke 22:42) for the same thing and was rebuffed.

The Matthew prayer continues, while the one in Luke (or the best reconstructed—or deconstructed—version of it) stops here. *Ahlla* in Matthew (second line of verse 13) is a strong "but": I might write, "But at least save us from the devil." At this point, the pleading descends to the ultimate pathos. Even as scholars have recognized the great likelihood that this is a personality, not evil in the abstract,* Western translators and church hierarchies have remained squeamish, and in Bibles and church services I still encounter an unlikely request for deliverance from a vague "evil" that speakers of the prayer may imagine to be the same thing as "temptation." But no, originally the children beg their father to save them from the monster.

Then, according to the most reliable manuscript evidence, even the Matthew prayer goes silent—and in the Catholic tradition it remains so. It is at this point much fuller than the Luke prayer, but still shows a chilly confidence in a dispensation that's on balance quite negative. Among very early Greco-Roman Christians, both prayers probably found resonance in stern pagan philosophical theories of the proper relation to the divine. It is unwise to pray for anything but "a healthy mind in a healthy body." The gods may haul off and slam you with the full punishment of fulfilling your wishes, with beauty that gets you raped, wealth that gets you robbed and murdered, and so on.

But it's *our* Bible; people added what they needed, and some added a whole verse's worth of words onto the prayer in Matthew. These words (a prolongation of verse 13 in the King James) are a

---

*This grammatical form of the words "the evil [one/thing]" does not allow certainty as to whether this entity is neuter or masculine, but in most places where the form occurs, the context dictates that it's masculine.

ring-compositional shift back to God's majesty and power, and in the King James are translated, "For thine is the kingdom, and the power, and the glory, for ever. Amen." ("Amen" is Hebrew for "truly.") We can expect to be saved from the devil because of this deity we invoked already, but now there is more of the deity: he has not only a kingdom but power and glory. In the Greek, his possessive pronoun shifts from the end (verses 9–10, lines 2–4) to the front, because these things emphatically belong to him. And God is not just an entity coming into manifestation, invisible in the sky but with a name to be blessed, a kingdom to arrive, and a will to be enacted. His kingdom, power, and glory simply *are,* now and through eternity—with an emphasis on eternity: the expression that means literally "into the ages of-the ages" is particularly fervent and poetic. The way the end of the prayer clings and prolongs itself makes me think of Genesis 32:26, in which Jacob says to the angel, "I will not let thee go, except thou bless me."

2

Magic Words: Vocabulary

Genesis 1:1–5
John 1:1–14

While I was waiting in a CVS for a prescription, I noticed a stand of religious books. Most were inspirational and didn't appeal—I dislike people's efforts to inspire me in the same ways they try to sell me time-shares or skin cream—but my eye fell on a paperback copy of *Foxe's Book of Martyrs,* which is a sort of anti-Catholic Lives of the Saints, from the mid-sixteenth century. I had heard about the book somewhere, so out of sheer curiosity I laid a copy down by the cash register beside my overpriced antacid.

It didn't turn out to be an antacid book. John Foxe *hated* popery and delighted in showing his Protestant heroes patiently suffering the gratuitous spite of the Romish clergy. But there is nothing tedious, nothing of the Letter to the Editor or the Complaint to Management in his screeds, but rather plenty of lively encomium and invective. Here is how Foxe depicts the dissenter (and early translator of the Bible) John Wycliffe first coming before an ecclesiastical court, at St. Paul's in London in 1377:

> At last, after much wrestling, they pierced through and came to Our Lady's Chapel, where the dukes and barons were sitting together with the archbishops and other bishops; before whom Wickliff [*sic*], according to the manner, stood, to know what should be laid unto him. To whom first spake the Lord Percy, bidding him to sit down, saying that he had many things to answer to, and therefore had need of some softer seat. But the Bishop of London, cast eftsoons into a fumish chafe by those words, said he should not sit there.

"Cast eftsoons into a fumish chafe"—the words were beyond wonderful to me. The first two were obviously on the Northern European side of modern English's heritage. I checked my *Compact Edition of the Oxford English Dictionary* (which has 4,116 miniaturized pages and comes with a little magnifying glass) and found that "cast" is from Old Norse; it replaced, for ordinary usage, a word from Old English for throwing, which we still possess as "warp."

"Fumish" is from the French noun *fume,* for "smoke," but also calls to mind the Latin source of that word, *fuma,* with which any educated man would have been familiar. Only a half-learnèd varlet would have associated the existing Old English–derived word "smoky" with the gaseous exhalations from internal "humors" that caused the Bishop of London to snarl at Wycliffe. But a cute thing about "fumish" is the Germanic ending (it would be *-isch* on a modern German adjective). The word is a high-flown but clumsy bit of evolution, like a pelican, which can resemble an industrial flange making its way through the air above a lagoon. "Chafe" comes from Old French, and originally the verb meant not "rub" but "warm" (as still signaled by "chafing dish"); by Foxe's time, it already had a long history as "excite" and "inflame emotionally."

We're before the time of Shakespeare here, and already even authors who weren't stretching for poetic effect could do all *kinds* of things with English vocabulary. In contrast, the vocabularies of the original Biblical languages, Hebrew and Greek, are tiny by our standards and monotonous to our ears and intellects. To some extent, it's obvious how a translator like me can make a credible effort. The roughly 170,000 words of currently used English have to be cannily deployed in representing languages that expressed their subtleties by other means than word choice, such as word order. I choose whichever English expression—and *Roget's Thesaurus* may offer pages' worth of choices under a single conceptual heading—seems most appropriate in a particular "context."

Take some of the most basic vocabulary that exists in any language, the terms for family relationships. In my *Roget's* I find five categories under the index heading "offspring," which covers a multitude of words from "tad" to "progeny." These resources have to be squared somehow with, first, Hebrew, which works the opposite way; it's not the array of words in one essential category but a lexicon's entry for a single essential word that's likely to look immense.

"Sons" may stand for children of both sexes or young men as such; "son" can be a descendant, a word of endearment, the young of an animal, or a member of any kind of group. The word is used in designating how old someone is. Often it is used metaphorically, and some translators render the Hebrew for "son" as "of"—which is at least convenient, because Classical Hebrew doesn't have a common word for "of," but rather usually constructs the concept out of grammar and syntax, as Greek does. So what on earth does it mean in Genesis that the "sons of God" mated with the "daughters of men" in Genesis 6:4?

Here is a combined Hebrew-Greek example of the role multivalent vocabulary played in the development of religious ideas, making great caution necessary for translation. The King James translation of Isaiah 7:14 goes, "Therefore the Lord himself shall give you a sign; Behold, a virgin shall conceive, and bear a son, and shall call his name Immanuel." The tale of the virgin birth is nowadays often traced back to a mistake in translating that verse for the Septuagint, the Greek version of the Old Testament: the Hebrew is supposed to mean simply "young girl," whereas the Greek is supposed to mean a physical virgin, with an intact hymen. This pseudo-scholarly urban legend, however, is based on the false notion that Hebrew and Greek words had the kind of narrow meanings characteristic of English words.

In reality, the Hebrew word (*ahlma*) concentrates on the sexual ripeness of a human female but doesn't indicate whether she's married or not, or even whether she's already a mother or not. The modern English "young girl" is actually too restrictive! The Greek word (*parthenos*) is about the female in question being unmarried, but it doesn't stipulate that she's had no sexual experience—the Greeks actually weren't too sure what a hymen was—and she, too, may be a mother already.

If, in such a murky sea of meanings, a reader strives to see this person in Isaiah more objectively with the help of the much touted *context,* she may find the confusion multiplied. What happens if the meaning of word A is contingent on the meaning of word B, but both meanings are uncertain? What is this "sign" Isaiah had in mind? Is it a mere "pledge" of blessings to come (as every hopeful pregnancy is—hence an old and widespread metaphor), or is it a "miracle" (an interpretation that would have solid literary support, too)?

Now I'm going entirely to the Greek side for a vocabulary conundrum. When exactly does *gunē* in Greek mean "woman," and when does it mean "wife"? It's the same word—as in Hebrew, French, German, and who knows how many other languages. True, in ancient cultures nearly all freeborn women married, but sometimes the distinction between married and unmarried is quite important. In 1 Corinthians, chapter 11, for example, Paul urges women/wives always to wear a veil when speaking in the religious assembly—so is he referring to the broader or narrower category of women? In my book *Paul Among the People*, I argue that it's all women without exception, including freedwomen and female slaves, even though current law and custom forbade all slaves to marry officially and perhaps both slave women and freedwomen to wear a veil anywhere. Paul's writings in general persuade me that he didn't mean to reserve this symbol of status, propriety, and protection for women who enjoyed it already.

However, it's just not possible to answer definitively a question such as "Woman or wife?" without strong context along the lines of "So-and-so [a female name] is the *gunē* of so-and-so [a male name]." You want to know what makes the question really annoying in 1 Corinthians, chapter 11? The same Greek word can mean both "man" and "husband," and that word appears here (in verse 3) in connection with *gunē*. So are we to understand that "the man is head/leader of a woman" or that "the husband is head/leader of [his] wife"?

On the opposite side of the vocabulary problem is the occasional word that is *too* specific, too special, too isolated. A limited amount of text frustrates translators here; if we had more text, we could see the word in a greater variety of environments and understand it better. The difficulty gets as bad as the *hapax legomenon* (Greek for "said once"), or word that occurs a single time. I see that the definition varies between "occurring once in a single author or text or corpus," on the one hand, and "occurring once in all of a language's extant literature," on the other; but, well, on the Hebrew side, given that we have just one small corpus of Classical Hebrew literature, it kind of amounts to the same thing.

Scholars can only speculate, for example, as to what was striking about Leah's eyes in Genesis 29:17. Were they an unusual color? Bicolored? Squinting? Nearsighted? Eye disease was rampant in the ancient world, so did *this* form part of the all-important contrast between Leah and her sister Rachel in Jacob's mind? Maybe it's not even a contrast, given the slipperiness of the Hebrew conjunction *v:* "Leah's eyes were [?], and/but Rachel was graceful and beautiful."

But the universal problem of ancient vocabulary is that it's just a different animal, with a different set of habits. In modern English, as a rule, you make sharply conscious, committed choices in wording, assisted by that massive vocabulary; you can be quite exact in getting your point across, but the loss is that you pick one meaning and ditch the others. That's unless you're being clever and ludic, making your readers puzzle and work and risking their irritation. Educated speakers of English, themselves trained for maximum precision, control, and accessibility in expository writing, are seldom in the mood to put up with the opposite qualities in somebody else's writing (unless they're handcuffed to this writing by its sheer beauty and authority, as in the case of James Joyce's *Ulysses*). Puns in this language deserve their reputation, as they tend to sound either childish or pretentious and are most successful if they're sparse. Such is the relative anomaly of reaching between words as compartmentalized as ours tend to be.

But in a typical important word in Hebrew or Greek Scripture, it's all there at once, effortlessly: the obvious meaning on the surface, and some other, altogether different meaning that nevertheless resonates in the context; often something plodding and prosaic that's inextricable from metaphysics. I know I'm on quicksand in asserting anything about the inner experience of the ancients, but I'm convinced that the audiences and readers did subconsciously, if not with conscious enjoyment, what scholars now do laboriously in hindsight, which is to map out large territories of meaning in a single word. On both the Hebrew and the Greek sides, punning could be pretty exuberant, suggesting that concern for the synthetic content of language had a status it no longer does. And everywhere, though performance of literature was important, it was also comparatively quite basic, with little or nothing visual being presented.* If people didn't sport with the words in their imaginations to the full

*The great exceptions, in the form of elaborate public and private dramatic productions, were strictly pagan; the Jewish hierarchy and the Church Fathers loathed the stage. Playacting had, apparently, nothing to do with Scripture during the entire long period I'm concerned with.

extent those words invited them to, they were getting only half or a quarter of a show. What were the still-evident patterns for, if not to offer a species of *whole* show?

In the original of some passages, such as the Genesis creation story and its startling revision in the first chapter of John's Gospel, protean meanings unfold through very few words. KJV Genesis:

> 1:1   In the beginning God created the heaven and the earth.
>
> 2   And the earth was without form, and void; and darkness was upon the face of the deep. And the Spirit of God moved upon the face of the waters.
>
> 3   And God said, Let there be light: and there was light.
>
> 4   And God saw the light, that it was good: and God divided the light from the darkness.
>
> 5   And God called the light Day, and the darkness he called Night. And the evening and the morning were the first day.

In its use of vocabulary, this account of creation is appropriately wide-open, because, well, it's about the origin of everything that exists. But in places it's narrow and specific, because it's also about the unique power of God.

I think it's worth considering, in connection to the first verse, how pared down in its applicability the word "beginning" is in English. The word is probably most resonant in this very passage and in uses associated with it. Still, there are no ready means within the word to dilate on the meaning of "beginning" as the creation of the world: the English term is just about things that start, that didn't happen or exist before. But in the typical way Hebrew does a great deal with a single common word, shadings of *reisheet* (roughly, "beginning") can touch on the social and political (as in "chief") and ritual (as in a firstfruits offering) as well as material (the best in quality). Critically, these meanings tend to overlap, as in commands that the choicest agricultural products, or the fresh, precious "first-fruits" available when the long-awaited harvest season or the birthing season among the herd animals started, be offered to God. I can imagine those closest to the texts, the authors, compilers, and early generations of readers, as well as the renowned Rabbis with their intricate commentary, saying, "What is this crap?" had they been

confronted with the likes of our lexicons, which segregate meanings in little office cubicles of definitions and suggest by that very
layout that there's always just one "answer" as a translation. In any
case, no one is going to convince me that a reader should treat this
Hebrew word as she would treat the English one, ignoring any possibility of an allusion to authority and superiority here, and slapping
her notebook shut after writing "at the earliest time" or something
like that—though the question of what a more nuanced translation
might be does boggle the modern mind.

Meanings in this Hebrew word beyond the most obvious are
even more strongly suggested in the Greek and Latin words used
to translate this passage (and to reflect on it in John, chapter 1—see
below): *archei,* in the Septuagint, is the word for "magistracy" as well
as for "beginning," and *principium* in the Vulgate brings to mind
the *princeps,* the first man or emperor of the Roman world. In fact,
one angle of *principium* is "the most honorable position, first place,
precedence," according to the *Oxford Latin Dictionary.*

Readers may be surprised about the verb in "In the beginning
God created the heaven and the earth." *Bara* is a special word to
depict *God* fashioning and transforming. He has a dedicated verb,
as his creative activities are unique.

As in Greek (and Latin), a single word (Hebrew: *shahma-yim*) is
used here for heaven and for the sky, and I like the way that excludes
from the proper imagery any hint of pearly gates, levitating blond
athletes, supermodels with harps, and so on. But the physical sky
and the defensible imagery of the "place" from which God operates
do share the apparent quality of infinity, so the definitions *should*
coexist. In this case, a translator has a pretty good out if she goes
backward to the archaic English "heavens," which both carries natural sky imagery and suits the technically plural form of the Hebrew
as well as the grammatical plural for "sky/heaven" (*ūrahnoî*) as sometimes (though not in the translation of this verse in the Septuagint)
found in Koinē Greek.

In Genesis 1:2, the earth's primordial condition before God's creative activity, "without form, and void," is shown by two rhyming words of two syllables each, with each word accented on the
first syllable. *Tōhū* and *bōhū* are an ironically harmonious pair, like
"helter-skelter" or "topsy-turvy" in English (though the elements of
these aren't used independently). The first word encompasses ideas

of formlessness, confusion, unreality, and emptiness, and the second concentrates on emptiness.

In English there are prevailing distinct expressions for these qualities, according to whether the qualities are physical, intellectual, or moral: for example, "void" vs. "inanity" vs. "vanity" (this latter from the Latin word for "emptiness"); or "turbulence" vs. "confusion" vs. "messed up." The different English words are by no means stuck fast in their particular frames of reference; a number of them can migrate back and forth, as when we speak of an agreement that's "null and void," or of "a moral void," as well as of "the void" of outer space. But the fact that we often have to include qualification when a word is off its home turf is significant: it *has* a home turf.

With these two Hebrew words, not so much. *Tōhū* seems to be an equally solid way to express the idea of a blank or chaotic space *and* a groundless argument or religious practice *and* moral depravity. *Bōhū* looks more like a physically descriptive word, but both its uses elsewhere in the Bible, also in pairings with *tōhū,* are deeply suggestive concerning God's judgment and his destruction of the land and its people as a punishment for heedless, morally degrading foolishness: the people must suffer in material form what goes on in their minds and hearts. In one case, that of Jeremiah 4:23, the verse immediately before reads, "For my people is foolish, they have not known me [God]; they are sottish [= idiotic] children, and they have none understanding: they are wise to do evil, but to do good they have no knowledge."

I'm going to wax poetic about the imagery of darkness in my Chapter 4, but here I'll just start by noting that *chōshek* (the word coming immediately after the black hole–ish *tōhū* and *bōhū* in Genesis 1:2) has as one of its definitions (in the *Brown-Driver-Briggs Hebrew and English Lexicon*) "extraordinary darkness" and as another "cosmic" darkness (in *The Hebrew and Aramaic Lexicon of the Old Testament* by Koehler and Baumgartner)—and I'm not surprised. Classical Hebrew literature has a particular interest in the lack of light, deploying several words for it, and these seem to have hardly any mundane content, as in recording when the sky naturally got dark, and how dark. The words depict darkness mostly as a divine intervention or as the mental darkness of ignorance or wrongheadedness. Darkness is, strikingly, one of the plagues visited on Egypt as punishment for the pharaoh's refusal to let the enslaved Hebrew people go; and the prophets endlessly register that the people of Israel and Judea are lost in inner darkness. At least implied in the word in Genesis 1:2 for the darkness before creation was a sort of super-nothingness, because the universe (if that term could even apply then) didn't yet know or obey God.

The darkness wasn't above some vague "deep" but above *tehōm,* subterranean water or an abyss, or the fathomless depths of the sea—in any case a horrifying place suggesting the roaring, numbing, consciousness-robbing, subduing underworld bodies of water or bottomless chasms in pagan mythology—as well, of course, as the place into which you disappear in the Psalms, if not for God's mercy. "Deep," as in the King James, is generally not an unpleasant English lexeme, whereas *tehōm* is not just emptiness or disorder but an ongoing primal catastrophe that preceded God's creative activity but was subdued by his power.

And here's my favorite part of Genesis, chapter 1, the end of verse 2, which in the King James reads, "And the Spirit of God moved upon the face of the waters." In the Hebrew, the spirit or breath or wind or life or disposition (the latter usually weighing toward agitated emotions like anger) of God—since the word *rūach* can point to any or all of these—doesn't just "move" over the water: it hovers or broods or cherishes, like a bird over its eggs or hatchlings. This word is perhaps the most specific in the whole passage, and must be comparing God to a natural nurturer of fresh life.

It's also in verse 2 that a mere common preposition comes alive, so to speak: the darkness is literally "on/above the face of" the abyss; then God is hovering "on/above the face of" the water. "Facing" is an ordinary Hebrew expression for being in the presence of or before someone or something—less often, for being above her or it. The abyss, of course, has no face, but the metaphor of a bird hovering implies faces (the word for "face" is, as usual, technically plural) below that turn up in expectation of food or comfort. The preposition "on/above" can have two seemingly contradictory connotations, of supervising and of serving; but aren't they harmonious when both applied to the care of a bird for its young?

The light that, according to verse 3, God creates by speaking* is

---

*The original speech act; see Chapter 1, pp. 18–19, concerning speech acts.

the usual word for "light" (ōr)—as if there could be anything "usual" about a Classical Hebrew word of such importance. Like words for darkness, it is very widely expressive; it is usually about the light of instruction, prosperity, favor, or salvation. Through "light," God acts to preserve what he created, especially the covenant with his people; they resist and retreat into the "darkness" of disobedience, where annihilation threatens.

A curious thing happens in the fourth and fifth verses of Genesis 1 ("And God saw the light, that it was good: and God divided the light from the darkness. And God called the light Day, and the darkness he called Night. And the evening and the morning were the first day"), a sort of literal mundanizing ("mundane" is from the Latin for "of the world") of terminology, a bringing of it into the hard categories of the universe experienced through the senses and through time. Tōv, for "good," in verse 4 is a notoriously broad term (encompassing both God's goodness and a woman's beauty, just to cite a couple of examples). After recognizing creation up to this point as "good," God begins parsing: he divides light from darkness, in a clause that in Hebrew requires a repeated preposition (literally, "between the light and between the darkness"): relative to the impression the English gives me, the impression of the Hebrew is that those entities are divided within an inch of their lives; they can never justifiably be confused again.

In naming the first creations in verse 5, God effectively narrows down definitions. Yōm, here always translated as "day," can have meanings other than one complete stretch of daylight hours, but God is clearly ascribing only that meaning to the time of light he has just created. "Night" (laila), also just now created, is likewise ipso facto the time when it's dark (though things that can go on during it, such as worship, weeping, or destruction, are important elsewhere in Scripture). Both the momentous darkness and the momentous light are thus cut down to size and made to serve in a way mortals can easily comprehend. "Evening" and "morning," signaled by relatively ordinary words for time, then seem to take shape on their own, and they enclose the simply but climactically named (literally in the Hebrew) "day one."

Even the verb for coming into being and existing is protean and powerful in this context. It occurs five times in this short passage ("the earth *was* without form" [verse 2], "*Let-there-be* light" and "*and-there-was* light" [verse 3], "*and-was* evening *and-was* morning" [verse 5]), which may seem a no-brainer, considering the topic. But a couple of things are noteworthy. One is the verb's use as a connective between a subject and a predicate in verse 2, like an English form of the verb "to be." Such a connective is rarer and more striking in Hebrew.* "Was in a state of" might be a more accurate translation. Or the stress might be placed somehow on long-past-ness, as the verb may be indicating that *before the creation,* the universe *used to be* like this.

Another thing worth noticing is that three out of these five instances of the verb for coming into being or existing are out of God's hands, so to speak, if not alien to his work: the first instance, there in verse 2, is about the *nature* of the universe (unordered but existing); and the fourth and fifth, in verse 5, are about things—morning and evening—that self-evidently and firmly exist, but without our reading explicitly that God created them.

But that pattern really works here. God does not in this narrative originate existence itself but rather fashions (that special verb in verse 1, *bara*) it to form a coherent universe. What he first brings into existence ex nihilo is only light (verse 3), but this is important, as it is through light that he begins to order all matter and energy. He deploys the light in such a way that, a couple of verses later, regular time—in the form of evening and morning—can be shown to exist without reference to him.

The universe is thus outwardly self-defining and self-sustaining, but only because it is infused with God's will, represented here by light. That will is a sort of divine principle (natural light is like that, very powerful and reliable yet mysterious at the same time). According to the Bible's account of creation, with its particular word choices and arrangements, the universe's arrangements—starting with time—are deeply and inviolably themselves *because* they come from God's special creative powers.

---

*The literal translation of this passage in Part Three shows that in these very verses, the connective is left out in places where an English speaker would use it, such as farther on in verse 2: "and-darkness on face." "My dog criminal" could in Hebrew be a perfectly correct clause.

*

The author of the New Testament Book of John, the Gospel with the deepest metaphysical concerns, certainly knew the opening chapter of Genesis and considered it in writing the exordium to his own work. But the John creation account is profoundly different from any Hebrew Scripture. In my Introduction, I stress the unknowability of God in Jewish belief and teaching; but an outright convulsion of mystery marked the advent of Christianity.

The religion arose, as I outlined above (pp. xxxii–xxxiv), when a small group of Jews became convinced that their leader, a poor and relatively uneducated man from the tiny town of Nazareth (a backwater of the backwater Galilee), whom the Romans had tortured to death as a troublemaker, had risen from the dead and ascended into heaven, thus delivering mankind from sin and death—and that this was the point of all existence in the universe. (As unscientific as it makes us seem, I and two billion–plus other people say, "Of course.")

Early Christians clearly had their theological work cut out for them; hence their increasing recourse to the authority of Greek philosophy (especially Stoicism and Neoplatonism). The influence of philosophical language on the opening of the book of John is glaring.

1   In the beginning was the Word, and the Word was with God, and the Word was God.

2   The same was in the beginning with God.

3   All things were made by him; and without him was not any thing made that was made.

4   In him was life; and the life was the light of men.

5   And the light shineth in darkness; and the darkness comprehended it not.

6   There was a man sent from God, whose name was John.

7   The same came for a witness, to bear witness of the Light, that all men through him might believe.

8   He was not that Light, but was sent to bear witness of that Light.

9   That was the true Light, which lighteth every man that cometh into the world.

10   He was in the world, and the world was made by him, and the world knew him not.

11   He came unto his own, and his own received him not.

12   But as many as received him, to them gave he power to become the sons of God, even to them that believe on his name:

13   Which were born, not of blood, nor of the will of the flesh, nor of the will of man, but of God.

14   And the Word was made flesh, and dwelt among us, (and we beheld his glory, the glory as of the only begotten of the Father,) full of grace and truth.

In John 1:1, the Greek rendering (*archei*) of the Hebrew for "beginning," as used in the Genesis creation account, could hardly be more precise: both words have shadings of sovereign power, and of excellence of several kinds. But then the New Testament passage starts to give its own distinct account of creation.

The word *logos* as the source of the English "Word"—what can I tell you? If there's any vocabulary broader than that of Hebrew words easily spanning the abstract and the concrete, it's the vocabulary of Greek intellectualizing. Just because I didn't want to go back to the more than two and a half large pages in tiny type in my Liddell and Scott *Greek-English Lexicon,* which is supposed to cover all the pagan, translated Jewish, original Jewish, and early Christian literature written in this language, I went to my tiny *Greek-English Dictionary of the New Testament.* That's the best index of commonsense and/or traditional meanings for Christian Koinē Greek. It said that in John's "Christology" *logos* is the "Word." Fine. Thanks a lot. Just take the easiest, most pedestrian received-wisdom interpretation possible, and capitalize it—everybody else does. And what more could any reader want?

Actually, "word," as in the letters forming a single independent semantic unit, is one of the few things *logos* seems pretty much never to mean, as far as I have the patience to investigate. At its roots, *logos* is a financial reckoning, but that meaning branched into argumentation, storytelling, all kinds of expression. Plato, the Stoics, and the Neoplatonists related the word to transcendent thought governing the universe. To all these people, *logos,* connected to mathematics, was about the perceived purity of thought itself, a concept quite at home in pagan philosophy, much of which was intent on separating the gross material world from the realm of sublime consciousness. But in John, chapter 1, the word may span the concrete-abstract gap by suggesting the literal context here: this *story* of Jesus that follows, this argument about his purposes, this set of evidence, as means through which the reader can come to know the ultimate reality of thought, the Truth.

In verses 1 and 2 ("In the beginning was the Word, and the Word was with God, and the Word was God. The same was in the beginning with God"), the repetitive, slow buildup of concepts seems a little comical, and it's tempting to refer to an audience that, as a whole, lacked sophistication or a high level of literacy. But a lot of ancient philosophical discourse worked this way, through the painstaking development of terms. One interesting thing is the preposition *pros* (in the King James: "with"), which is basically for motion toward or location near—but has many abstract meanings along the lines of "with regard to." Thematically, the ambiguity works: there's no graspable difference between an entity that's in God's presence and one that's associated with him in some other way. How would human beings define relationships with God well enough to put hard labels on them, even through such small details as prepositions?

Moreover, no clear difference appears in the Greek text between divine principle and divine personhood, no such boundaries to divine being. English translations are forced—because of English pronoun usage that pretty strictly divides, in the singular, persons, some animals, and deities ("he," "she") from things and abstractions ("it")—to decide whether *theos* or *logos* (God or the Word, both grammatically masculine) is the antecedent of the pronoun *autos* (also grammatically masculine, but translatable as either "he" or "it") in verse 3. "All things were made by *him;* and without *him* was not any thing made that was made" [my emphasis]—that's the King James choice, but it's just a choice.

This step on the logical stepladder of exposition (everything from this being, nothing apart from this being) introduces another element alien to Genesis, chapter 1—genesis! The Hebrew verb for "existing" or "coming into being" has no usual or characteristic connection with birth, but the Greek verb for "existing" or "coming into being," with the basic form *gignomai*—a verb to which the noun *genesis* is related*—certainly does. It is used three times in verse 3, where the King James has "were made," "was . . . made," and "was made." But the verb is really more properly about emergence than about being fashioned by another being.

The two meanings "to come into being" and "to be born" parallel each other and intermingle throughout Greek literature, and in many cases it wouldn't be absurd to say that the meanings coincide, rather than that one is excluding the other. The Greek translation of Genesis, chapter 1, in the Septuagint uses this verb, as it's the natural verb to use: the translator(s) would have had to stretch for another. But how particularly appropriate the verb is here in John, at the start of a book about the *son* of God. The Book of John loses no time, either, in bringing definite biological applications of the word into play. In John 1:6, John the Baptist is born/comes into being. In verse 13, in contrast, a different verb appears, the passive of *yennaō*, signifying *only* biological birth or growth. And in verse 14, the "Word" comes into being/is born "[as] flesh."

In John 1:4 ("In him was life; and the life was the light of men"), whether life is in God the person or in the *logos*/Word the abstraction (again, as you see, the King James has opted for an understanding of the pronoun as masculine) is unclear and probably unimportant—or the very lack of clarity may be part of the point. Another repetitious sequence begins here and continues through verse 5 ("And the light shineth in darkness; and the darkness comprehended it not"). Life, life, light, light, darkness, darkness. It's a sort of relay race, with backtracking. Light and darkness carry much of the broad significance they do in the creation as described in Hebrew in Genesis.

Verse 4 contains one of a great many testimonies to the folly of the controversy over gender in Bible translation. The roaring of traditionalists in favor of using the masculine is in vain when (as often) the masculine doesn't even belong. Here, this isn't "men" but "human beings"; it's grammatically masculine but refers to *both* men and women and in fact reflects indifference as to their gender. It's not even "a mixed group of men and women" but simply "human beings."

---

*The Old Testament books, whether originally Hebrew or Greek (the Apocrypha), get their standard titles in the Christian Bible from the Greek Septuagint.

In verse 5, two more protean words exert their power. The Greek verb behind "shineth" can also mean "appear" or "be manifest" in the intellectual sense.* This is fitting because the light, as verse 9 is going to start asserting, is the light of truth. Throughout ancient Greek literature, the verb behind "comprehended" travels between notions of physical and intellectual grasp. The darkness has not managed to "catch" the light and suppress it—but has also failed to understand it.

Verses 13 and 14—"Which were born, not of blood, nor of the will of the flesh, nor of the will of man, but of God. And the Word was made flesh, and dwelt among us, (and we beheld his glory, the glory as of the only begotten of the Father,) full of grace and truth"—force me into some nitty-gritty of the Greek vocabulary. These two verses are citing, and then, of course, going beyond, the essentials of legitimate family formation. Everything seems to cry out for the translation "a husband" and not the more abstract-sounding "man." This Greek word that's used never means "human being" (like *anthropos* in verses 4 and 6). This is instead an *anēr,* a manly man or a husband. And only "husband" makes sense, because in the Roman imperial world (including Palestine) illegitimate children weren't thought of as having a salient blood relationship with their fathers—and weren't even entitled to know who these were. Also, pretty universally in ancient literature, marital sex is about the will to have children.

I am ambivalent about the translation "grace" (John 1:14), because to the modern mind it suggests either a ballet dancer, a prayer before a meal, or a purely theological premise. For the Greeks, *charis* was instead the generous quality the universe could assume. Someone might give you a gift or treat you graciously when you hadn't merited it, or display unusual charm or beauty or eloquence to delight you. A longed-for son would normally be considered the very embodiment of *charis,* so the son of God embodies a sort of super-*charis.* Is *charis* "benevolence"? "A free gift"? "Divine favor"? "Life in death"? If *all* those are what it is, I'm not surprised that I can't easily describe it.

---

*Though that's usually in the middle and passive voices, not the active one, as here.

3

You Mean the Bible Has Style?

Ezekiel's Dry Bones (Ezekiel 37:1–14)
Revelation's Martyrs in Paradise (Revelation 7:9–17)

In writing about what the Bible is like, I know I'm expected to cite Erich Auerbach's *Mimesis: The Representation of Reality in Western Literature,* and also Edmund Wilson's writings on the Hebrew Bible. And though Auerbach may have been the most broadly sensitive yet meticulous reader of all time, and though Wilson was perhaps the twentieth century's most open-minded student of culture and ideology, the only writing about writing that doesn't send me climbing up the walls is about works I have no intention of ever sampling. I admire Virginia Woolf on Aphra Behn, and George Orwell on boys' weeklies, but exposition, no matter how good, of what's really good makes me feel like the guy in the *Legends of Caltech* photo who's duct-taped to a wall and watching a party go on without him.

Whereas I give Auerbach credit for describing the deep inwardness of his main example, the Binding of Isaac narrative in Genesis, chapter 22 (as opposed to the glimmeringly detailed surface world of Homer), and whereas I second Wilson in believing that, for instance, Hebrew expressions employing the infinitive absolute (which allows a sort of doubling of a verb) do mean something about ancient thought processes, I'm not going to give my account of the Bible through theirs. If this encourages some readers to take my attitude, ditch my own exposition, and go learn Hebrew or Greek or both in order to see for themselves, that's great. I know my third-rate place.

On the other hand, since as a translator I *am* on the toiling end of the literary enterprise most of the time—mopping that floor, stocking that salad bar—there are worse-informed people you could consult if you want to know what goes on in the kitchen. It's through my daily livelihood that I get a sense of the Bible's "style"—by which term I mean the large set of *choices* for expression, within the restrictions of the languages and the genres.

I hope I don't give offense by writing about style here, as if I were imagining the minds behind the Bible trying on different kinds of phrasing the way a person might try on hats at a mall, or the way a modern "writerly" author such as—oh, I don't know—Martin Amis drums up attention through cute word choices. As I stressed in my introduction, for the ancients, style was inseparable from subject matter. An impressive manner of writing was partly a certification of the right to write, an imprimatur of traditional knowledge; but much more important, that manner was both the design and the materials of the house that the author and reader (or listener) inhabited together.

Perhaps the readiest way to understand this is through ancient literature's varied repetitions. We do have some modern analogies. I remember standing on a beach in the evening with my sister, Gretchen—we must have been in our early teens—and singing all six verses of "The Battle Hymn of the Republic." I may have memorized every variation in the refrain—whether it was "His truth" or "Our God" or "His day," *vel sim.,* that was "marching on" after each verse. All the variations were important, I half-consciously knew, as each related to a certain nuance of the idea, developed from one verse to the next, of divine justice realized through human conflict. Julia Ward Howe's lyrics are set to the tune of the rather unedifying "John Brown's Body," and her hymn outcompeted any number of rallying and marching ditties by which Northern activists tried to perk up the largely racist and reluctant North for a very gory war of liberation (for other people), a war bungled for years by the Northern command. The great hymn won—and still wins—the adoption of its aggressively complex yet rhythmically repetitious beauty.

In the Bible, nobody repeats more, and repeats to greater effect, than the prophets. Below is the prophet Ezekiel's famous vision of a resurrected army. Ezekiel was of priestly descent, and was taken to Babylon in exile. To him are attributed many pronouncements about his nation's fate, including a prediction that the Temple would be destroyed. Other statements, however, are much more hopeful, as here in chapter 37 of the Book of Ezekiel.

1   The hand of the Lord was upon me, and carried me out in the spirit of the Lord, and set me down in the midst of the valley which was full of bones,

2   And caused me to pass by them round about: and, behold, there were very many in the open valley; and, lo, they were very dry.

3   And he said unto me, Son of man, can these bones live? And I answered, O Lord God, thou knowest.

4   Again he said unto me, Prophesy upon these bones, and say unto them, O ye dry bones, hear the word of the Lord.

5   Thus saith the Lord God unto these bones; Behold, I will cause breath to enter into you, and ye shall live:

6   And I will lay sinews upon you, and will bring up flesh upon you, and cover you with skin, and put breath in you, and ye shall live; and ye shall know that I am the Lord.

7   So I prophesied as I was commanded: and as I prophesied, there was a noise, and behold a shaking, and the bones came together, bone to his bone.

8   And when I beheld, lo, the sinews and the flesh came up upon them, and the skin covered them above: but there was no breath in them.

9   Then said he unto me, Prophesy unto the wind, prophesy, son of man, and say to the wind, Thus saith the Lord God; Come from the four winds, O breath, and breathe upon these slain, that they may live.

10   So I prophesied as he commanded me, and the breath came into them, and they lived, and stood up upon their feet, an exceeding great army.

11   Then he said unto me, Son of man, these bones are the whole house of Israel: behold, they say, Our bones are dried, and our hope is lost: we are cut off for our parts.

12   Therefore prophesy and say unto them, Thus saith the Lord God; Behold, O my people, I will open your graves, and cause you to come up out of your graves, and bring you into the land of Israel.

13   And ye shall know that I am the Lord, when I have opened your graves, O my people, and brought you up out of your graves,

14   And shall put my spirit in you, and ye shall live, and I

shall place you in your own land: then shall ye know that I the
Lord have spoken it, and performed it, saith the Lord.

You can all write to me about the amazing things my account
below misses in the repetitive but very effective working out of the
ideas in this passage, as I'm sure to be missing a lot. But I dare anyone to write to me about wasted words—at least, once she's seen the
Hebrew as represented in Part Three of this book. In the King James
Version, I count thirty-three words rendering the first verse, for
example, as opposed to the Hebrew's thirteen. With a language that
compact, that Lego-like, repetitive patterning is far less wearing.

More important, though, these repetitions express a quite intricate yet compelling progression of thought; they are gorgeously
functional. Take just the very similar images of God's physical interaction with the prophet in the first two verses. He put his hand on
me. He carried me out. He set me down. He led me beside. These
last three expressions are in the *hifil,* or causative mode, of Hebrew
verbs: He caused me to go out; He caused me to come to rest; He
caused me to pass by. In this way, the speaker rhythmically insists
that God's immediate presence and direct action brought him into
this vision, just as, later, with the repetition of the verb "to say" and
"to command" with God as the subject, the speaker makes clear that
he continued to be under God's guidance and to act on God's will.

In the Hebrew, there are even side-by-side repetitions, like "round
round" (verse 2), for being sent "round about" the plain with the
dry bones in it; and the "very very" great army that arises from
the bones (verse 10). But these are far from childish in their tone.
The first reinforces the speaker's deliberate, already repetitive depiction of himself as an instrument of God, amazed but still a consci-
entious personal observer of the scene. The diction is stretched out
like the investigative walk itself. The repeated "very" takes up and
contradicts the "very many" and "very dry" in verse 2: the new, resurrected army will be twice as large and mighty as the previous one
was large and dead.

Verses 2, 5, 7, 8, 11, and 12 each contain *hinnei,* an essentially
untranslatable word unusually rendered as "behold" or "lo"; but as a
professor I decline to name cogently suggested, it's really more like
"Shit. . . ." It's usually not about physically pointing out something
to a third party, but instead about an important (often surprised)

perception or realization. *Hinnei* is very thick on the ground here, indicating one arresting thing after another, a series of enlightening lessons. "Lessons" is a term I would vouch for, because of the way so many of these instances are closely followed up: God's knowledge is at issue in verse 3; God commands the bones to hear him in verse 4; and in verses 6, 13, and 14 the critical human knowledge resulting from the miracle of the rejoined and reanimated bones is emphasized and reemphasized: that he *is* God.

The repeated words setting out the most important themes fall into two clear-cut categories: the ones whose meanings remain stable, and the ones whose meanings change and can serve even for playfulness and wit. The most stable word is a name for God, Yahweh, repeatedly reinforced by the word that in fact replaced it for recitation purposes once Jews ceased saying the word "Yahweh" out loud: *Adonai,* or "Lord." "Lord God" is the traditional translation in English when both words appear together, rendering pretty accurately the way Jews avoid saying *Adonai Adonai: Adonai Elohim* ("Lord God[s]"). In any case, references to Yahweh, and to Yahweh But More So, crowd the passage. The clarity and certainty of the speaker's purpose grow, but it's the same deity infusing them. In parallel to Yahweh and *Adonai* is—in God's voice—the repeated *ben adam* (roughly, "son of a human being"), which suggests the visionary's very limited being and consciousness, and God's condescension.

Also remarkably stable are the words for saying, prophesying, and ordering, and not only because they are formulaic in character, normal means of setting up and structuring dialogue in Hebrew literature. It is unnecessary for the usual Hebrew verb "to say" to occur quite so many times (verse 3 [twice], verse 4 [twice], verse 5, verse 9 [three times], verse 11 [twice], and verse 12 [twice]), and for a clause about prophesying as commanded to occur at all, let alone twice (in verses 7 and 10), unless the communicativeness of both God and the prophet, and the prophet's obedience to God, were at issue.

As if the dance of speaking between the holy man and God were not formal and elaborate enough, it is prolonged and taken in an artificial, circular detour by God's question to Ezekiel as to whether the miracle is possible, and Ezekiel's pert or patient answer, "*You* [the technically unnecessary subject pronoun is used] know, Yahweh" (verse 3). In other respects, the verbal orchestration is complex:

the visionary quotes God's speeches and orders to himself, God's orders to be recited to the bones, and God's version of what the bones think or say. With standard modern punctuation (which I use in my literary translation of this passage in Part Two), the enclosing quotation marks cluster in as many as three layers, and the translator wonders, "What was that phone number in the commercial about learning to drive the big rigs in only six weeks?"

Among the less stable terms in the passage, the most arresting is *rūach,* which means spirit *or* breath *or* wind (among other things). The meanings in the Hebrew Bible tend not to be terribly confusing, because when the word is not attached to the divinity, it pretty reliably has a physiological or meteorological sense. The word in this passage is at first a sort of essence of God, perhaps metaphorically his breath, and what we might well call his "spirit"; it acts in concert with his "hand" (an image of his power), which fastens on and transports the speaker (verse 1: "The hand of the Lord was upon me, and carried me out in the spirit of the Lord, and set me down in the midst of the valley").

God promises twice (verses 5 and 6) that, with the help of Ezekiel's prophecy, he will put what must at least end up as the breath of life (*rūach*) into the bones. But when, in the next verse, they are reassembled,* they don't yet have breath (*rūach*) in them (verse 8). Then in verse 9 Ezekiel is told to prophesy to the wind (*rūach*) to supply this element, and it's uncertain when wind and breath become distinct, and whether it's about blowing or breathing into the inert bodies; but by the next verse these now do become animated and upright. However, the later promise, in verse 14, is that God will place his *own* spirit (*rūach*) in the whole nation.

*

Koinē, or Common Greek, in its compact, pointed repetition, is somewhat similar to Hebrew; in fact, the species of Koinē found in the New Testament owes much of its character to the Koinē of the then widely used Septuagint, the standard Greek translation of Hebrew Scripture. Christian utterances about the divine were thus to a certain extent predetermined according to Hebrew patterns

---

*Interestingly, the King James is literal here, "bone to his bone."

long before Jesus appeared or anyone wrote about him or quoted him in Greek, translating from his home language of Aramaic and from the Hebrew Scripture he cited.

Koinē is rhetorically quite unlike typical pagan literary Greek, with its great discursiveness, its color, its delight in the surface of the world, qualities that Auerbach notes. But as I showed in Chapter 1, Koinē shares both with the "more-sophisticated" incarnations of Greek and with Hebrew a massive amount of inflection (change in individual words to suit their functions), which allowed just a few words to do a great deal. Again: neither ancient Greek nor Hebrew usually requires, for example, separate subject pronouns ("I," "we," "you," "he," "she," "it," and "they") to go with verbs;* and neither has an indefinite article, like the English "a/an." Pithiness in expression and punch in repetition must have been easier to achieve in languages that are characteristically less wordy.

Here is another Biblical vision of resurrection, in the seventh chapter of the Book of Revelation. A devotee of Jesus purported to be named John (but whose historical identity is impossible to pin down) relates a vision of the world's end. For this speaker, the resurrected are not a nation but a hugely varied group, united only by their individual faithful endurance of a terrible persecution for the sake of their allegiance to Christ. John or "John" plainly draws on the language and style of Hebrew visions of salvation. The style of repetition with meaningful variation is in fact richest where the Hebrew Scriptural influence seems strongest.

9   After this I beheld, and, lo, a great multitude, which no man could number, of all nations, and kindreds, and people, and tongues, stood before the throne, and before the Lamb, clothed with white robes, and palms in their hands;

10   And cried with a loud voice, saying, Salvation to our God which sitteth upon the throne, and unto the Lamb.

11   And all the angels stood round about the throne, and about the elders and the four beasts, and fell before the throne on their faces, and worshipped God,

12   Saying, Amen: Blessing, and glory, and wisdom, and

---

*Independent subject pronouns are, however, more common in Koinē than in Classical Greek.

thanksgiving, and honour, and power, and might, be unto our God for ever and ever. Amen.

13   And one of the elders answered, saying unto me, What are these which are arrayed in white robes? and whence came they?

14   And I said unto him, Sir, thou knowest. And he said to me, These are they which came out of great tribulation, and have washed their robes, and made them white in the blood of the Lamb.

15   Therefore are they before the throne of God, and serve him day and night in his temple: and he that sitteth on the throne shall dwell among them.

16   They shall hunger no more, neither thirst any more; neither shall the sun light on them, nor any heat.

17   For the Lamb which is in the midst of the throne shall feed them, and shall lead them unto living fountains of waters: and God shall wipe away all tears from their eyes.

In the first verse of this passage, the tricky Hebrew *hinnei* (properly for a startling perception or realization) becomes, in Koinē Greek, a simple imperative, "Look!" That makes for *two* verbs of looking, the second literally urging the reader to share the speaker's vision (I saw, and now you see!). The King James renders the whole as "I beheld, and, lo."

An *ochlos* or crowd such as the one pictured in this verse can't be anything but a large number of people in the first place, so "big crowd" must be rather redundant. ("Great multitude" is a fine translation in the King James.) Furthermore, the speaker states, nobody could count these people. Then comes a picture of the crowd's variety, setting out categories of that variety we might think of as quite redundant and almost interchangeable, but which had real weight, especially in the Roman world with its imperial hodgepodge. Here's a rough account of the original Greek words, in order. An *ethnos* (King James: "nation") meant (approximately) a nation, but in this historical situation that entity was parallel to a modern American "Indian nation": a distinct people, but with limited political independence. "Tribes" is the now more common translation of the word (*fūla*) the King James renders as "kindreds": "*race, tribe,* or *class,*" says the lexicon; "race of women," Greek poets wrote. *La-oi*

(King James: "people") can overlap these previous two words but tends to be about a smaller, more visible, more functional group of people: an army, the people in assembly, a professional class or affiliation—as it happens, the group can also be either Jews or Christians. The "tongues" (*glōssai*) or languages point up cultural units; how important these could be is signaled in the story of Pentecost in Acts, chapter 2: Christianity could not cohere as an international sect until all its members could understand what other members were saying. Such a miracle as was reported from that early assembly proved unnecessary over time, because of the resource dramatized here in Revelation: Christians of many backgrounds could communicate in the lingua franca of Koinē Greek.

The assembly John pictures is, to me as a student of Classics, touching in a couple of ways. In Roman literature, a multiethnic array such as he describes with so much emphasis here is familiar mainly from depictions of military "triumphs": the various conquered nations, in all their (no doubt exaggerated) exoticism, had to parade in Rome in honor of the conquering general. Yet these figures wear not stereotyped ethnic costumes but white robes that stand for purity and prestige; and in the figures' hands is the evergreen foliage of palm trees, signifying eternal life and eternal glory. This set of imagery is thus associated with both subjugation and ascendancy: the conquered, the subjects of the Roman Empire, come together in a scene of ultimate triumph.

A note on the "lamb" on the throne this crowd surrounds: it's "little lamb," the diminutive form of the word. That diminutive does occur also in John 21:15, but Revelation has a flood of occurrences. There, Christ is only, and relentlessly, a "little lamb." I don't want to ride this distinction too hard, as diminutives seem naturally to replace ordinary words as languages evolve, and especially as literary languages grow more popular.* But say that (as is eminently possible) Revelation circulated early along with the Gospels and Epistles, so that the contrast of "lamb" and "little lamb" was noticeable. In that case, ordinary ancient readers themselves may have felt the heightened verbal staging of "little lamb" taken literally: this

---

*For example, a French knight, or *chevalier,* is, etymologically speaking, a man on a "little nag," since the French word for "horse" evolved from that Latin slang. Needless to say, that's no reflection on the dignity of French knighthood, nor should it ever impinge on translation.

lamb was smaller than the lamb cited almost everywhere else in these new religious writings. The huge crowd is standing "before" (literally [as Hebrew would phrase it, too], "in the face of") the throne *and* "before" the lamb. It's probably not a child-size toy throne, but an imposing one of the usual kind, so that the "little lamb" really is sitting "in the midst" of it (Revelation 7:17). Throughout the passage, the focus shifts dramatically among the immense, multiethnic throng (the representatives of the known world), other beings, the majestic throne, and the tiny animal on it.

Inspired by this sight, the crowd chants—in a contrastingly loud ("large") voice, emphasized with two verbs, one for crying out loud and one for saying, that salvation is to their God—to the one sitting on the throne—and to the little lamb (verse 10). Irony and paradox in the New Testament are important in overturning traditional expectations, especially those of a looming, thundering, punishing God. The imagery that modern Christians tend to digest unthinkingly, because it is so familiar, communicates in what would originally have been quite a startling way the essence of the faith. This tiny creature, like any of the thousands sacrificed every Passover, is the savior of the world. If Revelation postdates the destruction of the Temple in 70 C.E., then the difference is even more momentous: this little lamb is now the only Jewish sacrifice left in the universe.

Verse 11 continues with heterogeneous thronging, now of special denizens of heaven: angels, elders, and four heavenly monsters or "animals." (In the King James, it's the now rather off-putting "beasts.") The verse shows a heightened concern with their orientation toward the throne. They stand in a circle around it, fall down literally "in-face of" it onto their own faces, and their worship is a prostration "to-the God." According to the Greek verb chosen, they grovel before him. *Pros* ("toward") is part of two words here.

Their declaration to him is framed with two instances of the word "amen," Hebrew for "truly." What is thus represented as doubly true is a whole list of qualities ascribed and honors given to these speakers' God. Typically for a text influenced by Hebrew (if only by way of the Septuagint), there is noticeable compactness due to the absence of a "to be" verb, and it's likely that the King James is wrong about the subjunctive "[let] be unto": the worshippers are not wishing wisdom and other distinctions for God but declaring that he in fact has them; not commanding thanksgiving for him but performing an act of thanksgiving at this very moment. These are eternal attributes and recognitions of the deity, sealed at the end with the traditional (literal) "into the ages of the ages" as well as the second "amen."

The list in Greek (translated in the King James as "Blessing, and glory, and wisdom, and thanksgiving, and honor, and power, and might") is quite melodious, a series of feminine nouns, each with the definite article *hē* ("the") in front of it and with endings in this order: *–ia, -a, -ia, ia, -ē, -is, -us.* Some meanings of the words shade into each other beautifully, as their sounds do. To bless and thank God are similar, and both words start in Greek with *eu-* ("well": a super-literal version of the words would be "well-speakingness" and "well-giftedness/givingness"). My instinct was to write that, of the two words for "power" ending with the harmonizing *-is* and *–us* (*dunamis, ischus*), the first is a more abstract "power" and the second closer to physical "strength," but my lexicon tells me that the difference is not so clear-cut: here the meanings probably overlap to indicate God's omnipotence, and the words emphasize it far more effectively than could have been achieved by writing that God is "very" or "extremely" powerful, the way we would in English.

In verses 13 and 14, an emphatically expanded (if to modern ears rather silly-sounding) verbal exchange between a heavenly instructor and John about the sight before them affirms its reality. This somewhat resembles the exchange in Ezekiel 37:3, described above (pp. 55–56). Here in Revelation, one of the elders turns to the visionary, repeating almost exactly from verse 9 the designation of the martyrs as wrapped in white robes, but makes it into two questions—who are they, and where do they come from? In the Greek, there is the syntactical finger-pointing of *two* articles (instead of none, in verse 9), one before the noun, one before the adjective: "the robes the white [ones]." (You could do this in Greek, but it was far from universal; by the way, the same kind of repetition of articles occurs in verse 17 of this same passage, in, literally, "the lamb the [one] up [the] middle. . . .")

In practical terms, the very premise of the question is ridiculous, or maybe just condescendingly didactic. The elder is already an inhabitant of paradise, but he asks this witness, newly transported here, the identity of those he sees. The newcomer replies with perhaps overelaborate politeness. "My lord" (*kurieh mū*) includes the

same word as used for God, though this can also serve as a colloquial "Sir," as in the KJV. "You," the separate subject pronoun, is
probably emphatic in this sentence, suggesting something like "*You*
know," or "I guess you would know," or "I trust you to know."

"And I said" and "and he said" in verse 14 repeat the same verb
for saying, but with a contrast not visible in English: "I said" is in
the perfect tense, more like "I have said," whereas "he said" is in the
aorist, a simple past tense (when not an indication of timelessness).
The speaker places his speaking and the elder's speaking at different removes. This is, moreover, the same verb for saying as used
in verses 10 and 12, in quoting the crowd in its prayerful chants
("[and they were] saying"); but there the verb visibly shares the root
of the all-important term *logos,* or Idea (traditionally translated as
"Word"), which I discuss in the previous chapter (pp. 47–49).

Here, then, is how careful repetition in the Bible can be. Not
only is monotonous exact repetition of "ordinary" words avoided,
but the variants suggest that they are precisely deployed for the correct nuances. Is the still-living visionary's quotation of himself more
like a straightforward report of what he has just done? Does the
angelic elder's quotation of himself have, in contrast, the remote-
ness of heavenly authority? Do the words sung in heaven partake of
the eternal Idea? Perhaps the reason for the difference is much more
mundane, but there *is* a difference, which English Bibles typically
don't show; and I find it fascinating, as when I work in my garden
and ask, "Why did birds nest in *this* bush and not *that* bush?"

"These are," intones the elder in verse 14, here using the
far-from-automatic "to be" connective ("these in fact are"?—with a
stress on their real existence?), "the [ones] coming out of-the great
tribulation/disaster." The participle is in the present tense, almost
as if the martyrs have arrived in heaven this moment from a luridly
recent ordeal—though the same verb, used in a finite form in the
previous verse, was in the aorist tense, which would normally signal
the simple past (if, again, not timelessness): "Where did they come
from?" in ordinary English.

What the martyrs endured to arrive where they are is described
in a shattering metaphor: they washed their clothing in the blood of
the little lamb. The white-robed Temple priests, and certain pagan
priests, and other officials in ceremonial white garments no doubt
spattered themselves with blood while slaughtering animals at altars.

But this new sacrifice is a *cleansing* of garments: it renders them pure white, though they were dirty before. The martyrs, by sacrificing *themselves,* have washed away the blood of ordinary mortality.

Verse 15 contains the third and final "in-face of-the throne" in this passage, and the fifth and sixth out of seven occurrences of the word "throne." But all this hardly seems excessive in the Greek, which is in itself very spare but steadily expanding in meaning. Verse 16 is reminiscent of Psalm 121:6 ("The sun shall not smite thee by day . . ."), but it sort of knocks the wind out of me that "any heat/ burning" is the culmination of this list of mortal sufferings. Some martyrs were in fact burned alive: Nero tied a number of Christians to stakes coated with pitch and offered his populace this tormented, dying nighttime illumination.

Verse 17 is almost pure reversal: this tiny lamb in the center of the throne, like a toddler on a CEO's office chair, will now be the caretaker. This weakest and most dependent of herd animals will literally "shepherd" the deserving part of humankind, and lead them to—the expression looks like an awkward Greek version of a Hebrew construct chain, and can be literally rendered as "of-life springs/streams of-waters." At the very least, this scenario is a bizarre converse of the Twenty-Third Psalm's first half. God doesn't, like a shepherd, care for a single helpless sheep and ensure its comfort and survival; instead, a single tiny divine lamb cares for a very large number of human beings—and the lamb is so powerful because it was, at a critical moment in the past, weak and helpless and had its life annihilated in agony. And the stakes in this scenario are even higher: God's guidance and nurturance explicitly consist of eternal life, a life full of joy and free of sorrow and pain, with God wiping every tear away.

4

Poetry in the Bible: The Living Word of Everything and Nothing

The Twenty-Third Psalm
The Beatitudes (Matthew 5:3–12)

After thirty years as a translator of ancient poetry, I still have only one reason to be cheerful: nobody else has an organic grasp of this genre either. A lot of us can read it in the original languages, but who can say what it was *like*?

Here's the sort of thing that gets in the way. En route to an African hiking trail during my years overseas, I spent my first night in a campground on that continent. There was a shower facility with the usual glaring lights, and someone dropped me off beside it in the late evening, so I wasn't prepared to make my way back to my tent without a flashlight after complete, moonless darkness had fallen. Outside, it was as black as the inside of Zane Shawnee Caverns in Ohio had been when I was eight years old and the guide turned off the lights for a few seconds, just to show us what it would be like to be trapped in there. But this new darkness was on the earth's surface, and unremitting, and a light in my hand would have told me only that a bush was on this side, and long grass on that side, and maybe a pair of shining eyes behind me. As it was, I lost any sense of direction and might have wandered off toward a leopard's tree, had I not stumbled onto the gravel path again and shuffled my way to someone else's tent, which was luckily next to my own.

This is "darkness" for ancient herders. The "light" created at the beginning of the universe, according to the Bible, might have been imagined as a relief from this. The horrors of lightless space may have influenced the Greeks when they called the world "the inhabited [land]" or designated it with a word primarily meaning "orderliness"—that word is *kosmos,* by the way. Where you could not make your way from light to light after dark, you might well have a sense of the *chaos* before the world was created.

But on another trip, when I visited an astronomical observatory in the rural South African Free State on a night of the full moon, the stars (without any recourse to the telescope) were like a sea of ball bearings: crowded, three-dimensional, shedding an inexorable gleam—almost horrifying. It was evident why the Hebrews spoke of the "hosts" or "armies" of the sky, and why others among the ancients formed their ideas of fate around the shapes—the zodiac signs—of those heavenly bodies that most clearly stood out in this sublime mess. Here in Hamden, Connecticut, the night sky looks like a faded black suit with lint on it.

But even in Africa, I was only looking at the night rather than living in it. I have no idea what it would be like for such terror and transport to be ordinary, any more than the ancients would be comfortable in my mind, with its daily fear of another world war, but with Handel's *Messiah* often playing in the background: *O thou that tellest good tidings to Zion, get thee up into the high mountain . . .* (Isaiah 40:9).

The inability to get inside the words of Classical Hebrew and Koinē Greek obtains all across the Scriptures, but the poetic passages are especially hard to penetrate, because the elements that keep them from being prose are so different from the elements in English that create this distinction.

Hebrew poetry—the "tribal" verse and other insets in Biblical narratives, the Psalms and the Songs of Songs (or Song of Solomon) and Lamentations, a great deal in the Prophets, and much of the philosophical writings such as Job—is easily distinguished from prose, and both Hebrew texts and English translations like to set it apart by segregating lines, and often by creating distinct columns. Yet this doesn't reflect any consistent system of sounds. In our literature, a reader can refer to many fixed classifications of forms (which make "formal" verse formal), saying, for instance, "That's a Petrarchan sonnet," or "That's a heroic couplet," but Hebrew poetry is unable to acquire labels like those; there's nothing to hang them on, such as meter or rhyme.

This tells me that the Westernization of Hebrew poetry in translation is unnecessary and in fact counterproductive, like the bombing of civilians—and if that comparison seems overly harsh, just check out the Puritans' *Bay Psalm Book:*

> To waters calm he gently leads
> Restore my soul doth he
> He doth in paths of righteousness
> For his names sake lead me.

Hebrew poetry's structure is mainly in the content, not the form. The content's patterns are quite intricate and supply a lot of charm in themselves. The typical arrangement of Hebrew poetry is called "parallelism," meaning that the images and ideas in each line tend to be strung out with counterpoint and rephrased repetition; when in the text the line is physically divided in two, the gap in the middle typically separates the initial assertion and another version of it, or two assertions that still form some kind of tight pair.

A native English suggestion of how Hebrew poetry achieved this effect can be found in, of all places, a poem of the early nineteenth-century essayist Charles Lamb:

> I have had playmates, I have had companions,
> In my days of childhood, in my joyful school-days,
> All, all are gone, the old familiar faces.

> I have been laughing, I have been carousing,
> Drinking late, sitting late, with my bosom cronies,
> All, all are gone, the old familiar faces.

> I loved a love once, fairest among women:
> Closed are her doors on me, I must not see her—
> All, all are gone, the old familiar faces. . . .

Sonorous and striking, no?—even though the meter is not clip-clop, clip-clop?

It might, then, be assumed that translators are on relatively firm ground with parallel *content,* not to say with *any* content. It is, after all, notoriously easier to transfer an idea, like "He hath set me in dark places" (Lamentations 3:6), from one language to another than to come up with analogies of the sounds in speech and the shapes in the line that originally conveyed that idea.

But—hem!—what *about* darkness? The question of imagery ought to undermine any reassurance translators of Hebrew poetry feel. The look—and smells, and sounds—of night in ancient Palestine, and the pressures of those kinds of paths beneath those kinds of sandals, and the itch of those fleas, and a great many other sensations are unrecoverable (as long as our own clean, safe, polyurethane civilization holds, at any rate). Even when one word in an ancient and another in a modern language are the only logical counterparts to each other, their relationship is still maddeningly incomplete—much unlike the *converging* images in our globalizing era, when we can more and more easily experience for ourselves something of what foreign-language speakers in the most diverse cultures are talking about, through looking at photos, for example.

But problems of content, huge as they are, don't define the task. It's not as if, in the absence of the rather monotonous formalism that has dominated ancient Greek and Roman and modern Western verse, Hebrew poetry lacks form; the form is merely individualized and selective. There are all kinds of devices such as chiasmus (interlocking word order), internal rhyme, alliteration, mirror images of consonant and vowel order—it's an endless variety, and extremely artful. Here's something I noticed in a passage of Lamentations: long polysyllables, which are fairly rare in the language, sometimes cluster at the ends of lines. In English this pattern can speed up the line ending dramatically, almost like a vehicle peeling out—but it's usually a solemn sound: "To vanish in irrevocable night" is a line of Edward Arlington Robinson's about the transience of shallow poetry ("Songs without souls, that flicker for a day"), in the poem "Oh for a Poet—for a Beacon Bright." In Edwin Markham's "The Man with the Hoe," "immedicable woes" ends a line about the obscure and endless suffering of the poor. The following is one way some lines from chapter 3 of Lamentations (a series of laments over the Babylonian conquest of Jerusalem) with (in the Hebrew) a couple of long polysyllables at the ends of lines can be rendered, without conventional English meters, to give a more precise poetic effect than in the King James (which I place first).

60   Thou hast seen all their vengeance and all their imaginations against me.

61   Thou hast heard their reproach, O Lord, and all their imaginations against me;

62   The lips of those that rose up against me, and their device against me all the day.

63   Behold their sitting down, and their rising up; I am their musick.

60   You have seen all their rancor toward me, all their
          connivances.

61   You have heard their taunts, Lord, every one of those
          contrivances—

62   The whispers, the mutterings my attackers rehearse at me
          the whole day;

63   They sit, they stand, only to aim at me their chanting
          caricatures.

Below, I'm going to try to suggest how formal nuances work with the theme in the most famous piece of Hebrew poetry, the Twenty-Third Psalm. Everyone who writes feverish books about the degradation of Western culture during the past two or three or four centuries can come pelt my house with distaffs and dueling pistols for suggesting that the King James version isn't perfect. Here it is, anyway:

1   The Lord is my shepherd; I shall not want.

2   He maketh me to lie down in green pastures: he leadeth me beside the still waters.

3   He restoreth my soul: he leadeth me in the paths of righteousness for his name's sake.

4   Yea, though I walk through the valley of the shadow of death, I will fear no evil: for thou art with me; thy rod and thy staff they comfort me.

5   Thou preparest a table before me in the presence of mine enemies: thou anointest my head with oil; my cup runneth over.

6   Surely goodness and mercy shall follow me all the days of my life: and I will dwell in the house of the Lord for ever.

The King James *isn't* perfect. In the first verse, the traditional "shepherd" as a translation may be quite wrong, as the word isn't a straight noun. Classical Hebrew contains very few such nouns for occupations. For crafts, menial tasks, and most other work, a participle is commonly used: "[the one] doing such and such a thing"—here, "[the one] pasturing." This makes a lot of sense for a society in which there was little specialization—beyond divinely ordained roles such as "king" or "prophet"—but in which certain people did certain things habitually, because of age or social status or gender or some other reason. Some people did make their living from herding, but in the Twenty-Third Psalm, the usual Hebrew wording for a vocation fits in really nicely with a sheep or goat's point of view, which is oblivious of human institutions such as jobs: "the one pasturing me" is the one who, among many who conceivably could, takes this responsibility. It's a relationship. (But for short, I'll keep referring to a "shepherd.")

Nor would it, pace Malcolm Gladwell in *David and Goliath,* have indicated a lowly status that someone was entrusted and left alone with the family's main wealth, its herds. In 1 Samuel, chapter 17, David finds himself in this role merely because he is young and his older brothers are needed in the army resisting the Philistine invaders. His brothers are upset that he has left the herd with a mere servant, someone with no property interest in the animals, in order to come up to the front lines. But David is astutely insistent that his skills against the wild animals that threaten his charges at home can meet a military challenge, too, against a foreign giant. The Twenty-Third Psalm is one of those labeled "To/for/regarding [here pretty much an impossible word to translate] David."

The shepherd was the ultimate metaphoric protector, and as many Biblical annotators state, a frequent symbol for kingship both in the Middle East and southeastern Europe. But this poem is unusual in the face of expressions such as "shepherd of peoples" for Agamemnon in Homer. Here a single sheep or goat, as if not part of a browsing or moving mass of livestock, but as if instead a beloved individual, is speaking of his own, personal caretaker. This kind of imagery leads naturally to Jesus's Parable of the Lost Sheep in Luke 15:3–7: there may be a hundred in the flock, but a good shepherd—or a good king or a good deity—rescues whichever one is in trouble, so that each of them can feel the same confidence that a cherished household pet would feel. (And lambs *were* kept as pets: see 2 Samuel 12:3.)

Accordingly (and see the literal translation in Part Three, as usual), the sounds of the Psalm are heavy with *-ee* and *-nee* for first-person pronouns ("me" or "my") tacked on at the end of verbs and nouns, indicating direct objects (the shepherd's good treatment of me) and possession (he acts benevolently toward what belongs to me, defiantly toward what threatens me). Sometimes these pronouns are instead pronounced *-ai*, as in "try," and two instances of that in this poem are, tidily, both in Psalm 23:5, and in the same Hebrew line of the verse, the first one ("Thou preparest a table before *me* in the presence of *mine* enemies"). With the addition of affixes for "your" (*-ka*) in the second line of verse 4, plus, later, the *-ta* ending characteristic of second-person singular verbs in this category, plus other rhymes, the pattern becomes very intricate indeed. Here's part of what's going on in verses 4 and 5:

> "Because (*kee*) you (*ahtta*) with-me (*imma-dee*), rod-your
> (with *-ka*) and-staff-your (with *-ka*), these comfort-me
> (*-nee*). . . .
> You-have-anointed (with *–ta*) with-oil head-my (with *-ee*).
> Cup-my (with *-ee*) has-abounded (with *-ya*). "

But let me back up a little. In verse 2, "maketh me to lie down" doesn't seem apt. Perhaps the King James phrasing, in the era when it was adopted, was less suggestive of force, but in any case the New Revised Standard Version translators shouldn't have changed that phrasing simply to "makes me lie down," as in "My parents make me go to military school." The Hebrew verb form is the *hifil*, about causing something to happen, but it is often used of gifts, care, service, and helpful commands. The *hifil* certainly doesn't have to imply compulsion—and that would be bizarre in this case. The verb itself is a special one for stretching out and relaxing, and is often used of animals in their proper places of rest, such as stalls and dens; another usage, for lying down beside the dinner table, is related nicely to the theme of human hospitality in the second half of the Psalm. I prefer something like "He will invite me to stretch out." The "green pastures" in which this is going to happen are not just green, but they are full of "fresh shoots"; this is spring.

There really is great stress on restfulness in verse 2. In the Hebrew, the second verb ("leadeth" in the King James) is a very particular one, "to guide to rest or water," obviously an important act for a pastoral people in a dry climate. And the water is not "still waters" but "the water of rest." I don't see the rationale of leading "*beside* the still waters"; the sheep is literally led "to" or "into" the water—no need for the plural in English, by the way: in Hebrew, "water" is normally plural, so that form has no highfalutin tone, as the English "waters" does. The full translation of verse 2 should be more like "He will guide me to a place of rest, where I can quench my thirst, and where the water is at peace."

In verse 3, it isn't the "soul" being "restored" (whatever that would mean for a sheep), but the "life" or "life force" that is "caused to return." (There's the *hifil* or causative verb form again.) We're talking about the real pastoral enterprise here, not the scenic, carefree world of so-called pastoral literature (composed by comfortable urbanites), with a lovely shepherdess beaming in every fragrant glen, and nothing to do but court her. Herding is exhausting, full of hardships and dangers, and redeemed only by periodic moments, such as the arrival at a good watering place, when survival and comfort seem assured.

The "paths of righteousness" on which the Lord leads the speaker in verse 3 are really nothing so bland as "paths": they are deepened "wagon-tracks"; and the word for the justice that characterizes them is linked to traditional imagery of right weights and measures, an unchanging standard of looking out for the vulnerable as they obtain food. The image is of sheep following a shepherd, maybe not even being able to see over the sides of a path made for another purpose—but the shepherd makes sure everything is safe, "for his name's sake," (loosely) "just because of who he is": "name" stands in for the deepest, most solid identity.

The Hebrew of verse 4 is actually uncertain. In a tentative literal sense, it goes, "Also, though I walk in the valley of/in the midst of darkness-death, I will not fear evil." I favor the picture of a valley, a hollow passage where the primordial darkness, the darkness of impending annihilation, is especially thick, to produce an especially creepy fear of what might be in there—but it's certainly not my friend. It's trite to refer, in such a connection, to a child's fears of the closet or the space under the bed, but that's the basic psychology here.

There's plausible folk-etymological play with the clause *lō eera ra* (literally, "not I-will-fear evil"). The sound *ra* is repeated as the last two syllables of the clause, and it looks as if the verb "fear" is being associated with the noun "evil" (and perhaps placed in counterpoint to the sound *rō-ee,* for "shepherding-me" in verse 1; that participle comes from the verb with the basic form *ra-a*).

Furthermore, in what the King James translates as "for thou art with me," "you," the rare separate subject pronoun, appears right beside "with-me," the pronoun-plus-preposition, without any verbal or other connective: the syntax represents the message literally, as "you with-me"—you stand right beside me, with nothing in between. This is the point at which the poem becomes even more personal and the shepherd begins to be addressed directly, in the second person.

The comforts derived from the shepherd's "rod" and "staff" at the end of verse 4 are of two special kinds. The "rod" (which is etymologically associated with "smiting"), such as a king symbolically carries, is a kind of long club, a visible threat to chastise mischief makers, and in fact no shepherd worth the trust placed in him would be out there without a weapon against predators and bandits and the strength and skill to use it. The "staff" is more ambiguous, a word generally used for the cane that "supports" (that's the relevant etymology here) the old and infirm. Since such a condition wouldn't characterize a working shepherd, this is either mountain-climbing gear, or more probably—because otherwise why is the sheep focused on it (literally, "these comfort-me"; the "these" is a longer form of the demonstrative pronoun)?—a staff with the classic crook used to pull sheep from places they are stuck or about to fall from: it gets or keeps *them* on their feet.

Here, alas, is the trouble, at least according to my father, whose family raised several kinds of livestock to get through the Great Depression: sheep are the dumbest creatures God made. A sheep with her head stuck loosely between two slats of a fence will just stand there, frozen with terror, and without intervention will starve. It could, granted, be a goat's view from which Psalm 23 is imagined, but goats are, for their part, more full of hell than any other livestock and need a sturdy crook for the good of everyone concerned. I remember, as a child, looking across the highway and seeing that the two goats our neighbors had acquired to raise for an African development project had escaped their pen and climbed up onto a new sedan in the driveway, and were inspecting the roof and hood for edibility. In either case, sheep or goat, this Psalm is an apt representative of humankind's need for close supervision.

Abruptly, though, in Psalm 23:5 ("Thou preparest a table for me in the presence of mine enemies: thou anointest my head with oil; my cup runneth over"), the speaker of the poem is humanized and playing a role in another great Biblical motif of love and care, hospitality. In the Hebrew, the deity doesn't just "prepare" the meal on the table but "arranges it," a verb used for both physical arrangements of food and for the alignment of soldiers for battle. The image is far more significant than that of just slapping down a meal, especially since those encroaching on the speaker (here's another participial form: they're not abstract "enemies," but those who "vex" or "harass") are right there. Even the prepositions are more heightened here than a translation could reasonably make them. In Hebrew, what the King James renders as "before me" is actually "in my face." And the rather bureaucratic-sounding "in the presence" is more like "directly in front" or "opposite."

The ultimate indulgence at a feast is anointing. Oil was of course used in cooking, so there needed to be a substantial amount to spare for external application to be practical. The main method of application was probably a species of bathing. Until the Roman Empire spread the use of public bathhouses, it wasn't usual to be able to bathe regularly in water. But it is likely that a cleaning expedient we know of best from the ancient Greek world was common: oil was applied and then wiped or scraped off. (Try some vegetable oil on dirt or grease on your hands if you don't believe me.) The use of oil as a toiletry was apparently linked with feasting in both Europe and the Middle East: this was one more comfort offered to guests after their journey on a dusty road.

The greatest luxury for personal grooming was expensive, imported perfume oil. Psalm 133:2 celebrates God's blessings of community as being like precious oil that runs down through the beard and onto the clothes. Anointing of the head with oil certified kingship—David was God's anointed—and even more: the savior who was to arrive would be "the Anointed One," the Messiah, and the word was translated in Greek as *Christos*.

It should be noted, though, that in Psalm 23, it's a different verb for anointing—a bathing-type word—than the one from which "Messiah" was derived. But that doesn't critically diminish the importance of the Psalm 23 image. In John 12:3–5, a follower of Jesus named Mary is said to have "anointed" (not connected to *Christos*) his feet and wiped them with her hair, using spikenard, a costly oil from India, and rousing the anger of Judas. To complete the picture of ease and plenty in the feast of Psalm 23, the cup doesn't messily overflow, but "abounds": it is filled again and again.

The final verse ("Surely goodness and mercy shall follow me all the days of my life: and I will dwell in the house of the Lord for ever") suggests wit, with the archetypal "goodness" and "care/kindness/compassion" perhaps not just "following" the speaker—the verb is seldom used in a positive sense—but "dogging" or "persecuting" him: he could not escape God's care, even if he wanted to. The emphasis on length of time is stronger than translations indicate, and pointed up by a neat repetition: "all the days of my life" is quite correct, but in the next segment it is not simply "forever" but "for the length of days," a series of days pictured stretching on and on. They normally refer to a full human lifetime.

*

Even on the surface, the poetic parts of the Greek New Testament—mainly hymns and prayers—look more regular than Hebrew poetry in their sounds and other formal effects. But so heavily worked is *most* Greek literary language that what a modern reader considers commonsense and essential divisions between prose and poetry don't necessarily apply. That's the case with the Beatitudes ("Blessingnesses")—"Blessed are the poor in spirit," and so on. Matthew 5:3–12 contains the longer, better-known version that I will explore here. Metrically, it doesn't appear to be a poem, but it is certainly more than "prosaically" composed. The Nestle-Aland Greek edition of the New Testament, which indents the lines (the first line of each verse a little, then the second—along with further lines, where there are any—a little more), backs up the classification of the passage as a poem. I merely keep the lines separate in my literal translation and transliteration in Part Three. But here is the King James:

3 Blessed are the poor in spirit: for theirs is the kingdom of heaven.

4 Blessed are they that mourn: for they shall be comforted.

5 Blessed are the meek: for they shall inherit the earth.

6 Blessed are they which do hunger and thirst after righteousness: for they shall be filled.

7 Blessed are the merciful: for they shall obtain mercy.

8 Blessed are the pure in heart: for they shall see God.

9 Blessed are the peacemakers: for they shall be called the children of God.

10 Blessed are they which are persecuted for righteousness' sake: for theirs is the kingdom of heaven.

11 Blessed are ye, when men shall revile you, and persecute you, and shall say all manner of evil against you falsely, for my sake.

12 Rejoice, and be exceeding glad: for great is your reward in heaven: for so persecuted they the prophets which were before you.

Here are, first of all, some of the images and related concepts that the plays on sound serve to create or deepen. "Blessed" is necessarily a rather bland translation of *mahkarios;* the Greek word means "happy," but that happiness was thought to have a special connection to immortal life. The word was one of the few means by which pagans imagined their dead as having a further existence that was worthwhile, instead of a miserable one in a dank, dark, and oppressive underworld. What Jesus is represented as saying here—insistently, in all these repetitions with careful variation—is that every most important human need, longing, suffering, and worthy aspiration is, by its very existence, rewarded by the eternal happiness that best satisfies or soothes it. The complete suitability, the loving adaptation of each transcendent fate to each kind of person, is driven home by correspondences and counterpoints in sound.

The "poor in spirit" of verse 3 ("Blessed are the poor in spirit: for theirs is the kingdom of heaven") may be worse off than poor. According to this word choice in Greek, these do not seem to be ordinary low-income people, but more like beggars: grisly victims of imperial upheavals and brutal economic shakeouts of the period, who would have been pictured as diseased, emaciated, and ragged mendicants, or uprooted peasants failing to scrape by as day laborers, perhaps even losing their children to slavery on account of unpaid debts. But it's good to be cautious when reading a language that has developed into a lingua franca, as Koinē had. Previously colloquial or crude expressions tend to become ordinary expressions, a prominent example in the New Testament being the verb *laleō,* or "speak"; in Classical Greek, it's "jabber" or "prattle," but in the Gospels and Epistles it has no pejorative tinge—it's really just "speak."

These people are poor in respect to "the spirit"; yet it isn't "holy spirit" or "spirit of God," or any other elaboration on that word.* It's tempting to translate "spirit" as "disposition," *their* spirit—in other words, they're spiritless—and to speculate that they're depressed and discouraged. But given that this word means "life force" or "breath," too (the Hebrew *rūach,* which *pneuma* represents in Greek translations of Jewish Scripture, has roughly the same array of meanings), I have another proposal—though I admit it's a stretch: these are "beggars as to their breath/life"; they have absolutely nothing. It would be fair in the big religious picture (if quite unexpected in the mundane course of things) that they get an actual kingdom in the afterlife.

"They that mourn" of verse 4 ("Blessed are they that mourn: for they shall be comforted") are not just those afflicted by grief. To be widowed or orphaned or to lose a son could easily mean starving and becoming homeless—hence the urgency of commands throughout the Bible to help such people, and the poignancy of the story of Ruth and Naomi. "Comfort" in such a situation couldn't have been mere words ("I can't say how sorry I am; I know it's hard for you to believe this, but you won't always feel so bad—is there any more of this cheese dip, by the way?") but had to include something more solid, as when David "comforts" Bathsheba with sex and gives her another child (2 Samuel 12:24), who will grow up to be king and assure her safety and prosperity even when David is gone. God will replace what helpless, desolate mourners have lost.

---

*I'm discounting the possibility that they are supposed to be "blessed . . . in spirit," as that seems to separate "blessed" too far from its qualifier; and, by qualifying "blessed" at all, the verse would be out of whack with the rest of the Beatitudes.

The "meek" (King James) or "gentle" of verse 5 ("Blessed are the meek: for they shall inherit the earth") resemble the "beggars" or "poor" of verse 3 in that they look to be a very lowly type; yet they will get a most unexpected and, in worldly terms, unsuitable reward—in this case, the earth as an inheritance—just for being what they are. The word for this second humble group, in *Classical* Greek, is often used for animals being "tame." Thus, perhaps people with the same tractability as oxen or dogs will have the powerful, very human privilege of inheriting land, and apparently not one parcel, but all the land that exists. But again, it's good to read Koinē with an awareness of what I've decided to call the "jazz phenomenon": a word for "jism" (slang for "ejaculate") came to mean for us a kind of music the Air Force Band can perform on Memorial Day Weekend, and lost every trace of its association with the brothels where both sex and a new style of piano playing were available. It's unlikely that even the first readers of Matthew pictured a well-behaved dog or a working ox here—but really, there's no saying.

Verse 6 ("Blessed are they which do hunger and thirst after righteousness: for they shall be filled") may contain an actual joke: my big lexicon shows that the Greek verb normally translated "be filled" is commonly used of farm animals, and the primary definition is "feed, fatten." A correctly nuanced English translation might be "they will pig out [on justice]" (not of course that Jesus would have compared his followers with an unclean animal) or "they will be fed [on justice] as if for slaughter."

As to sharing this at Wednesday night Bible Study, better you than me. Here, however, I'm going to rebel from caution about the jazz phenomenon and point out that in the New Testament, this verb is used for feasting, and that a common subject of the verb is "everybody"; only in James 2:16, as far as I can see, does the verb concern the filling of the individual stomach as a matter of need on one side and duty on the other. At Christmas and Thanksgiving with my cousins in rural Ohio during my childhood, I experienced both literal images of "pigging out" and a sense of merry license, as we stole the best pies for our own table in the laundry room and practiced "aerobic eating." Celebrations used to be like this, instead of a mere impetus to tell the world at large that being at the table with your extended family is the worst durance of your life. In the ancient world, you happily ate and drank on command, mocking the very suggestion that God's community would ever lack ridiculous abundance.

In verse 7 ("Blessed are the merciful: for they shall obtain mercy"), the Greek basis for the English "shall obtain mercy" is a single-word extension, a verb-ization if you will, of the noun meaning "mercy": almost "will-be-mercy-ed." "Mercy" isn't a popular modern concept, but I believe it's wrongly elided rather than outdated. Where the King James translates "servant," the Greek usually reads "slave." A soldier among civilians could do more or less as he liked. The rights at law of the poor and outsiders were largely theoretical. The head of a household ruled it almost absolutely—and so on, and so on. That was then; but because I lived in Africa for many years, I won't ever be able to forget that a lot of people are at my mercy in the modern world. That helped motivate me, in my literary translation of the Beatitudes in Part Two, to decide against the relatively bland "compassion" and stick to the notion of life-or-death power I believe is contained in the original text.

Verse 8 ("Blessed are the pure in heart: for they shall see God") has another one of those words that span the mundane and the ideal: the word the King James renders as "pure," *kahtharos*. It also means "clean," as in clean clothes. In this case, there's no doubt about an operant blurring of categories. Ritual purification of the body was enjoined in God's law; and moral uncleanliness, the curse of guilt in God's eyes, wasn't a metaphor: it was considered a fact, as real as physical dirt. Hence in part the Bible's motifs, from the fall of humankind story onward (Genesis 3:7–11), of drawing back and hiding from God out of shame. But as a reward for an inner life that is "clean" in God's eyes, a mortal will be able to see God in turn—not at all a common privilege, according to Hebrew Bible stories (see Genesis 33:10 and Exodus 33:11).

Who are these "peacemakers" in verse 9 who "shall be called the children of God"? This is one of only five instances of the word "peacemaker" I find in my Greek lexicon, and I don't know of any historically confirmed ancient mediation or negotiation aimed at peace as a priority. Diplomats represented states and armies but, as far as I can see, powerful people never allowed any compromise of their own interests in the name of nonviolence. How would real peacemaking happen? But the idea is highlighted here. "Son of God" is a lofty honorific in Hebrew literature.

In verse 10 ("Blessed are they which are persecuted for righteousness' sake, for theirs is the kingdom of heaven"), the word the King James translates as "persecute" has some much more specific associations than mere terrible, unfair treatment; it's often about legal prosecution, and such an interpretation would seem historically sound. By the time this Gospel was written, persecution of Christians had probably already established its normal basis: believers were hauled into hearings before magistrates and, if they would not recant and sacrifice to the Roman emperor's image, were put to death.

This process, an entirely legal one, supplied brutal spectacles in the arena (Christians were a much handier, cheaper resource for public abuse than bandit gangs perilously tracked down, trained gladiators, trapped local or imported exotic animals—or even criminal slaves, who were, after all, property and could be put to some long-term use), so "for righteousness' sake/because of justice" may have a certain tang: the Greek word is obviously formed from *dikē*, meaning "trial," "prosecution," and "verdict," as well as "justice." Justice, the real thing, was what Christians died for; the trappings—kangaroo courts—sent them to die.

Both verse 6 and verse 10 have the Greek word for "righteousness/justice" at the end of their first lines. Maybe in the first case the justice associated with hunger and thirst is the crucial material fairness the poor require: they are in need because they have been cheated—a common circumstance of the time, when elites controlled what was left of local institutions and connived with the Roman Imperial administration in exploiting the poor.

According to verses 11 and 12, assuring a "great . . . reward in heaven" to those persecuted and abused in the name of the new faith, three related actions—insult, persecution/prosecution, and slander must bring on a strong but paradoxical reaction, expressed by two verbs in the imperative, which the King James renders as "rejoice, and be exceedingly glad." This second verb (subsuming the English adverb "exceedingly") connotes having a real hoot (sometimes at someone else's expense).

Let me show how all this was emphasized, by pointing out a few persistent sound effects I believe are thematic in the Greek, a full representation of which appears, as usual, in Part Three. A "to be" verb is not included in the first line of a verse until verse 11, at which point the verb is in the second-person plural, "you-are" (not the third-person plural, "they-are," as it would have needed to be earlier), indicating that the speaker is changing to direct address. Until then, the list begins and continues in the pattern "Blessed the beggars. . . ." This means the Beatitudes have a Hebrew type of syntax, short on "to be" connectives.

Overall in the Greek, in fact, there is a great paucity of verbs where they are not strictly necessary and would not do any real work. The verbs that do appear are artfully placed. The second lines of each of verses 3–10 all contain verbs, most of them quite long verbs, and most placed at the emphatic line end. Four of these verbs are passive, creating a pattern.

Whereas in English the Beatitudes are a rhythmic nullity, the Greek text is quite different. In the first lines of verses, the article *hoi* ("the") is unaccented, and in combination with the four-syllable *mahkarioi* ("blessed/happy"), with its single accent on the second syllable, yields one accent for the five syllables. With the help of the four short vowel sounds (even the final *-oi* is short in this position), the effect is light and quick. Likewise, *estin* ("is") and *este* ("[you] are") have no accents of their own in verses 3, 10, and 11, helping create considerable springiness at the beginnings of their own lines. The pounding comes in the second halves of the Beatitudes' lines, until there are no longer any distinct lines.

To go from the beginning concerning another feature of the Greek: in rapid succession, there are four *p* alliterations in the naming of the first two categories of blessed people and the reasons they are blessed. Later, alliterations of *d, e,* and *k* take their turns. Also, several of the "Blessed . . ." clauses nearly match the following "for/ because . . ." clauses in number of syllables.

I probably could not mimic most of these features in the original forms without creating doggerel ("Spiritually poor people"? "They are cared for by Providence, for they possess paradise"?), but the forms are fascinating to consider. Remember that, in this case, we know that they reflect a performance, the Sermon on the Mount given by Jesus in Aramaic to a large crowd. The wording must have been memorable; Jesus is uniformly depicted as sharp and witty. But it's not a wild-eyed speculation that whoever composed the New Testament passage was influenced more by the highly formal hotdogging of literary Greek than by quotation of the Aramaic. And Greek-speaking people in the wider Roman Empire very likely experienced this passage as a sort of chant. In an age long before pop music and advertising came to supply most of the rhythmic language that sticks in people's heads, the sheer catchiness of these words—it's easy to imagine—helped them to be adopted as instruction in Christian faith and practice.

5

Authorship or Rhetoric
or Voice or Something

Ecclesiastes on the Fragile Joys of Life (Ecclesiastes 9:7–11)
Paul on the Love of God Through Jesus (Romans 8:31–39)

Among many other blessed dispensations of the Scriptural tradition is the muted, communal role of most authors (but I should in fact write "authors," with those qualifying quotation marks): they left their names off, ascribed inspiration to God, edited respectfully, amalgamated, and, as the canon formed much later, weren't there to plead for themselves or hear what people thought of them and their work.

Take creation stories—the approaches, the tones, the structures and purposes. For contrast, on the one side I can adduce the Greek poet Hesiod and the Roman satirist Juvenal, and on the other the two creation stories in Genesis.

Hesiod is actually the first firmly identifiable author (an individual recording his own thoughts under his own name) in the West. Around 700 B.C.E., he was a farmer in an obscure town (Ascra, in mainland Greece) whose avocation was poetry, and who won a recitation contest on perhaps the only journey he ever took out of his own district (to Chalcis, on the island of Euboea).

Hesiod uses some material that is plainly traditional, and his *Theogony* or *Birth of the Gods* sounds in part like an old oral account of the universe's early history. But in this poem, he does not merely invoke the Muses, as the legendary figure "Homer" does: instead, they meet him while he is pasturing his flock and give him a laurel staff to certify his personal calling. In another poem, *The Works and Days,* Hesiod grouses in highly personal terms. His hometown, where his father settled as an immigrant, is a total dump. Women will do a man in despite his backbreaking efforts to make a go of a farm. They wag their bedizened bottoms and clean out a chump's storehouse. And just imagine a pampered young girl in the middle of winter, luxuriating in a warm house and taking a bath, no less—nothing for *her* to do, nothing for *her* to worry about!

Hesiod unblushingly integrates his own experiences and attitudes into his version of what the entire world is about from its inception. What had happened to first spread suffering? He has two versions of the same story, one in the largely mythological *Birth of the Gods,* but the more memorable one in the more intimate *Works and Days.* In sum, trouble and disease came from womankind, as a punishment for the theft of fire from heaven by Prometheus for human benefit. The gods ganged up to construct Pandora, the slutty, sinister bitch who opened the canister of evils. There was probably an older folktale in which both partners have their motivations, but in Hesiod we see only the malignant gods huddled around their new creation, instructing her and dolling her up and corrupting her like teenagers about to send a young sibling to carry out some hideous prank. It's a wantonly stacked narrative deck, but Hesiod got away with it; there is no sign that anyone even tried to splice in a more moderate account later. A persuasive author could write what he wanted, and it would stand.

Another European author of a creation story is the Roman satirist Juvenal, active around the beginning of the second century C.E. When Jewish Scripture was quite well established and the New Testament was coming together, Juvenal was at the end of an opposite line of literary development. His is the ultimate individual voice: sophisticated, cynical, committed to nothing but merciless social criticism and contemptuous competition with other authors. He will have nothing to do with a creation story, that very basic part of a worldview, except in lampooning it.

Hesiod solemnly recites the grim story of mankind's decline from innocence, starting in the Golden Age, when there was no crime and no agriculture: people ate the wild produce of the land and lived in peace, health, and happiness. Juvenal, to preface his seven-hundred-line tirade against women, concedes that, right, in the Golden Age there was no adultery, but he insists that this was because the women were too ugly: they didn't look anything like the famous (married) girlfriend of the Roman poet Catullus, playing with her cute song-bird; no, these women's breasts were the kind for "hefty babies to guzzle," and wives were "often hairier than their acorn-belching husbands." Juvenal's goal, like that of any self-respecting modern author, was not to smooth over differences but to annihilate the competition and have the last word—and in misogyny, his victory stands uncontested after nineteen hundred years.

The Biblical scribes, with care, reverence, and mutual defer-ence, kept the two creation stories concerning humankind in Gen-esis (1:26–29 and 2:7–25) in tactful parallel to each other, though that meant ignoring the big differences that remain. In the first, God envisages the world almost as a single farm, with the male and female human beings, created together, husbanding it together and commanded to breed abundantly, as the animals themselves breed and fill it. This is all one tight narrative. In the second story, verses about the creation of man and of woman are widely separated by a description of the Garden of Eden (including its broad geogra-phy, with some mining and trade information thrown in!) and the instructions about the forbidden fruit, and then by Adam's naming of the animals. At last, after his productive surgery, Adam punningly names "woman."

The comfort with which people—like the Biblical scribes, along with most of their readers throughout the ages—handle incompat-ibility, ambiguity, and even nonsense in traditional texts makes me think of the way children handle the "Mondegreens" they create from phrases in hymns, prayers, and Christmas carols. (Among my favorites are "While shepherds walked their fox by night" for "While shepherds watched their flocks by night," "Pity mice implicitly" for "Pity my simplicity," and "Goddamn sinners reconciled" for "God and sinners reconciled"—this last one was my father's, from rural Ohio in the 1930s.) That the young and unlettered misinterpret the abstractions and images from ancient stories presented to them in lofty, archaic language is hardly phenomenal. What's more interest-ing to me is the normal way of accepting, placidly remembering, and reciting distortions year after year.

But that doesn't allow me to discount the individual voices in the Bible, the distinct urgings of special viewpoints. In the Hebrew Bible, that's certainly the case for Ecclesiastes or Kohelet (both traditionally translated as "Preacher"), whose author flirts with nihilism. Here are some verses from Ecclesiastes, chapter 9.

7 Go thy way, eat thy bread with joy, and drink thy wine with a merry heart; for God now accepteth thy works.

8 Let thy garments be always white; and let thy head lack no ointment.

9 Live joyfully with the wife whom thou lovest all the days of the life of thy vanity, which he hath given thee under the sun, all the days of thy vanity: for that is thy portion in this life, and in thy labour which thou takest under the sun.

10 Whatsoever thy hand findeth to do, do it with thy might; for there is no work, nor device, nor knowledge, nor wisdom, in the grave, whither thou goest.

11 I returned, and saw under the sun, that the race is not to the swift, nor the battle to the strong, neither yet bread to the wise, nor yet riches to men of understanding, nor yet favour to men of skill; but time and chance happeneth to them all.

The writer of Ecclesiastes (or the writer of—perhaps—all but chapter 12's pious coda, which is almost certainly tacked on by another hand) has an impressively different point of view. I don't think it's that of the bored, disaffected princeling of some Middle Eastern literature; Epicureanism seems a more likely influence. This philosophy didn't advocate overindulgence or sensuality but the opposite: the calm enjoyment of ordinary pleasures such as plain food, friendship, and family life.

In the first three verses of Ecclesiastes set out above, the pleasures are by and large simple ones, including the company of a single mate,* not of a powerful and arrogant man's floozies. Bread was a staple food, wine the default drink at meals. White garments were posh and could be ceremonial, as I've pointed out in my discussion of the martyrs of Revelation (pp. 61–62); and oil as a toiletry at the table signaled the good life, as the Twenty-Third Psalm makes clear

---

*In Hebrew, the perfect (= semi-past) aspect of the verb for the speaker's feelings for her may signal the youthful passion that, though it hasn't endured as such, hasn't been forgotten or replaced.

(pp. 73–74). But there's nothing here about hordes of animals, as in stories of the patriarchs, or about a whole suburb of idle, partying progeny, as in the story of Job (1:2, 4). As Epicurus would recommend, this is to be quiet, thoughtful, and not excessive enjoyment.

The famous verse Ecclesiastes 9:10 ("Whatsoever thy hand findeth to do, do it with thy might; for there is no work, nor device, nor knowledge, nor wisdom, in the grave, whither thou goest") suggests an individual's willful creation of meaning in the activities he devotes himself to—because, apparently, there is no other meaning to be had, none available from tradition or clan or nation. This is really pretty far out when set against the background of Scriptural Judaism.

But the ultimate intellectual rebellion follows in verse 11 ("I returned, and saw under the sun, that the race is not to the swift, nor the battle to the strong, neither yet bread to the wise, nor yet riches to men of understanding, nor yet favour to men of skill; but time and chance happeneth to them all"): whatever passion or energy you put into your endeavors may very well not pan out. Neither God nor other people nor the universe can be counted on to reward you—fine; but you won't necessarily be able to reward yourself either. This gloominess goes beyond Epicureanism, which never claimed that you couldn't "win" in life if you tried, only that conventional "winning" wasn't worth it.

This passage has a marvelously idiosyncratic combination of matter and manner. For instance, it lifts mannerisms from other Scripture and uses them for the opposite of their original purposes; but does so seriously, with only sad irony, and without a trace of parody.

"Walk/go" is normally a command to get off one's butt, not onto it, as in verse 7. Moreover, "Get up and go" is a lot more intuitive than "Go [sit or recline] and eat." But for all its strangeness, this verse ("Go thy way, eat thy bread with joy, and drink thy wine with a merry heart; for God now accepteth thy works") is nicely harmonious in the Hebrew. There are two expressions using *beh* ("with" in the King James) and a noun for enjoyment (the "joy" and the "merry heart"), each right before the noun for what is to be enjoyed (the bread and the wine); to each of these two words, the affirming possessive is attached: might as well enjoy it—it's yours. That same "your" (= -*ka*) comes at the end of the next poetic line, and there it is attached to a word for "works," so that enjoyment and work blend sonically as well as ethically. Here is the literal translation and the transliteration:

walk/go   eat with-joy   bread-your || and-drink with-[a]-heart
leik   ekōl beh-simcha lachmeh-ka || ū-shahtei beh-lev

  good [= cheerful] wine-your
  tōv   yeineh-ka

because   already   is-pleased-with || the God(s)   (direct object marker)
kee   kevar   rahtsa || ha-elōheem   et

  works-your
  ma-aseh-ka

The passage employs a pretty extreme amount of repetition, which is paradoxically both flowing and expressive of certain ironies (and to which the notes to my full literary translation in Part Two, along with my full technical version in Part Three, offer detailed guidance). There are several expressions for continuing time, starting at the beginning of verse 8 ("at-every time") and extending through the construct chain "all [the] days ([of the] life) [of] evanescence-your" that occurs *twice* in verse 9. Similarly, the repeated "under the sun" (twice in verse 9, once in verse 11) is a vivid expression for "on this earth," or "everywhere the sun shines," the great *spatial* extent of humankind's possibilities. God has given all of these days and all of this space—the universe belongs to us to be enjoyed. But then the reader is brought up short: at the end of verse 11, "time" (the same word as at the start of verse 8, when the addressee is told to be spruced up for feasting "at-every time") and "chance" are forces of limitation, the forces that "happeneth" to us to make all our endeavors losing ones.

If this worldview can be described at all by modern analogy, perhaps it is an Epicurean asceticism or a mystical nihilism. In Ecclesiastes, time and space do not really *belong* to people, as in the English expression "your time on earth." They are just the vast arena in which we are set down, without pagan parameters of "fate" or Jewish ones of the national covenant or Christian ones of personal redemption. What does belong to us, and is in fact joined with "life" in the longer "construct chain" in verse 9, and reserved for the stronger last position in both chains in that verse, is what the King James calls "vanity" and what I call "evanescence."

Hebrew *loves* these expressions of physical insubstantiality given moral or intellectual meaning (which I discuss in Chapter 2, pp. 41–42). The *thing* at issue here is a wisp of vapor or a puff of wind; but it's a thing that's gone, blended back into the air, before you can even focus on it. It's not self-conceit but the inability to establish *anything,* let alone inordinate pride. Quite ironically, in verse 9 the word cluster for "your evanescence," *hevleh-ka,* nearly matches in sound the word *helkeh-ka* in the same verse, or what you get by law, custom, or reward (in the King James, "thy portion"). This could be your inheritance, the plot of land or number of sheep or other wealth set aside for you—which you ought to be able to rely on as a matter of right. Too bad: it's no more solid than the morning fog, because in time, over life, as Ecclesiastes has drummed in from its first chapter, there's no relying on anything—including property—except as a source of exasperation, or "vexation of spirit," as the King James repeatedly translates it. All the Scriptures' heroic amassers of livestock for benefit of their children shouldn't have bothered, apparently.

Accordingly, the words in the passage for what should be advantages in life show in the Hebrew an extraordinary number of puffy, insubstantial sounds, which can be traced throughout the transliteration in Part Three.

In the famous verse about a variety of pointless endeavors (athletics, war, etc.), there's also an especially trailing or drawn-out style. This verse has *five* poetic segments (halflines, that is), in syntactic parallel, for dismissing as many broad categories of human effort and ability. The addition of "also" (KJV: "yet") three times suggests that merely making the list is tedious.

Over the course of the list, the vagueness of the attributes increases, and the connections to the rewards expected grow more fuzzy. Why should shrewd people get bread, in particular, or knowledgeable people popularity? What's more, two items from the peppy verse 10, the exhortation to work that comes immediately before this verse, are taken up here in personalized forms—"shrewdness" becomes "shrewd [people]" and "knowledge" becomes "knowledgeable [people]"—and are in their turn declared useless; not unreliable, not less than a guarantee, but a wash, once people try to enact and embody these ideals of achievement. Modern Westerners are fond of misquoting this verse as saying that "the race is not always to the swift," and so on. There's no "always." The speaker saw that the winners were *never* who they ought to be.

Ecclesiastes is ravishing in its irony. On the one hand, what's the point to anything? Worse, is there ever an end to life's failures and disappointments? Apparently not. On the other hand, the world has magnitudes of things you can enjoy—just contemplating them is wonderful. Most wonderful of all, you can share your impressions in unforgettable, eternal language that belies everything you claim about the fragility of human aspiration.

*

My friends know better than to get me started on Paul of Tarsus. He is the only real author in the Bible, if a definition of "author" as an undoubted historical figure undoubtedly writing under his own name prevails. He is also the strongest link between the Old and New Testaments, as a Jew learned in Scripture who also outlined (if he didn't actually come up with) the essentials of Christian theology. Six or seven of the New Testament books of Epistles (or "Letters") come from him. These testify that during his missionary career he was welcomed in some quarters and reviled in others for trying to reconcile Palestinian Jewish and pagan European culture under a new monotheism with benefits. Sorry, but if Jews are allowed to make Jewish jokes, a Christian should be allowed to make Christian ones, acknowledging the strangeness of the belief in the incarnation and crucifixion as the source of salvation.

Paul was possessed by the urge to spread the word, and his success seems to have owed a great deal to his skill in Greco-Roman rhetoric. In his Diaspora upbringing, he had evidently passed through the standard public-speaking curriculum and then some, the refinements of philosophical discourse. Here he is before the tribunal of theology, in Romans, chapter 8:

31 What shall we then say to these things? If God be for us, who can be against us?

32   He that spared not his own Son, but delivered him up for us all, how shall he not with him also freely give us all things?

33   Who shall lay any thing to the charge of God's elect? It is God that justifieth.

34   Who is he that condemneth? It is Christ that died, yea rather, that is risen again, who is even at the right hand of God, who also maketh intercession for us.

35   Who shall separate us from the love of Christ? shall tribulation, or distress, or persecution, or famine, or nakedness, or peril, or sword?

36   As it is written, For thy sake we are killed all the day long; we are accounted as sheep for the slaughter.

37   Nay, in all these things we are more than conquerors through him that loved us.

38   For I am persuaded, that neither death, nor life, nor angels, nor principalities, nor powers, nor things present, nor things to come,

39   Nor height, nor depth, nor any other creature, shall be able to separate us from the love of God, which is in Christ Jesus our Lord.

I had heard this passage again and again from the pulpit in English, and it left little but "Yeah—fine—okay" in my mind. This was just Paul on salvation, right? But when I started to consider the Greek, from the first clause on a remarkable personality delivering a remarkable message with remarkable skill hit me.

The passage is rich in the rhetorical question, that audience-involving device. The first question ("What shall we then say to these things?") had me saying to myself, "Huh! I've seen that all over the place." I conducted a quick electronic search of the most famous Greek orator, Demosthenes, and sure enough, "What shall we say then?" (though not in the same exact words in Greek) popped up right and left. This is technically aporia, a feigned expression of doubt. The speaker pretends that he doesn't know where he's headed, and ideally he dramatizes an outreach to his listeners at the same time: they're supposed to sense the correct train of thought as well as he does. In the Greco-Roman world, where ornate writing and display oratory were treated as sports, a public figure could not get away with talking down or writing down, could not play the expert. He had to construct a virtual conversation.

A second question ("If God be for us, who can be against us?") contains an antithesis, or highlighted—perhaps artificial—contrast. The practical answer to this question is obvious: God may indeed be for us, but that doesn't stop scary majorities of mortals from being against us everywhere we go. Paul means, of course, that ultimately and in the ways that matter, there is no human being against us; but this very compact opposition of terms makes that idea quite punchy.

Verse 32 ("He that spared not his own Son, but delivered him up for us all, how shall he not with him also freely give us all things?") with its switched-around syntax demonstrates prolepsis, or anticipation. One impression is that the speaker is excited and so dwells a little on the main source of the excitement before proceeding to his argument. In Matthew 6:28, the lead-in to Jesus's illustration of why his followers should not worry about the necessities of life is endlessly cited as an example of prolepsis, and it's really the perfect example. "Consider the lilies of the field, how they grow" is nicely set up to delay the lesson and places at the front of it an image of spring fields and large white flowers—like posh bleached festival or ritual clothing. In this verse of Paul's, it's first, and lingeringly, an image of a father giving up his own single beloved son, a superlative appeal to emotion in that era.

This verse also contains sharp antitheses: begrudging, surrendering, giving for free; God's own single son, everything that exists. The three verbs are a progression, by way of paraprosdokia, or surprise, toward a climax. Anyone would naturally hold back his son (his most precious relation, according to ancient values) from anything not in his best interests; but the verb for surrendering that's used here (*paredōken* is the form in which it appears) is often about indifferently or cynically (if not under force) turning someone over or in—a slave (for torture as a witness to a crime), a hostage, a criminal, a betrayed friend or countryman. The word is repeatedly used of Judas "handing over" Jesus to the authorities. Yet this exercise is, bizarrely, aimed at the giving of everything good, to everyone who wants it, gratis.

As an added ornament, in Greek "us all" (for whose sake the son has been given up) and "all [things] to-us" (the ultimate gift) form a

neat chiastic (= interlocking) word order; in Greek, moreover, they
are four words of two syllables each and so have a tidy rhythm:
heimōn pahntōn and *pahnta heimin.*

Bolstering my hunch that *paredōken* is about judicial proceed-
ings, verse 33 ("Who shall lay any thing to the charge of God's elect?
It is God that justifieth") launches into a full-blown spoof of foren-
sic defense oratory, stock themes of which are the accuser's gall in
bringing charges, and the impropriety of the trial in general. In the
Greek, there is sound and semantic play between *enkahlesei* (KJV:
"lay . . . to the charge") and *eklektōn* (KJV: "of [God's] elect"), and
sound play between both of these and *dikaiōn* (KJV: "justifieth" =
technically here, "the [one] judging/sentencing/acquitting"). This
word choice points up the absurdity of hauling *into* (*en*) court those
who are singled *out* (*ek*) for a friendly verdict by the judge himself, God. The ultimate joke is stressed by the anadiplosis (the same
word that ends one clause begins the next) of the word for "God"
in the Greek (literally "who will-bring-charges against chosen [ones]
of-God God [is] the [one] judging"). A prosecution of the faithful is
pretty stupid, because who sits in judgment (of everything, in fact)
but God?—and in case you don't get that, I'm repeating the word
"God" without a break. We're talking about God here. God God
God God God. The metaphysical fix is in.

Verse 34 ("Who is he that condemneth? It is Christ that died,
yea rather, that is risen again, who is even at the right hand of God,
who also maketh intercession for us") is in the Greek a masterpiece
of isocola, or segments of words of the same or roughly the same
length succeeding each other. The segments are ten, eleven, eleven,
and ten syllables long, respectively. Identical or near-identical beginnings of segments are called anaphora, and this verse has plenty of
that:

tis hŏ ("Who [is] the-one") . . .
hŏ ("[It is] the-one") . . .
hos kai ("who even/also") . . .
hos kai ("who even/also") . . .*

*At the end of segments, repetition is antistrophe—some of that in this passage,
too: not the kind of thing we sweated in school at the age of fourteen, but Paul and
his classmates did.

Within this virtual stanza, Paul continues the courtroom drama to great effect. Who would dare convict? Jesus is actually the one who died—and so is the alleged victim according to this farcical murder trial. Or rather, he came back to life. More than that, he's sitting on God's right hand (on the tribunal?); and more than that, he's the one making an appeal on our behalf!

Verse 35 ("Who shall separate us from the love of Christ? shall tribulation, or distress, or persecution, or famine, or nakedness, or peril, or sword?") is a rhetorical question full of polysyndeton, or the repetition of conjunctions (here, *ei* or "or") in a series of coordinated segments. This is a long polysyndeton, but a rapid-fire one, as words, not phrases or clauses, form the list.

The list is quite interesting. The second item, "distress," literally "narrowness," sounds like expressions in the Psalms for the distress in which the speaker is (if I put it colloquially) "jammed" or "stuck," but on the whole the situations and conditions in Paul's list are the kind the poor dread, and the voice of the Psalms is not that of a poor man. Even this word for "peril" was one often associated with legal troubles, fearsome to the less well-to-do who lacked the influence, skills, connections, and rights, as well, of course, as the material resources they needed to come out well in this arena, and who faced grimmer outcomes. (Exile was the worst punishment someone of the citizen class would normally suffer under the law.)

In verse 36 ("As it is written, For thy sake we are killed all the day long; we are accounted as sheep for the slaughter"), Paul makes one of his frequent recourses to quoting the Scripture (here, Psalm 44:22). Scriptural references were much more frequent in pious Jewish discourse than literary ones were in Greco-Roman rhetoric, but in both, quotation was a mark of learning, a certification of authority. More or less all the time, Paul appears unable to quote on target to save his life; right now, he just swipes a verse from a Psalm about the fate of the nation seemingly abandoned by God and exposed to military defeat. But had misquotation not been routine—not to say useful and well-regarded—the Bible never could have come together in the first place, let alone expanded and changed.

Verse 37 ("Nay, in all these things we are more than conquerors through him that loved us") has a handsome hyperbole, a very rare verb that should mean something like "we are über-winners." Perhaps the operant metaphor is, if not one of legal victory, then one of war (to which the Psalm quotation properly alludes); but more probably this has to do with athletics, favorite imagery of Paul's. (See, for example, Galatians 5:7 concerning faithfulness as a foot-race.) It is a joke—and also not a joke—to compare the religious life with what went on at the Olympics and the other Great Games. Athletic competition had essentially nothing to do with traditional Jewish culture, but was bound up in pagan religion itself and very highly regarded in Italy, Greece, and elsewhere as military, civic, and moral training. Victorious athletes were much glorified.

Verses 38 and 39 ("For I am persuaded, that neither death, nor life, nor angels, nor principalities, nor powers, nor things present, nor things to come, nor height, nor depth, nor any other creature, shall be able to separate us from the love of God, which is in Christ Jesus our Lord") are like the finale of a fireworks display. A mechanical translation of the opening would read, "I am in the present and enduring state of having been persuaded." The verb tense is the rare and special perfect; this is a true passive verb (whereas the English "I am persuaded" or "I am convinced" doesn't express much more than "I am of the opinion"); and the verb is "persuade," evoking the immense prestige and importance of rhetoric in Greco-Roman society (there was a goddess Persuasion) yet turning the idea of verbal competition—in which Paul himself has been engaged this whole time!—on its head. The losers—the tractable, the persuad-able, the humble—are the winners in this new religion; the reader should be persuaded by Paul not because Paul is a hotshot with words but because Paul himself has been persuaded. The power that acted on him beginning on the road to Damascus, and not his personal cleverness and skill, speaks through him to others. Most important of all, this verb has the same root as the noun for "faith": Christians are persuaded, they trust, they have faith, they surrender their intellectual authority to God in the name of their inexplicable salvation.

There follows a mass of polysyndeton with the connective "nei-ther" (*úteh*). (Compare the polysyndeton with *ei* ["or"] in verse 35.) In this list, *dunahmeis* ("powers") cleverly echoes *duneisetai* ("shall be able"): power itself has no power to get in the way of love.

The ultimate, pulling-out-all-the-stops climax is the designation of love's source. Not just the love of the Anointed One, Jesus (see verse 34), and not just the one who loved us (verse 37), but love,

God, the Anointed One, Jesus, our Lord—these are the reasons for joy and confidence. In the Greek, the possessive "of-us" gets the very last word: *our* savior, *our* sacrifice, *our* gift. The passage's exposition of what is and isn't done, can and can't be done *to us,* is joyfully resolved in our new possession, God made man, and God given to us to keep.

6

Scripture as the Big Conversation

The Ten Commandments (Deuteronomy 5:6–21)
The Parable of the Good Samaritan (Luke 10:25–37)

One day, while I was living in South Africa, two young black men jumped me outside Cape Town's Quaker House, pushing me down onto my back and grabbing my backpack in the same moment. I thought of the copyedited manuscript inside, and the days it would take to redo all that work, and I hung on to a strap, shrieking and peeing. Both men were standing at my upturned toes, pulling for all they were worth. One lifted in hesitant threat the knife with which he had begun sawing at the backpack strap. I shrieked louder, and they were suddenly gone, running, a security guard after them. But he stopped after about twenty yards and strolled back to me. The muggers got into a white car at the end of the block and departed, not at a conspicuous speed.

It occurred to me later: I had sort of won. In a two-to-one tug-of-war I had hung on just long enough. I was pretty strong, and it was a pretty badly planned attack. I was, as it had played out, a match for them. I started to turn over the incident like a shoddy foreign handicraft: "Pathetic. It's as if they've got no self-respect at all. My grandma on her worst day could have done a better job."

Nobody laughed or shook his head at this take on it. A partner in an up-and-coming software firm said, "You did the right thing. You can't give in. When I'm downtown, I just walk like, 'Hey, come on, try it!' and they stay away." I also knew, especially from the journalism I was doing, that it could be better to die than live as a victim around here. Get held up or roughed up a couple of times without getting your own back—which could include not only a bullet or two of yours in the fuckin' kaffirs, but perhaps even a well-armed expedition into the local squatter camp to literally get your own back—and you might not be grateful to survive. You might in fact die anyway, from a prolonged, undiagnosed, but clearly stress-related illness, or from depression-induced suicide. Or they might, after finding someone nice and vulnerable, not stop coming back until they got everything, and you'd be unlikely to survive *that*.

So stand up for yourself—or get out, go to New Zealand along with the toddler-clutching families and the frail aunties and the bombed-out liberals. "Africa is not for sissies," goes the pop song. Win—you *have* to win. It doesn't matter how. Show the bastards you're not going anywhere.

That was on the weekend. Then it was Tuesday, and Lucy came from the black township to clean the house. She traveled two hours each way by bus, and a few months before, when the minibus taxi barons had hired thugs to shoot up the buses, she kept coming, though I offered her full pay to stay home. All that restrained me from giving her three times instead of twice the standard pay was the certainty that she wouldn't spend it on herself but pass it on, because she couldn't stand to see anybody in need. If I and other white people were stressed, what must *she* feel, *out there,* watching the *township* crime victims hitching their way across the road on makeshift crutches? I sobbed in shame and horror.

Because of all this, I care what the Bible has to say about our possibilities for getting along with one another, and I've thought a lot about what the Ten Commandments and the Parable of the Good Samaritan managed to do, when and where they were written, and adopted, and embraced. I believe few historians would dispute that those were times and places with more fear and hatred prevailing, with more violence threatening, than we're used to in post–Civil War America. Yet—well, even here and now people are hardly getting along to any whiz-bang extent.

What interests me most as a translator is the interactive way the Bible handles the interactions of conflict. In my book so far, I've been stressing the power of the texts in the original languages to charm and persuade listeners and readers; but the ultimate power the texts can manifest is to come fully into our hands and help us toward our own achievement of more goodwill and orderliness and equality than human beings can usually muster, a worthwhile future for human society against the human odds—as if God cared for us and would bear with us to the end and beyond.

Perhaps I can explain this impression best by circling in on a single word of Hebrew used in the Ten Commandments, *rei-a* (more or less "other"—but that's a major "more or less"), and also its translation and deployment in Greek in the Book of Luke. I'm going to explore how its very ambiguity may have led to challenge and renewal.

Let me start (and I promise I'll get where I'm going) by describing the Hebrew of the Shema or Sh'ma (literally, the "Hear"), which (in the King James Translation) announces, "Hear, O Israel: The Lord our God is one Lord: And thou shalt love the Lord thy God with all thine heart, and with all thy soul, and with all thy might" (Deuteronomy 6:4–5).

Appearing together here, the words "heart," "soul," and "might" signal that devotion to God must have no conceivable limit: if you think you can delineate it with a word, then have another think—in the form of another word. The result is a broad, circular, overlapping description of the most vital human capacities. The word translated as "heart" subsumes the definitions "mind" and "will." The "soul" word (literally, "neck") is a much more earthy description of inner life than the English "soul," and can be related to physical strength and health. "Might" is also greatness, muchness: this is the vaguely immense potential owed to God. The word for "thy" or "your" in the Hebrew is here, as normally, a possessive pronoun (-*ka*) attached to the end of the nouns, so that the list is more harmonious than English translations; it's readily chantable. Do *this* for God, and *more* for God, then *more* for God.

But the next two verses command no dramatic act of devotion, no worship, no sacrifice—nothing directed at God at all.

> 6   And these words, which I command thee this day, shall be in thine heart:
> 7   And thou shalt teach them diligently unto thy children, and shalt talk of them when thou sittest in thine house, and when thou walkest by the way, and when thou liest down, and when thou risest up.

The hearer must take the words of the law in thoroughly. Here's "heart" again. He is required to make the words *part of himself,* and the outward pledge of this is that he teaches them to the young and ignorant and discusses them at every opportunity. What you were supposed to do with the law was embrace it with all of your abilities. You were not supposed merely to follow it.

Understood this way, even the most thunderous, solemn law, such as the Ten Commandments, looks in detail less like what we would recognize as statute—I picture for comparison the text of typical legislation, or the signs in parks listing municipal regulations—and more like a basis for expansive discourse, or the beginnings of that discourse itself. And the text of the law itself tends to bear this out. In fact, the Greek-derived name for the Ten Commandments is the Decalogue, "Ten Words/Ideas,"* based pretty faithfully on the Hebrew heading for these items, literally the "Ten Words/Matters." For the sake of keeping my discussion within the same Biblical book for now, I'll quote the version of the Ten Commandments that appears in Deuteronomy, chapter 5, shortly before the Shema (and not the Ten Commandments as set out in Exodus, chapter 20).

6 I am the Lord thy God, which brought thee out of the land of Egypt, from the house of bondage.

7 Thou shalt have none other gods before me.

8 Thou shalt not make thee any graven image, or any likeness of any thing that is in heaven above, or that is in the earth beneath, or that is in the waters beneath the earth:

9 Thou shalt not bow down thyself unto them, nor serve them: for I the Lord thy God am a jealous God, visiting the iniquity of the fathers upon the children unto the third and fourth generation of them that hate me,

10 And shewing mercy unto thousands of them that love me and keep my commandments.

11 Thou shalt not take the name of the Lord thy God in vain: for the Lord will not hold him guiltless that taketh his name in vain.

12 Keep the sabbath day to sanctify it, as the Lord thy God hath commanded thee.

---

*See Chapter 2 on John, chapter 1, concerning the Greek word *logos,* pp. 47–49.

13   Six days thou shalt labour, and do all thy work:

14   But the seventh day is the sabbath of the Lord thy God: in it thou shalt not do any work, thou, nor thy son, nor thy daughter, nor thy manservant, nor thy maidservant, nor thine ox, nor thine ass, nor any of thy cattle, nor thy stranger that is within thy gates; that thy manservant and thy maidservant may rest as well as thou.

15   And remember that thou wast a servant in the land of Egypt, and that the Lord thy God brought thee out thence through a mighty hand and by a stretched out arm: therefore the Lord thy God commanded thee to keep the sabbath day.

16   Honour thy father and thy mother, as the Lord thy God hath commanded thee; that thy days may be prolonged, and that it may go well with thee, in the land which the Lord thy God giveth thee.

17   Thou shalt not kill.

18   Neither shalt thou commit adultery.

19   Neither shalt thou steal.

20   Neither shalt thou bear false witness against thy neighbour.

21   Neither shalt thou desire thy neighbour's wife, neither shalt thou covet thy neighbour's house, his field, or his manservant, or his maidservant, his ox, or his ass, or any thing that is thy neighbour's.

When I drive modern theocracy and Bible-thumping out of my mind, this sounds a lot more like half of a conversation between a demanding but not ruthless parent and a rather backward child. As in such a conversation, what is not immediately obvious is explained. First (verse 6, which is expanded on in verse 15) comes the basis for (if not absolute monotheism, then at least) God's absolute superiority: he has a long-standing relationship with his people; they are under a great obligation to him. Other rationales for obeying come later in the passage. Particularly interesting is God's warning description of his own personality, in verse 9: he is jealous, so do not provoke him with straying worship.

The Sabbath is explained at length (verses 12–15), obviously for a reason: this was an imported foreign custom, like many others. Israelite society was full of influences from a variety of neighboring and intermixed peoples. The character of the Scripture that emerged must have had a lot to do with that: these writings *built* and *justified* a special identity, instead of dictating one from on high—which no document could have managed to do in such a contentious and changing cultural mix. From this comes a lasting impression of living voices working things out.

Decent treatment of parents is not only enjoined but also encouraged by the promise of rewards (long life and well-being in this God-given country—verse 16), and this makes a good deal of sense. The cherishing of children is mainly about instinct and not (in spite of much blather to the contrary in the American media) heroism: there's a normal gut-wrenching need to save that small mortal who came out of your own body. In contrast, older parents have served their evolutionary purpose, passed on their genes, and propped up their offspring, who are now able to reproduce and raise their children in turn. Aging weakness is far from viscerally compelling, and the gut says, "Ditch 'em." But in the Ten Commandments, God's mention of long life and prosperity as rewards for honoring parents suggests the consideration that will recur to a civilized child: I am in ongoing debt for my life and everything good in it.

The Tenth Commandment (verse 21), the ban on coveting, is to me the most interesting one. By now we are well beyond any evidence that the passage was most at home in a tribunal. The instructions for keeping the Sabbath (the Fourth Commandment, verses 12–15) has moved the discussion (if you will) beyond religion per se to worthy relations between people, and after the stricture on honoring parents (the Fifth Commandment, verse 16) and straightforward prohibitions of some of the worst crimes (the Sixth through Ninth Commandments, verses 17–20), the list winds up with feelings we are not supposed to feel. Killing? Committing adultery? Stealing? Lying formally to gain an advantage? How about not even allowing yourself to think about thinking about any of these? Don't let yourself have the desire for something that isn't yours, a desire that could lead you to all sorts of bad behavior. In modern terms, take a step back from the situation in which you're emotionally entangled and examine your motives.

So much for a lightning bolt carving the Ten Commandments in a stone slab with a fearsome *ZOT* sound, as in a cartoon. In fact, so digressive, so humane was the basic Scriptural Law in structure and essence, that a general law about *human* love came to run a close second to the Shema's urging to love God with the fullness of being: the command to "love thy neighbor as thyself." By Jesus's time this command was rattled off after the Shema as if it were originally part of it (Luke 10:26–28), or were a "second" command (Matthew 22:36–40), whereas in the Hebrew Bible it occurs in Leviticus 19:18, in a passage bursting with miscellaneous rules. That is, the command seems to have originated in quite a different context and tradition.

There, neighbor-loving is counter to all kinds of dirty tricks that can be played in a community. But the stricture must have taken wing—as it was quite free to do, according to conventions of quoting and commenting established already in antiquity—as a perfect criterion by which to regulate one's behavior: "Would I do that to my precious self?"

So what does any of this have to do with translation—let alone with a big picture of the Bible's gifts to and from civilization? Well, in my view the Hebrew *rei-a*—usually rendered in English as "neighbor"—is helpfully, dynamically untranslatable.

First, to recap: the *rei-a* is the person to be loved as one loves oneself (Leviticus 19:18), and not betrayed by a false oath (Deuteronomy 5:20, the Ninth Commandment, about not "bearing false witness" against a "neighbor"), and not subjected to jealous scheming (Deuteronomy 5:21, the Tenth Commandment, about not coveting a "neighbor's" possessions). But who the heck is the "neighbor"?

The word seldom carried the idea "location of one person's house close to another's." Yet I can't readily offer any alternative translations except the gratuitously gender-specific and ludicrously rhyming "the man at hand," the flat "another person," the pompous (and again, gratuitously gender-specific) "your fellow man," and the almost flip "someone else." (See, in Part Two, a hapless collection of my further attempts.) *Rei-a* is in fact one of those maddeningly vague words such as I discuss in Chapter 2, words that can mean practically anything within a certain wide sphere. It's "fellow," "friend," "equal," "companion," "member"—even a throwaway "other," as in "People in the crowd were all saying such and such to each other." The type of person is restrictive perhaps only in that a *rei-a* tends to be a member of the same group or community: he or she is someone already there. This is significant for the Jewish law, which was not ordinarily shared with foreigners.

But through my irritation at my helplessness as a translator, I recognize the genius of the Hebrew Bible. Like so much vocabulary there, this word was protean, meaning what it needed to in a given context—and never plopping into any single hard category and staying there. Or I could even say it had a complex shape, inviting both scholars and ordinary people to see multiple dimensions, to debate what the meaning should be, and to change that meaning over time without resorting to any kind of revolt against Scriptural authority and thus against the foundation of their own identity. Jews seem never to have lost the sense of interactivity that their most important texts invite, whereas Christians—don't get me started.

Anyway: the ambiguity of the word *rei-a* must have been quite tantalizing to the Jews. Having memories of secure hegemony only in the remote past; trampled from every direction during the historical period; fighting to preserve at least their religion when everything else was threatened or destroyed; and yet led by that religion's idealism to intuit its universal applicability and to take seriously its appeal for many pagans, Jews had to ask how far their obligations went, how exactly they should treat outsiders, how to negotiate their survival while maintaining their integrity.

*

In one passage of the Gospels, in chapter 10 of Luke, Jesus is shown exploring the meaning of the word *rei-a* along these lines.

> 25   And, behold, a certain lawyer stood up, and tempted him, saying, Master, what shall I do to inherit eternal life?
>
> 26   He said unto him, What is written in the law? how readest thou?
>
> 27   And he answering said, Thou shalt love the Lord thy God with all thy heart, and with all thy soul, and with all thy strength, and with all thy mind; and thy neighbour as thyself.
>
> 28   And he said unto him, Thou hast answered right: this do, and thou shalt live.
>
> 29   But he, willing to justify himself, said unto Jesus, And who is my neighbour?

30   And Jesus answering said, A certain man went down from Jerusalem to Jericho, and fell among thieves, which stripped him of his raiment, and wounded him, and departed, leaving him half dead.

31   And by chance there came down a certain priest that way: and when he saw him, he passed by on the other side.

32   And likewise a Levite, when he was at the place, came and looked on him, and passed by on the other side.

33   But a certain Samaritan, as he journeyed, came where he was: and when he saw him, he had compassion on him,

34   And went to him, and bound up his wounds, pouring in oil and wine, and set him on his own beast, and brought him to an inn, and took care of him.

35   And on the morrow when he departed, he took out two pence, and gave them to the host, and said unto him, Take care of him; and whatsoever thou spendest more, when I come again, I will repay thee.

36   Which now of these three, thinkest thou, was neighbour unto him that fell among the thieves?

37   And he said, He that shewed mercy on him. Then said Jesus unto him, Go, and do thou likewise.

In the prelude to the confrontation with the lawyer, Jesus is shown joking about the superiority of simpleminded faithfulness. In Luke 10:21, he prays, "I thank thee, O Father, Lord of heaven and earth, that thou hast hid these things from the wise and prudent, and hast revealed them unto babes." The Greek words for "you have hidden" and "you have revealed" are end-rhymes with identical beginnings, too, *ahpekrupsahs* and *ahpekahlupsahs* (a real singsong), and the "babes" are apparently the disciples, returning from their preaching and healing journeys with the excited news that, yes, this works. I read a sigh into Jesus's thanksgiving: Yes indeed, Father—this is in fact what seemed best in your judgment.

The gentle irony about lack of perceptiveness seems important in that Jesus's encounter with a learned man that follows isn't at all—as it's usually been understood—about the simpleminded assertion of right-thinking virtue foiling wily sophism. Both parties are deeply attached to the Scripture, and both feel licensed to debate its meanings word by word. Jesus makes strong points about prejudice and officialdom and corners the lawyer into a startling answer to the central question "Who is my neighbor?" (that is, what does the word mean?), but it's hardly a definitive answer; and I would claim that this is part of the point.

Jesus's narrative reply is indeed a shocking one, which must have gotten everyone's attention. The hero of his story is a Samaritan. Samaritans claimed to be the only valid inheritors of the Abrahamic law and covenant. They had had their own sanctuary (which was reportedly destroyed in the second century B.C.E.) in the northern Palestinian city of Samaria, the capital of a region with the same name.* But in the tight confines of Palestine, members of different religious groups did cross each other's paths. See Jesus's tense encounter with the Samaritan woman in John, chapter 4.

Rather than contempt, other Jews must have felt for Samaritans the venomous fear that people reserve for in-their-face claimants to their own tradition. Substantial populations of Shiite and Sunni Muslims sharing modern nation-states might be comparable. Such a situation isn't about exploiting a servile race or telling far-fetched stories about a distant, sometimes hostile one; it is about mutual loathing constantly confirmed and renewed.

Perhaps it's fitting, then, that a fairly rare verb describes the Samaritan's feelings when he sees the alien traveler lying naked, bruised, and bleeding by the side of the road: pretty much literally, "he felt it in his guts" (Luke 10:33). There is no reason for him to stop—on the contrary; he is nonetheless overcome by his sense of what it would be like to be that man. He experiences a raw physical sensation that he simply follows up on: in verse 34, he nurses the man and takes him to an inn.

The priest (in Greek, his name comes visibly from the word for "holy") and the Levite (who was supposed to be a descendant of Jacob's son Levi, and so was an inheritor of an important religious office) who walk by on the other side of the road (verses 31–32), leaving the traveler near death from his beating, may not be simply

---

*The names of the Northern and Southern Kingdoms, after the division of Israel, were Israel and Judah, respectively; under Roman rule at the time of the events with which the New Testament is concerned, these places were called Samaria and Judea.

hypocritical or indifferent. They may think that the man is dead already or might die while they tend to him. Handling a corpse would violate their ritual purity.

The Samaritan, on the other hand, appears to be an ordinary layman, free to answer the call of pity if he wishes. Jesus, whose contempt for officialdom, especially the clergy, is plain elsewhere (most of all in Matthew, chapter 23, Mark 12:35–40, and Luke 11:37–54), may be pointing to a dividing line beyond the national or religious one. He may be pointing to the multiple agenda of officialdom in the face of need, and to the freedom of outsiders to act.

Another dimension of the story is what the Samaritan and the man he saves are up against, simply as travelers in the ancient world. Not only are the main characters exposed—the Samaritan further exposing himself voluntarily—but the stakes are extremely high. All over the Roman Empire, the violence a solitary traveler risked was terrible, and strangers' indifference to a victim went largely unquestioned. Inns were strongholds of a sort, but innkeepers were bywords for lowlifes and chiselers.

A single episode from the Roman novel *The Golden Ass*, written within a few decades of the Book of Luke, gives a harrowing demonstration of these points. In the novel, a merchant is traveling when a band of robbers attacks him. They rough him up but leave him his clothes—they were more decent, he remarks later, than the female innkeeper to whom he then managed to make his way. Her initial kindness is only a way to ensnare him. She quickly casts a love spell on him and makes him her sexual slave. For her sake, he even sells his clothes and goes to work as a day laborer, dressed in filthy rags, while his faraway wife and children give him up for dead and start a new life in which he would be unwelcome if he ever returned. He ends up murdered by the innkeeper and her fellow witch as he attempts to escape, and the old friend who discovered his plight and tried to help him never dares to go home himself. He abandons his family, settles in another province, and marries another woman. The Parable of the Good Samaritan makes for a remarkable contrast to this story.

So what is the parable doing to answer the lawyer's question about semantics and the applicability of fundamental law? The Greek translation of the Hebrew *rei-a* is quite apposite, except that the Greek word is even more open. A *pleision* is literally someone close by; it could be someone in a house down the street (though this isn't the proper Greek term for neighbor, *geitōn,* which the New Testament does use, so we know that at least a couple of the authors were familiar with it), but there are other situations in which physical closeness can be more significant, as in a battle line: in the hoplite army, holding the line with the help of the man next to you, your *pleision,* protects both of you and the entire commonwealth.

But sometimes being "close" is merely accidental: the word also applies to objects and can function as an adverb or even a preposition—as appears in the Greek of the lawyer's question in Luke 10:29, most literally, "And/but who is next to me?" It's *pleision* (neuter), as everywhere in the New Testament, not *pleisios* (masculine)! It's a location, not a person! Jesus, in turning the question back on the lawyer after the story, in verse 36 ("Which now of these three, thinkest thou, was neighbour unto him that fell among the thieves?"), uses the word in this way. But the story has, of course, knocked even this basic meaning galley-west: the lawyer may have meant "on my level" or "personally or culturally close to me"; Jesus seems to shift the basic significance to one of mere coincidental location. The Samaritan was "there for" the man in trouble.

In this way, Jesus in the Greek text is *shown* answering an even more challengingly worded query than likely would have been put to him in Aramaic about the Hebrew text, and he answers in a much more challenging fashion than he likely would have or could have. As shown in the Gospels, he is interested in expanding the circle of obligations—see especially Matthew 5:43–47 and Luke, chapter 6—but not in any facile, brotherhood-of-mankind way. He is, notably, no Samaritan- or Canaanite-hugger. The cosmopolitan Gospels soft-pedal his attitude toward the Greeks and Romans, but not to the extent that you could imagine him signing notes to them with "XXXOOO." "Gentiles," literally "those of the races," have no God-given law or covenant to discipline them. They can be called undeserving dogs to their faces when they seek healing; but in the course of events, a significant connection may happen nevertheless. Jesus makes an about-face in Matthew 15:21–28 and Mark 7:24–30: he goes from a protest that it's not his problem, and from the dog insult, to commending the woman and promising a cure.

Even Jesus does not know at first the inner worth of everyone he encounters—much less, as he shows in his story told to the lawyer, can an ordinary Jewish traveler predict that members of his own religion's hierarchy will leave him to die but that a detested outsider will come to his rescue. The man who shows saving mercy at first happens to be physically close, and then unaccountably *makes* himself close in the best conceivable sense of the word. He turns out to be a transcendent illustration of the law; and God delivers such illustrations any way he wishes.

The important lesson, therefore, is not about Samaritans or, really, anyone or anything specific within the story. The important lesson is that this *is* a *story,* a *narrative* constructed out of a scholarly or political or theological question, a movement from abstraction to life, through literature. In crude terms, in the course of events you find out who your friends are; how it all unfolds isn't under the control of any fixed equation. (If I've got one message as a translator, it's "Just try to nail down Scripture that way.") You, a man of law, are supposed to be living the law, so go out and live it, keeping it in your heart but letting yourself be taught it in further dimensions by the unexpected things that happen to you (recall Deuteronomy 6:7: you must wake and sleep, stay home and travel with it on your mind). Yes, *even you:* the "and" (*kai*) in Jesus's concluding statement (Luke 10:37), and the separate subject pronoun, beg for translation—translators usually ignore both.

7

Let Your Mind Alone: Comedy

The Book of Jonah (Chapter 3)
Paul on Circumcision (Galatians 5:1–12)

Nowhere is the Bible's tight bond between form and content more important than in humor. Style is, in fact, universally more crucial in humor. In plenty of incontinence-inducing performances, style *is* the substance. Jonathan Winters's voice and facial expressions, not the content of his jokes (which on paper seem pretty flat), allowed him to set records for volume and duration of laughter invoked. Among his most famous moves, he imitated his dog's smirking, sidelong gaze when she saw him naked; the *Jack Paar Show* clip may be the best thing on YouTube.

Tragedy, in contrast, seems always to be grounded in events that are tragic in themselves. There's nothing inherently funny about a dog watching as you come out of the shower; if she likes to stick close to you anyway, you may barely notice her. But death and injury and disease and abandonment and all the rest are inherently sad, at least to civilized people. We talk about "tragic" events and "tragic" works of art both, but not about "comic" things that just happen; and those we call "funny" may just seem strange to us. Though some events are potentially more comic than others, humor is in essence an artifice. So what would it be doing in a sacred book?

But I hotly defend Biblical humor as an uplifting manifestation of the Bible's joy. Axiomatically, tragedy is about separation, humor about reconciliation. Just to take a couple of examples: in the Book of Jonah's spoof of prophetic adventures and in Paul's sardonic ranting against his rival missionaries (who demanded that gentile converts to the worship of Jesus be circumcised), the powerful theme is God's mercy, his absurdly forthcoming, undiscriminating welcome to a loving relationship with him. If that's a joke, it's a good one, in every sense of "good."

In the Book of Jonah, everybody seems more ready for a relationship with God than does the prophet himself (who is, nevertheless, not irrevocably punished, as he deserves according to commonsense human reckoning): the apparently God-fearing heathen sailors on the ship with him, during the storm that halts his flight from God's assignment to convert heathen Nineveh; the "big fish" immediately obedient to God in swallowing Jonah and then in regurgitating him; the king and people of Nineveh itself, once the fish delivers Jonah to them as a proselytizer—even the Nineveh animals, who together with their owners cry out in repentance while fasting, dressed in sackcloth, and smeared with ashes.

Wordplay, pointed repetitions, and personification of the world around Jonah—even of the ship he's on—highlight the cartoonishness of the story. Here in Jonah, chapter 3, in the King James Version, Jonah (whose name in Hebrew means "Dove"—a bird associated not with peace but with flightiness and cowardice) is, after the fish episode, reinstated on his mission, which proves fabulously and almost effortlessly successful (but for that very reason will send him, in chapter 4, into a melodramatic, infantile sulk):

1   And the word of the Lord came unto Jonah the second time, saying,

2   Arise, go unto Nineveh, that great city, and preach unto it the preaching that I bid thee.

3   So Jonah arose, and went unto Nineveh, according to the word of the Lord. Now Nineveh was an exceeding great city of three days' journey.

4   And Jonah began to enter into the city a day's journey, and he cried, and said, Yet forty days, and Nineveh shall be overthrown.

5   So the people of Nineveh believed God, and proclaimed a fast, and put on sackcloth, from the greatest of them even to the least of them.

6   For word came unto the king of Nineveh, and he arose from his throne, and he laid his robe from him, and covered him with sackcloth, and sat in ashes.

7   And he caused it to be proclaimed and published through Nineveh by the decree of the king and his nobles, saying, Let neither man nor beast, herd nor flock, taste any thing: let them not feed, nor drink water:

8   But let man and beast be covered with sackcloth, and cry mightily unto God: yea, let them turn every one from his evil way, and from the violence that is in their hands.

9   Who can tell if God will turn and repent, and turn away from his fierce anger, that we perish not?

10   And God saw their works, that they turned from their evil way; and God repented of the evil, that he had said that he would do unto them; and he did it not.

Just to trace, in this one passage, one of the many repetitions that carry ridiculous ideas and images through the whole Jonah narrative, I'd like to discuss "big" things. It's a single Hebrew word, *gedōl*, for physical size (as of the fish in Jonah 1:17), simultaneous size and importance (Nineveh is a "great" city from its first mention in 1:2), and human authority and position (the people the King James calls "greatest" in 3:5 above, and then the ones it calls "nobles" in verse 7). But small things—a bush, a worm, Jonah's pettiness—will take over the story in chapter 4.

This casts humorous suspicion on a highly unusual and puzzling use of the word "big" in Jonah 3:3 above. Where the King James says, "Now Nineveh was an exceeding great city of three days' journey [across]," the Hebrew actually designates a "city big to-G/god(s)," which I render "a God-awful big city." I'm sorry if that sounds irreverent; it isn't meant to be.

Let me back up a little. There's a thematic running joke in the Book of Jonah, a confusion between the technical, grammatical plural of this Hebrew word for "God," and the actual polytheism of people around Jonah in this story. It isn't clear exactly whom the sailors picture they're fearing and deferring to in Jonah, chapter 1, when they find out Jonah is fleeing a holy mission, agonize over what to do with him, and at last piously throw him overboard. They *do* the right things, but why? Is it their own traditional "gods," or the Hebrew "God" they refer to? Are they instantly converted, as the population of Nineveh is going to be, or are they just better people, polytheism and all, than God's chosen prophet? Likewise, are the extravagantly repentant king and people of Nineveh clear on the monotheistic concept? The "God" the king refers to in Jonah 3:8–9, in his eager cooperation in what he supposes are God's wishes, and in his hope of escaping destruction—he sounds a lot like the sailors—is that same technically ambiguous plural.

Like the sailors, the "big to-G/god(s)" or maybe "G/god(s)-big" city of Nineveh is pagan; its material power is reflected in the number of its gods and the extravagance of their temples and their worship. Yet Nineveh converts, and right away: the King James phrasing in Jonah 3:4 is confusing as Jonah starts his assigned declamatory trek across the city, but the Hebrew must mean that as soon as he's set foot within the walls and opened his mouth, the mass conversion begins and roars ahead on its own.

Therefore, at the least, there's a bizarre contrast between how big and powerful this heathen city is—so that we would presume a propensity to ignore or persecute the true God's prophet—and how completely and humbly it accedes to the truth. It belongs to God in the first place. (The *l* or *leh* preposition for "to" in "city big to-G/god(s)" can be a possessive.) Or its greatness in regard to its own gods is a mere joke. Basic to humor is surprise, but it has to be surprise that makes sense.

*

Christian Scripture is comparatively unfunny. Jokes it certainly has, but sustained humorous dramas it doesn't. That said, Paul of Tarsus was a bitterly witty writer who deserves less timid, more accurate representation of his sallies. A series of them in the Book of Galatians (chapter 5) that I particularly like concerns circumcision. Here is the King James:

> 1   Stand fast therefore in the liberty wherewith Christ hath made us free, and be not entangled again with the yoke of bondage.
> 2   Behold, I Paul say unto you, that if ye be circumcised, Christ shall profit you nothing.
> 3   For I testify again to every man that is circumcised, that he is a debtor to do the whole law.

4   Christ is become of no effect unto you, whosoever of you are justified by the law; ye are fallen from grace.

5   For we through the Spirit wait for the hope of righteousness by faith.

6   For in Jesus Christ neither circumcision availeth any thing, nor uncircumcision; but faith which worketh by love.

7   Ye did run well; who did hinder you that ye should not obey the truth?

8   This persuasion cometh not of him that calleth you.

9   A little leaven leaveneth the whole lump.

10   I have confidence in you through the Lord, that ye will be none otherwise minded: but he that troubleth you shall bear his judgment, whosoever he be.

11   And I, brethren, if I yet preach circumcision, why do I yet suffer persecution? then is the offence of the cross ceased.

12   I would they were even cut off which trouble you.

Such is the general literary insensibility to Paul that I almost suspect some Christian doctrine of having arisen out of mere misunderstanding of his moods—particularly his exasperation. He traveled over much of the known world preaching the crucifixion, the resurrection, and salvation, and he seems to have loathed the distraction and frustration of having to answer strictly observant Jews who challenged his authority, and converts and potential converts who piped up, "The other missionaries say we have to be circumcised—and that we can't eat with our families or friends anymore unless we all adopt the entire Jewish law."

It's pretty clear to me from the Greek of this passage that Paul's main hurt is personal. As converts, the Galatians have been very dear to him. In this same letter to them (Galatians 4:15), he complains, "Where is then the blessedness ye spake of? for I bear you record, that, if it had been possible, ye would have plucked out your own eyes, and have given them to me." It's no contradiction that throughout the document he cajoles, vituperates, and scolds. He's treating these followers as wayward children.

The core of his argument is that if they no longer believe that the crucifixion and resurrection are enough, they cannot be serious or committed followers of Jesus: as to their conversion in its original terms, they must fish or cut bait. But this challenge to them is plainly mixed up in his mind with the acceptance or rejection of his own personal authority—so in rather personal terms, he harangues and threatens them.

Among his snide remarks in this passage comes a—here, supremely ironic—Jewish saw, in Galatians 5:9: "A little leaven leaveneth the whole lump": that is, if the baker is careless (say, in using unwashed implements) in making Passover bread, it will rise like ordinary bread and not be acceptable for the festival. Ritual minutiae are thus alluded to: for Passover, houses were cleaned punctiliously to remove crumbs that might contain yeast, and prayful pardon was asked in case a crumb had been missed. Paul, however, is using this analogy to argue in the opposite direction, for the *spiritual* correctness of faith as canceling out all traditional ritual requirements. Converts to the Way of Jesus must avoid the taint of doubt, revisionism, complications—anything that will distract and hamper their commitment to the divine love and sacrifice that change everything.

But the really amusing thing in this passage is Paul's sarcasm about circumcision itself. It's a venerable rite and one he takes very seriously, being circumcised himself (Romans 3:1–2, Philippians 3:5). But in this present context, with converts from paganism in a panic over the rite and not realizing that it's merely the most concrete form of an ancient culture they cannot practically adopt wholesale and do not need to adopt anyway—it's a joke: it's reduced to its physical terms. This is the purport of Paul's rhetorical question in Galatians 5:7 (the King James: "Ye did run well; who did hinder you that ye should not obey the truth?"); in the Greek, it's not "hinder you," but "cut you in" (= "cut you off") in your race. The climactic joke, in verse 12 (the King James: "I would they were even cut off which trouble you") is the wish that the interfering missionaries will be "cut off," as in castrated.

As to "trouble" in that same verse, Galatians 5:12, these missionaries are referred to by a present active participle, probably from the verb *anastatoō,* which is used in pagan literature, the Septuagint, and the New Testament for (illegitimately) "rousing" people—usually for civil unrest. But the participle would be easy to confuse with that of the verb *anastateō,* which (though very rarely, and only with late attestation) may mean "lead off," as in "seduce." Is Paul combining the meanings, or perhaps landing on the second one? That would be an understandably snarky crack, implying that the real interest of the Judaizing missionaries isn't in circumcision as a divine behest, but in the erotic possibilities opened up through the regulation of penises.

PART TWO

POSSIBILITIES PUT FORWARD

Mainly, the Passages Retranslated

I

General Principles for Translating Vai-hee *("And It Was/Became/Happened") in the Story of David and Bathsheba (2 Samuel 11–12:7)*

LITERAL EQUIVALENCE

The value of this in actually settling any translation questions is exploded as easily as a terrorist cell would be if it hoisted a placard visible from space to identify itself. The value is much more easily exploded in the case of ancient literature, with its vanished context, tiny vocabulary, and alien grammatical and syntactical forms, all making a single literal meaning itself very hard to get at.

This is why I often use forward slashes in the literal translations I show for the sake of convenience—as in the title of this section. Here we're not necessarily talking about something even as specific as "events," but maybe about a whole immense set of circumstances, or even a sense of "the way things are" that emerges and reemerges in human lives. (Note that the English "essence" is related to the Latin verb "to be," and that there is a similar connection in Greek philosophical vocabulary.) Since in Hebrew Bible narrative a sort of ultimate way things are usually emerges to vindicate justice in the end, and since the verb "to be" is associated with an important name for God (Yahweh), it's perhaps not absurd to suppose that an element of the idea "God" is inherent in this verb used in the construction *vai-hee.* I'm just saying.

BROAD CONTEXT

Vai-hee is a formulaic element—too basic to be called an actual formula, but nevertheless occurring very widely as a bridge in narrative (which is the way many formulae work), and having (for us, anyway) a sort of cozily traditional look, like "Once upon a time." That tells English speakers that a fairy tale is beginning. The King James's mechanical "And it came to pass" communicates to us that we are in the Bible or related writing. So why then not just keep it?

The best answer I can come up with is that this isn't how the Bible *works.* If I may be allowed a contemporary (nominally) secular analogy, formulaic Biblical style was probably like baseball pitching. To an outsider, unfamiliar with the game's intricacies, pitches are pretty much indistinguishable. But every pitcher is different, and every pitch thrown has its particular results and meaning in the vast culture of the game. That's why, pace the King James's beauty and authority, it isn't okay to cut and paste "And it came to pass" or any other single representation of *vai-hee* throughout a Bible translation. The translation has to be varied with care and sensitivity.

NARROWER CONTEXT

Here we get closer to the nitty-gritty. Reading the story of David and Bathsheba, it's easy to feel how the action turns at the spots conspicuously marked by *vai-hee,* and to vary the translations there according to the different kinds of turns.

To start with, the story is to some degree discrete; *vai-hee* has a special function just in beginning it. A translator could intervene there as forcefully as to write, "But now a new episode began" at the start of 2 Samuel 11:1. I would be tempted to write (but probably wouldn't dare) at the start of verse 2 (in which the footloose King David, having stayed home from the war, first sees Bathsheba bathing on her rooftop), "And it just so chanced that . . . ," loading into the clause the strain I sense between chance and choice, a strain maybe amounting to irony.

The *vai-hee* of verses 1, 2, and 14 *all* lead into time references (campaigning season, evening, morning), thus forming a triplet, whereas *vai-hee* in verse 16 leads straight into an action: Joab's reconnoitering the city, action that is now part of the actual murder plot being carried out. Perhaps here the contrast with the previous verse should be drawn very sharply, as now agency comes to the fore: "It followed that, as Joab spied out. . . ."

I hate to mention this completely different, quasi-scientific consideration, but what about an amalgamated text, one cut and pasted (as it were) early in antiquity from two or more traditional stories (which is demonstrably the way a lot of Biblical narration came together)? The repetition of a normally transitional formulaic element four times in a fairly short passage, in two pairs, suggests multiple versions fitted together, with the seams showing. One story would have started with verse 1, and one with verse 2; one would have conceived a major turning point at verse 14, and another at verse 16. That's "why" the arrangement is as it is. All I can say as a translator is that that seems a rather pitiful way to *read* the Bible; and as a poet that a couple of the best lines I've written in my life were accidents. What's the point of where exactly something comes from? The only worthwhile question is "Can it live?"

AESTHETICS

One source of pain in joining a clause like *vai-hee* to the clauses coming after it is that, to the pretty much on-the-money "It happened" must be added a "that," which is wordy and alien to the Hebrew diction. To hesitate over such a good option with such hypersensitivity may seem downright decadent. But the character of the original language does have certain rights, as well as a profound beauty—and the character of that beauty does have a lot to do with the compactness I harp on in Chapter 3. Going in the other direction, however, toward "Then," is a vote for truly radical compactness (50 percent fewer syllables than the Hebrew has got!); moreover, "then" isn't even a clause; it's just one little ordinary word, with nothing formulaic or otherwise special about it.

Why, after all, am I being so fussy about details like this? I can only assert again that in ancient composition, the medium was the message to a degree hardly imaginable now. The authoritative rhythm of a formulaic expression (for example) shouldn't be dispensed with in translation, or the message will be "This is not traditional literature." A formula, *as a formula,* was so important that it didn't even necessarily have to make sense. A Homeric hero is "wily"—if that's his regular epithet—when he's making a total fool of himself, and a woman can have "beautiful ankles" no matter what she's up to, including stuff that should make the beauty of her ankles of no interest to anyone but her fellow psychopaths. But how to adapt to English, a language that eschews formulae and related phrasings as archaic clichés?

PROPRIETY

"Propriety" comes from a Latin word connected to ownership and tends to mean that something belongs in a particular place and time and to particular people. I could snottily turn "propriety" into a question of who "owns" the Bible, and answer that it's everybody equally, so that I'll do whatever I want in translating it. But then why would anyone who loves the Bible and has studied it deeply pay any attention to such a disrespectful commentator? Why would anyone unfamiliar with the Bible but intrigued by it not ignore me—and everyone else—on the grounds that one interpretive whim is as good as another?

Here I give a self-pitying sniff over my scholarly transition from secular to sacred literature. In translating a Latin novel, I rendered a semi-formulaic transitional element like *vai-hee* as "And now guess what" and "And get this" when I thought the context demanded it, and no one complained. Now, like Johnny Cash once he was off drugs and married to June Carter, I have to walk the line.

SHEER PIGHEADED EGOTISM

Well, yes, there's that, too. It is awfully uncommon among Biblical translators; but I bring from the translation of pagan literary works a great reluctance to write what everybody else has written, commonsensical and well supported as it may be. But one benefit of retranslation—the business I'm in—is the potential to get readers to look again at a familiar text and perhaps see it more clearly or sympathetically.

The Two Lord's Prayers

THE LORD'S PRAYER OF MATTHEW (MATTHEW 6:9–13)

The King James Version

9 . . . Our Father which art in heaven, Hallowed be thy name.

10 Thy kingdom come, Thy will be done in earth, as it is in heaven.

11 Give us this day our daily bread.

12 And forgive us our debts, as we forgive our debtors.

13 And lead us not into temptation, but deliver us from evil: For thine is the kingdom, and the power, and the glory for ever. Amen.

My translation

9 . . . Father, our father* in the heavens above,
   Spoken in holiness must be your name.

10 Into the world must come your kingdom,
   And into being whatever you have willed,
   In heaven the same way as here on earth.

11 The loaf of bread, our every next loaf, give it to us today,

12 And free us from our debts,
   Once we have—just as we have—set our debtors free.

13 And don't, we beg you, take us into the ordeal—
   No, save us, save us from the Evil One.

THE LORD'S PRAYER OF LUKE (LUKE 11:2–4)

The King James Version

2 . . . Our Father which art in heaven, Hallowed be thy name. Thy kingdom come. Thy will be done, as in heaven, so in earth.

3 Give us day by day our daily bread.

4 And forgive us our sins; for we also forgive every one that is indebted to us. And lead us not into temptation; but deliver us from evil.

My translation

2 . . . Father,
   Spoken in holiness must be your name.
   Into the world must come your kingdom.

---

*My repetitions are an attempt to reproduce some of the original text's rhythms and emphases.

3   The loaf of bread, our every next loaf, give it to us day by
       day,
4   And free us from our sins
     As long as we free everyone who owes us,
     And, we beg you, do not take us into the ordeal.

2

Genesis 1:1–5

The King James Version

1 In the beginning God created the heaven and the earth.

2 And the earth was without form, and void; and darkness was upon the face of the deep. And the Spirit of God moved upon the face of the waters.

3 And God said, Let there be light: and there was light.

4 And God saw the light, that it was good: and God divided the light from the darkness.

5 And God called the light Day, and the darkness he called Night. And the evening and the morning were the first day.

My translation

1 It was God who inaugurated the heavens above and the earth below.

2 The earth at that time was suffused with confusion as bad as a void, and darkness loomed over the abyss; but the will of the living God came to brood over that helpless water.

3 And God said, "Let light come into being," and light came into being.

4 And God saw the light, and how beautiful* it was, and
   he separated light and darkness.†

5 And God named the light "day" and the darkness
   "night"; and evening arose, and morning arose, and this
   was the first day.

John 1:1–14

The King James Version

1 In the beginning was the Word, and the Word was with
God, and the Word was God.

2 The same was in the beginning with God.

3 All things were made by him; and without him was not
any thing made that was made.

4 In him was life; and the life was the light of men.

5 And the light shineth in darkness; and the darkness comprehended it not.

6 There was a man sent from God, whose name was John.

---

*Why "beautiful"? Well, first of all, because I can: the Hebrew word *tōv* (normally
translated as "good") can easily mean that. Secondly, the English "good" is quite
susceptible to ethical and pragmatic meanings, which hardly apply to a newly created universe (well, a newly ordered and dynamic one—there was some kind of
matter and energy in existence before). What's more, the English "good" isn't all
that suggestive of the deep spiritual comfort or wonder *tōv* can allude to. Here,
God is impressed with his own creation, so it must be impressive indeed. Moreover,
I think Saint Augustine is right: God is "beauty" and creates and presides over
"beauties" less beautiful when subjected to the degraded human will and judgment.
"Beautiful" is hence a letting-go sort of description on the human level: "What
a sublime, inexplicable thing to exist. It's so beautiful. Only God could have
done that."
   The more specific Hebrew word for "beautiful," by the way, wouldn't have been
considered by the author of this passage: it means beautiful in a quite limited way,
as in a young girl's prettiness.

†In the hope that attention to such nuances won't get me yelled at as pedantic:
darkness and light are here on the same syntactical footing (as in the Hebrew).
There's no "light divided from darkness" like wheat from chaff; neither entity looks
privileged in this verse. Though God began creation itself, according to verse 3, by
creating light, presumably to get the better of darkness (or proto-darkness), he is
now just evenhandedly making the basic arrangements of time and space, and this
includes assigning a limited darkness its proper function, and light its own, likewise.

7 The same came for a witness, to bear witness of the Light, that all men through him might believe.

8 He was not that Light, but was sent to bear witness of that Light.

9 That was the true Light, which lighteth every man that cometh into the world.

10 He was in the world, and the world was made by him, and the world knew him not.

11 He came unto his own, and his own received him not.

12 But as many as received him to them gave he power to become the sons of God, even to them that believe on his name:

13 Which were born, not of blood, nor of the will of the flesh, nor of the will of man, but of God.

14 And the Word was made flesh, and dwelt among us, (and we beheld his glory, the glory as of the only begotten of the Father,) full of grace and truth.

My translation

1 First was the Living Idea, and the Idea was with God, and the Idea was God.

2 He was first with God.

3 Everything came into being through him, and apart from him not even a single thing arose. What has been born*

4 in him was life, and the life was the light of humankind.

5 And the light still appears radiant in the darkness, which did not take hold of it.

6 There was born a person, sent with a purpose by God,† and his name was John.

7 He came to give testimony, to attest to the light, so that everyone could believe through him.

8 But this person was not the light; instead, he came to testify about the light.

*Notice the difference between sentence division here and in the King James Version. Verse divisions are modern, so scholars in some cases rethink them.
†This is the same verb that generated the noun we know in English as "apostle," so I thought it should have a more pointed translation than just "sent."

9   The light was the true light, which gives light to every
    human being coming into the world.*

10 The light was in the world, and the world was born
    through him, but the world did not recognize him.

11 He came into what belonged to him, but the people
    who belonged to him did not take him for themselves.

12 But to all those who accepted him, he gave the right to
    be born children of God, if they trusted in his name.

13 These are the people who have been engendered not in
    blood relationships, and not from what the body wants,
    and not from what a husband wants, but from God.

14 And the Idea became a body, flesh and blood, and
    pitched a tent and sojourned† among us, and we gazed
    on his splendor, the splendor that a father's only son
    has, full of benevolence and truth.

---

*It is unclear whether the light or the human being is coming.

†"Lived in his tent." The word choice nicely reflects the patriarchs' way of life and
at the same time emphasizes that Jesus lived on earth only temporarily. There is also
the "tabernacle" (which is from the Latin for "tent"), the holy tent in which the Israelites are said to have worshipped prior to the Temple's existence. Also, tent-pitching
has some metaphorical, metaphysical, philosophical background: see Sirach 24:8.

Ezekiel's Dry Bones (Ezekiel 37:1–14)

The King James Version

1 The hand of the Lord was upon me, and carried me out in the spirit of the Lord, and set me down in the midst of the valley which was full of bones,

2 And caused me to pass by them round about: and, behold, there were very many in the open valley; and, lo, they were very dry.

3 And he said unto me, Son of man, can these bones live? And I answered, O Lord God, thou knowest.

4 Again he said unto me, Prophesy upon these bones, and say unto them, O ye dry bones, hear the word of the Lord.

5 Thus saith the Lord God unto these bones; Behold, I will cause breath to enter into you, and ye shall live:

6 And I will lay sinews upon you, and will bring up flesh upon you, and cover you with skin, and put breath in you, and ye shall live; and ye shall know that I am the Lord.

7 So I prophesied as I was commanded: and as I prophesied, there was a noise, and behold a shaking, and the bones came together, bone to his bone.

8 And when I beheld, lo, the sinews and the flesh came up upon them, and the skin covered them above: but there was no breath in them.

9 Then said he unto me, Prophesy unto the wind, prophesy, son of man, and say to the wind, Thus saith the Lord God;

Come from the four winds, O breath, and breathe upon these slain, that they may live.

10   So I prophesied as he commanded me, and the breath came into them, and they lived, and stood up upon their feet, an exceeding great army.

11   Then he said unto me, Son of man, these bones are the whole house of Israel: behold, they say, Our bones are dried, and our hope is lost: we are cut off for our parts.

12   Therefore prophesy and say unto them, Thus saith the Lord God; Behold, O my people, I will open your graves, and cause you to come up out of your graves, and bring you into the land of Israel.

13   And ye shall know that I am the Lord, when I have opened your graves, O my people, and brought you up out of your graves,

14   And shall put my spirit in you, and ye shall live, and I shall place you in your own land: then shall ye know that I the Lord have spoken it, and performed it, saith the Lord.

My translation

1   On me was placed the hand of Yahweh, and it partook of Yahweh's spirit in bringing me out and setting me down in the middle of the valley, and this valley was full of bones.*

2   And he led me past all of them, around and around, and I was astounded at how very many there were, spread out in the valley, and how very dry they were, too.

3   And he said to me, "Mortal man, can these bones you see come to life?" And I said, "Lord Yahweh, this is something only you know."

4   And he said to me, "Prophesy to these bones, saying to them, 'Dry bones! Listen to Yahweh as he speaks to you!

5   "'Here is what the Lord Yahweh has said to you, the

---

*This scene is historically tantalizing, especially because of the definite article's use with "valley": it's "*the* valley." The author does seem to be picturing a real valley and the long aftermath of a real battle—but it is impossible to tell with certainty which.

bones here: "Here I am, yes, breathing the spirit of life into you, so that you will live.

6 " ' "And I will put muscles on you, and grow flesh on you, and cover you with skin, and blow breath into you, and you will live; and then you will know that I am Yahweh." ' "

7 And I prophesied in the way I was commanded, and while I was still prophesying—I could hardly believe it—there was a noise, and a shaking, and the bones came together, every bone in the right place.

8 And I watched as—truly—muscle and flesh grew on them, and skin covered over the muscle and flesh; but the breath of life was not in them.

9 Then he said to me, "Prophesy to the wind, prophesy, mortal man, and tell the wind: 'This is what Yahweh the Lord has said: "Come from the four quarters, wind, and blow your breath into these men who have been cut down, so that they will live." ' "

10 And I prophesied just as he commanded me, and the breath of the wind came into them, and they came alive and stood up on their feet as a great, a very great army.

11 And he said to me, "Mortal man, the bones you see here are the whole house of Israel, and here in your hearing they are saying, 'Our bones are dried out, and our hope has perished; we are hacked away from ourselves.'

12 "This means you must prophesy, saying to them, 'Here is what Yahweh the Lord has said: "It is me, truly in your presence, about to open your graves, and I will raise you out of them, my people, and bring you into the land of Israel.*

13 " ' "And you will know that I am Yahweh because I open your graves and raise you up out of them, my people.

14 " ' "And I will place the breath of my spirit in you, and you will live, and I will settle you in your own

---

*At this point (if not earlier), the prophecy seems to center on the return from the Babylonian Exile.

land. And you will know that I myself, Yahweh, have spoken it, so that I will fulfill it. This is the decree of Yahweh." ' "

Revelation's Martyrs in Paradise (Revelation 7:9–17)

The King James Version

9 After this I beheld, and, lo, a great multitude, which no man could number, of all nations, and kindreds, and people, and tongues, stood before the throne, and before the Lamb, clothed with white robes, and palms in their hands;

10 And cried with a loud voice, saying, Salvation to our God which sitteth upon the throne, and unto the Lamb.

11 And all the angels stood round about the throne, and about the elders and the four beasts, and fell before the throne on their faces, and worshipped God,

12 Saying, Amen: Blessing, and glory, and wisdom, and thanksgiving, and honour, and power, and might, be unto our God for ever and ever. Amen.

13 And one of the elders answered, saying unto me, What are these which are arrayed in white robes? and whence came they?

14 And I said unto him, Sir, thou knowest. And he said to me, These are they which came out of great tribulation, and have washed their robes, and made them white in the blood of the Lamb.

15 Therefore are they before the throne of God, and serve him day and night in his temple: and he that sitteth on the throne shall dwell among them.

16 They shall hunger no more, neither thirst any more; neither shall the sun light on them, nor any heat.

17 For the Lamb which is in the midst of the throne shall feed them, and shall lead them unto living fountains of waters: and God shall wipe away all tears from their eyes.

My translation

9   Next, with my own eyes I saw a giant crowd, of
countless people from every nation and tribe and
community, and speaking every language in the world,
and they stood facing the throne, and facing the little
lamb who sat on it. They were draped in white robes,
and palm branches were in their hands.

10 And with a giant voice they shouted these words:
     "Salvation belongs to our God, who is sitting on the
     throne, and to the darling lamb."*

11 And all the angels stood in a circle around the throne,
the elders and the four strange animals† with them,
and they all fell on their faces in front of the throne,
prostrating themselves to God, 12 with these words:
     "Truly, blessedness and glory and wisdom and all
     merit and honor and power and strength belong to
     our God, age after age and forever—truly!"

13 And one of the elders responded, speaking to me with
these words: "These whom you see draped in their
white robes—who are they, and where did they come
from?"

14 And here is what I said to him: "But *you* know, my
good sir." And he said to me:
     "These are the ones coming out of the great ordeal,
     But now they have washed their robes;
     But now they have bleached their robes white in this
       little lamb's blood.

---

* *Variatio,* or the translation principle of rendering the same word differently over
the course of a passage even when this is unnecessary for the sense, is not just a
way to avoid boring and irritating modern readers with repetitions uncongenial
in their own language: *variatio* can also heighten expression. Here, where we're
looking at a glorious but paradoxical scene, to change the way the "little lamb" is
designated is to invite the reader to picture this animal afresh again and again and
insist that—yes—it is tiny and pet-like.

† This is the only way I can find to express that these creatures are both mon-
strous and heavenly—not an easily digestible combination, given the anodyne,
Hollywood-type images of heaven that prevail in the modern West. But this might
help: *monstrum* (source of our word "monster") in Latin can mean both a miraculous
sign and a bizarre aberration—both are supposed to come from the supernatural.

15 "Because of this they stand facing the throne of God,
And they serve him all day, and they serve him by
night in his sanctuary.
And the one sitting on the throne will build a shelter
over them in the desert.

16 "They will never go hungry anymore; they will never
be parched anymore;
The sun's heat will not assault them, no burning heat
will strike them.

17 "Because the tiny lamb there in the middle of the
throne will be their shepherd;
And he will lead them on the paths to springs
flowing with water that gives them life,
And God will wipe away every tear from their eyes."

4

The Twenty-Third Psalm*

The King James Version

1 The Lord is my shepherd; I shall not want.

2 He maketh me to lie down in green pastures: he leadeth me beside the still waters.

3 He restoreth my soul: he leadeth me in the paths of righteousness for his name's sake.

4 Yea, though I walk through the valley of the shadow of death, I will fear no evil: for thou art with me; thy rod and thy staff they comfort me.

5 Thou preparest a table before me in the presence of mine enemies: thou anointest my head with oil; my cup runneth over.

6 Surely goodness and mercy shall follow me all the days of my life: and I will dwell in the house of the Lord for ever.

*Without making a long historical digression into the Psalms: these lyric poems were commonly imagined as originating in the court of David (tenth century B.C.E.), but it is obvious that all the extant versions are much later. They were sung liturgically in the Jerusalem Temple, they were important in Jewish learning and discourse, and they could have a deep personal meaning to individual Jews. In an index of my Greek New Testament are more than four double-column pages in small print of Psalm citations. Even some of the authors who must have known that they were changing their branch of Judaism beyond recognition as Jewish, or even discarding Judaism as such, quoted the Psalms like maniacs.

My translation

1 The Lord is the one pasturing me:
     I will never go without.
2 He will always invite me* to stretch out in pastures full
        of green shoots;
     He will not fail to guide me to a place of rest, where the
        water is at peace.
3 He will bring my life back to me.
     He will lead me along wagon-tracks of fair dealing—he
        would not be who he is if he did otherwise.†
4 I tell you, though I have cause to walk through the valley
        of deadly darkness, there is nothing fearsome there,
        nothing for me to fear,
     Because of you, you there with me. Your weapon and
        your crook—I see them, and I know I am safe.
5 You arrange a feast on a table where I sit, though my
        enemies loom on the other side.
     You refresh my head by bathing it in oil; you fill my
        cup again and again.
6 Certainly goodness and unfailing mercy‡ will chase after
        me everywhere I go, as long as I exist,

---

*"Imperfect" forms of verbs dominate the poems, suggesting "never" and "always in the future."

†This may seem like a wild expansion of "for his name's sake," but names in the ancient world operated in such a way that I think I'm justified. For the Hebrew God the five most common ones are *Yahweh, Adonai, Ya, El,* and *Elohim* (technically the plural of *El*); his descriptive epithets are legion. All this blatant evidence of a polytheistic past must have made monotheists nervous, especially because names were normally so critical in defining someone. (There wasn't a long document trail, or a huge material and technological superstructure, or a culture of self-definition to do this. What a hoot the ancients would have found the notion of a person going to court to change her name and thus acquire a modified identity.) No wonder the custom began among pious Jews of verbally calling God *HaShem,* "The Name." Jews could imply something like "God's real, unvarying, essential, holy, singular self—he has many names, but he really ought to have only one."

‡The Hebrew word *chesĕd* is one of the most important in Scripture, yet at the same time one of the vaguest. I don't care much for the modern rendering "kindness," preferring the old-fashioned "mercy" wherever it can work, and maybe adding a heightening adjective, as I did here. I say, "Oh, you're too kind," to the nice man who lets me have the window seat. If I said, "Oh, you're too merciful," I would be implying another sort of relationship altogether: the sort that weak, unworthy humankind has with the omnipotent and benevolent deity.

And I will live in the Lord's house through all my
length of days.

The Beatitudes* (Matthew 5:3–12)

The King James Version

3 Blessed are the poor in spirit: for theirs is the kingdom of heaven.

4 Blessed are they that mourn: for they shall be comforted.

5 Blessed are the meek: for they shall inherit the earth.

6 Blessed are they which do hunger and thirst after righteousness: for they shall be filled.

7 Blessed are the merciful: for they shall obtain mercy.

8 Blessed are the pure in heart: for they shall see God.

9 Blessed are the peacemakers: for they shall be called the children of God.

10 Blessed are they which are persecuted for righteousness' sake: for theirs is the kingdom of heaven.

11 Blessed are ye, when men shall revile you, and persecute you, and shall say all manner of evil against you falsely, for my sake.

12 Rejoice, and be exceeding glad: for great is your reward in heaven: for so persecuted they the prophets which were before you.

---

*"Beatitudes," from a Latin noun based on an adjective originally meaning (mainly) "fortunate" and "rich," is a late designation of this passage that exemplifies the impossibilities a translator faces. The ancients defined happiness quite narrowly, as wealth, other conspicuous endowments or good luck in prescribed spheres, the special favor of the gods, or eternal life. (They didn't have, as far as I know, a word for "personal fulfillment." But that's what we tend to mean by "happy," and "blessed" is to us a rather vague or prim word.) But the Beatitudes in the original Greek wouldn't work nearly as well if the significance of the Greek *makarios* (mainly "in heaven," "lucky," and "prosperous"; transliterated in context as *mahkarios*) were not fairly specific in several directions, so that it could be defined differently (and startlingly or even ironically) accordingly to each of the human needs and merits shown in each verse. I won't even try to retranslate the title "Beatitudes."

My translation

3   Happy those who beg in the spirit, who beg for their very
      breath,
    Because theirs is the kingdom of God above.

4   Happy the bereaved and destitute,
    Because they will be restored.

5   Happy the pliant people,
    Because they will be privileged heirs of the land.

6   Happy those starving and parched for justice,
    Because they will feast to the fullest.

7   Happy those who show mercy,
    Because they will be shown mercy.

8   Happy those with spotless hearts,
    Because they will see God with their own eyes.

9   Happy the peacemakers,
    Because "sons of God" will be their title.

10 Happy those persecuted for the sake of "justice,"
    Because theirs is the kingdom above.

11 Happy are all of you, when they insult you and hound
    you and slander you in every way for my sake.

12 Laugh yourselves giddy with joy, because the wages you
    will receive in heaven are generous. This, you see, is
    how they hounded the prophets who came before you.

5

Ecclesiastes on the Fragile Joys of Life (Ecclesiastes 9:7–11)

The King James Version

7 Go thy way, eat thy bread with joy, and drink thy wine with a merry heart; for God now accepteth thy works.

8 Let thy garments be always white; and let thy head lack no ointment.

9 Live joyfully with the wife whom thou lovest all the days of the life of thy vanity, which he hath given thee under the sun, all the days of thy vanity: for that is thy portion in this life, and in thy labour which thou takest under the sun.

10 Whatsoever thy hand findeth to do, do it with thy might; for there is no work, nor device, nor knowledge, nor wisdom, in the grave, whither thou goest.

11 I returned, and saw under the sun, that the race is not to the swift, nor the battle to the strong, neither yet bread to the wise, nor yet riches to men of understanding, nor yet favour to men of skill; but time and chance happeneth to them all.

My translation

7 Come, eat your bread with joy, and drink your wine with
      a light heart,
   Because God is already content with your work.*

---

*To try to work out the right register for this passage is of course futile: nothing so casually beautiful can come from modern didactic English, and the earnest translator risks sounding like a self-help tome. Little more can be done, really, than to modernize archaisms and to avoid psychobabble and triteness.

8 In every part of the time you have, wear clothes that are
   spotless white, and never spare oil for bathing your
   head.*

9 Take in the pleasures of life alongside your beloved wife,
   through every day of your evanescing life,
   Which is given to you under the sun, every last day of
   your evanescence,†
   Because these pleasures are doled out to you in this life,
   for all the toil you have taken on under the sun.

10 Everything your hand finds to do, put your whole heart
   into it,
   Because there is nothing to do, or devise, or know, or
   understand in the Pit,‡
   Which is where every step is taking you.

---

*I hope to be pardoned for my little flight in expanding "at-every time," in order
to have a fuller English expression than "always." I want to parallel the Hebrew, to
avoid the flat and vague "every time" and the officious "on every occasion"; and also
to riff on the passage's thematic repetitiveness of the word "time."

In the rest of the verse, I've tried to balance out the tone by being precise about
the ethereal mundaneness, so to speak, of the advice: the white clothes and the
(scented?) oil are not about showiness or self-indulgence but about the ordinary
pleasurable care of the body that is a gift from God. This took more trouble than it
does now. In ancient moral and philosophical literature, the miser's "dirt" is a syn-
onym for "moneygrubbing" ("picking up a penny from manure with one's teeth" is
an expression I love from the Roman novelist Petronius); and since dining alone was
anomalous and denigrated, being dirty and unfit for a banquet meant withholding
the good things of life from others, including people unable to procure them on
their own.

†I render a little more variously the expression that in this verse occurs twice in
almost identical form (both in the Hebrew and the King James): "all the days of
the life of thy vanity" and "all the days of thy vanity." Once more, I invoke the
ancient rhetorical principle of *variatio,* which says that stylistic concerns can dictate
whether, and how much, verbal repetition is proper; in modern English, not very
much can sound pretty dippy.

‡"The Pit" is a conventional way out of the bind here. "Sheol" was pictured as a real
place—that's a proper noun (probably based on the root for "hollow"). Here's how
I understand it, and please forgive the rather wispy reconstruction: this is nightmare
stuff, and the ancients didn't lay it out all that clearly themselves.

As in the pagan world, where Hades comprised the dominant set of images, the
Hebrew concept of the afterlife's horrors seems to have been influenced by the fate
of corpses no one took care of. People who died at sea were sucked down into an
unknown abyss; cadavers of the very poor, the homeless, and the losers in battle
were in general not washed and tidied up and ritually disposed but thrown away
like garbage, sometimes along with it, and a dump or pit was a convenient place

11 I made my way back to the beginning, and I saw under
the sun

That the race is not won by the fastest, or the battle by
the strongest.

And no, men of understanding don't get bread, or men
of discernment wealth,

And men with knowledge aren't popular. They all meet
up with the randomness of time.*

Paul on the Love of God Through Jesus (Romans 8:31–39)

———

The King James Version

31 What shall we then say to these things? If God be for us,
who can be against us?

32 He that spared not his own Son, but delivered him up
for us all, how shall he not with him also freely give us all
things?

33 Who shall lay any thing to the charge of God's elect? It is
God that justifieth.

---

for this. There, the proverbial dogs and carrion birds could rip them apart, or they
would smolder and stink after halfhearted attempts to tidy the place up. But Kohelet, or Ecclesiastes, with the mention of Sheol, must be emphasizing the futureless-
ness of individuals, not any torments they will suffer or degradation they will be
aware of; the author does appear to share the Epicurean view that death means the
annihilation of consciousness.

*Here's where I want to throw up my hands: "time and chance" (the King James's
exact rendering of the Hebrew)—what's that phrase supposed to mean? Well, if
the author is influenced by the Greek-speaking world's Epicureanism, he could
also partake of its common rhetorical tropes; this could be a hendiadys, a "one
through two": the words would be not two separate semantic units but one, something like "chancy time." This impression is strengthened by the clause the King
James translates as "happeneth to them all"; the Hebrew is more like "stumble onto
everyone"—anyway, it's another expression of chance. People think they're in control, racing or fighting or discerning for all they're worth, but their whole active lives
are an unwitting encounter—no, a clash—with time, which is inherently random.
In the absence of perfection anywhere under the sun, people *never* get what they
should (even that "should" is a stretch in this context; Ecclesiastes doesn't use such
moralistic language), but what their opportunities—or their health or their mood
or the weather or whatever—at particular moments give them.

34   Who is he that condemneth? It is Christ that died, yea rather, that is risen again, who is even at the right hand of God, who also makes intercession for us.

35   Who shall separate us from the love of Christ? shall tribulation, or distress, or persecution, or famine, or nakedness, or peril, or sword?

36   As it is written, For thy sake we are killed all the day long; we are accounted as sheep for the slaughter.

37   Nay, in all these things we are more than conquerors through him that loved us.

38   For I am persuaded, that neither death, nor life, nor angels, nor principalities, nor powers, nor things present, nor things to come,

39   Nor height, nor depth, nor any other creature, shall be able to separate us from the love of God, which is in Christ Jesus our Lord.

My translation

31   So what can we say about these things? With God on our side, who can be on the other side?

32   The God who didn't begrudge his own son, but surrendered him for the sake of us all—how then will such a God not freely give us everything else, along with him?

33   Who will bring charges against those God has chosen to be in his charge? God is the one passing judgment!

34   Who's the one rendering us guilty? It is Jesus the Anointed who died—no, who came back to life— and who is at God's right hand—and who actually intercedes for us!

35   Who will separate us from the love of the Anointed One? Will it be any pressure put on us, or the tightest place imaginable, or persecution, or starvation, or the inability to put clothes on our backs, or danger, or execution?*

*Following the judicial theme, I take it that "the sword" stands for beheading, a well-known form of execution. (Paul himself is said to have died this way at Roman government hands.) Here in the King James English "the sword" unhelpfully suggests warfare, and that's not at issue. The Roman Empire was widely at peace dur-

36 To quote the Scriptures:

Because of you, we are dying all day long.
We are counted off one by one like sheep for slaughter.

37 But in all these things we are the victors over the
    victors, thanks to the one who has loved us.

38 I have been persuaded, you see, to believe that neither
    death nor life, nor angels, nor the authorities on
    earth, nor things that are here now, nor things that are
    coming, nor supernatural powers,

39 nor the highest nor the lowest thing in the universe, nor
    anything else in creation* has the power to separate us
    from the love of God in the Anointed Jesus, our Lord.

---

ing this period, and military service (largely for peacekeeping functions) was quite
prestigious.

*This list, as traditionally translated, is painfully in need of clarification. It's beau-
tiful enough, and the words of the King James and its successors here strengthen
many of us, but until I read the Greek original it never emerged for me that this
was a sort of map of the universe. Angels are the functionaries of heaven; these
"principalities," the functionaries on earth (as the Greek means "magistrates" or
"magistracies"). Since the highest temporal powers are named thus, I think that
the King James's "powers," named next, are miraculous ones; miracles themselves
are subordinate to God's omnipotent care for us—a characteristic Pauline thought.
(See, for example, 1 Corinthians 1:22–23.) God rules even over inexorable-seeming
time, so whatever is or will be unites us with God—it doesn't *separate* us. Depth was
associated with the annihilation of death (see the footnote on pp. 140–41), height
with both heaven and human exaltation. "Creature" is the old-fashioned word for
"created thing": nothing that such a God created could in itself conceivably separate
us from God.

6

The Word Rei-a *("Other," etc.) in the Ten*
Commandments and the Great Commandment
(Deuteronomy 5:6–21 and Leviticus 19:18)

Since no part of my goal is to cite as many academic works as possible, and since a major part of my goal is not to go insane, I tend to zero in on as few lexical categories of a word as I can get away with in deciding what the word means in a given context. Fortunately, in Classical Hebrew a single common word tends to be used in such widely varying ways that a translator can fairly quickly put aside the great majority as irrelevant.

In this case, there is any number of ethical connotations of the word, but I'm concerned here with *fundamental* ethics, and almost by definition there's never a whole lot to those. *Rei-a,* or "other," is enshrined within them really only in the final two of the Ten Commandments, and in Leviticus 19:18, as it came to be associated with the Shema's commandment to love God (Deuteronomy 6:4). Respectively, false witness against the "other" and envy of what belongs to him are forbidden, and the "other" is to be loved as oneself. What translation can fit into these ideas and still be readable (whatever that means) in modern English? (I've already discounted, in my Part One exposition, the stupidest stuff that came to mind.)

I don't like "other," to start with. It smacks of psychobabble and, more important, is historically misleading. When *we* discuss treatment of the "other," we mean the unfamiliar, the different, the outsider. Jews were enjoined to treat outsiders humanely* but not like

---

*And they were so enjoined in the Ten Commandments themselves: see Deuteronomy 5:14, in which the privilege of rest on the Sabbath is extended to them.

themselves or one another—just the opposite; there are bans too numerous to cite here on marrying foreigners and on sharing their worship. Yes, it would be wrong to lie formally about a foreigner to disadvantage him; but requirements for the right *feelings* tend to be restricted to members of one's own community. Leviticus 19:18, in fact, forbids malicious behavior toward (literally) "sons of your people" before enjoining love for them.

"A fellow Jew"? I'm not willing to negate in this way the Hebrew Bible for use by Christians. Anyway, it's quite a translation stretch to specify so powerfully what's unspecific in the original. "Another Jew" sounds positively denigrating.

"Any member of your community"? This suggests a promo for a PBS documentary on local arts.

"Your fellow citizen"? I was nonplussed to see this in a lexicon as an option. "Citizenship" evolved as a Greco-Roman concept, and the privileges and obligations it entailed would have baffled Jews, unless they were Diaspora cosmopolitans—no such thing at the time of Deuteronomy's composition.

"A friend" or "a companion"? Too wishy-washy! And unnecessary!* "Comrade," though it can suggest mere membership in the same nation or other institution, has shades of Bolshevism.

Okay, then, why not just stick with "neighbor"? Well, I think it's by now too heavily weighted with the distractions of specifics. "Neighborliness" evokes down-home, small-town helpfulness, and "neighbor" itself is understood too concretely by most of us: the family across the street or down the hall. In my generation, primary school teachers spoke of our "neighbors" as those sitting next to us in class or in the auditorium, to whom we must not whisper or pass notes. And "neighborhoods" can be a politically correct word for "ghettos."

I think chickening out is underrated. I'm not translating this passage, so I don't have to make a call. And I'm quislingly calling on Jesus's authority (see the second part of my Chapter 6, and the account immediately following here) in leaving the word's meaning in suspension.

---

*Jesus certainly thought so. See Matthew 5:43–44.

The Word Pleision *in the Parable of the Good Samaritan*
(Luke 10:25–37)

———

Heh, heh! In Greek, as usual, there's a clear basic image to be traced through an incredible variety of literature, most of it non-Scriptural and so providing chances for vigorous cross-checks. *Pleision,* the Gospels' Greek translation of the Hebrew *rei-a,* means "near" or "next to." Both usages in this passage are in the neuter, and so are more like prepositions than adjectives. So what translation might capture this in the scene between Jesus and the "lawman"—if I go ahead and discount the translations of *rei-a* I rejected in my Part One exposition and in the discussion of the Ten Commandments immediately above?

"Peer" is heavy-handed as to the interpretation of the lawman's motives and personality and does nothing to suggest a joke about proximity. And the word is rather inert; Jesus can't be shown handily turning it in any other direction.

"Fellow" has possibilities. "Who's *my* fellow man?" Jesus, at the end of his story, might be translated as asking. "Who was in fellowship with the man who fell among thieves?" Far from perfect, but could be worse; fellowship is a sort of proximity. Also, the word "brother" might function somewhat similarly, given the Hebrew and Christian uses of that word in contexts of fellowship, uses now reinforced by our images of both limited "brotherhoods" and the "brotherhood of mankind": a play between the narrower and the wider application is possible.

Better yet would be "at hand" or "on hand" or "within reach" (though I ruled out from the start the dumbsily rhyming "man at hand"). Everyone in such a position must be loved. Well, who's *at hand* or *on hand* or *within reach* for me? The lawman: Who's ready, like a tool, to serve my preconceived notions and uphold my privileged position? I'm happy to "love" that person. Jesus: Ah, but what about the person who's *on hand* or *at hand* or *within reach* when you're unexpectedly in trouble, and will send your notions in the new direction God chooses?

7

The Book of Jonah (Chapter 3)

The King James Version

1   And the word of the Lord came unto Jonah the second time, saying,

2   Arise, go unto Nineveh, that great city, and preach unto it the preaching that I bid thee.

3   So Jonah arose, and went unto Nineveh, according to the word of the Lord. Now Nineveh was an exceeding great city of three days' journey.

4   And Jonah began to enter into the city a day's journey, and he cried, and said, Yet forty days, and Nineveh shall be overthrown.

5   So the people of Nineveh believed God, and proclaimed a fast, and put on sackcloth, from the greatest of them even to the least of them.

6   For word came unto the king of Nineveh, and he arose from his throne, and he laid his robe from him, and covered him with sackcloth, and sat in ashes.

7   And he caused it to be proclaimed and published through Nineveh by the decree of the king and his nobles, saying, Let neither man nor beast, herd nor flock, taste any thing: let them not feed, nor drink water:

8   But let man and beast be covered with sackcloth, and cry mightily unto God: yea, let them turn every one from his evil way, and from the violence that is in their hands.

9   Who can tell if God will turn and repent, and turn away
from his fierce anger, that we perish not?

10   And God saw their works, that they turned from their
evil way; and God repented of the evil, that he had said that
he would do unto them; and he did it not.

My translation

1   And once again the Lord's word came to Flitillary Joe,
     to wit:

2   Now get yourself up and step it to Nineveh, that
     giant city, and cry out to it in the way I am personally
     instructing you.

3   So up Joe-Nothing got and walked to Nineveh, just
     as the Lord said to do. Now, Nineveh happened to be
     a God-awful big city, and it took three days to walk
     across.

4   Busterfly just started on a single day's walk in the city,
     crying out the message, "Forty days more, and Nineveh
     will be turned upside down."

5   But hence the men of Nineveh came to believe in
     God, and criers announced a fast, and everyone—the
     big, important people clear down to those of little
     consequence—dressed in burlap bags.

6   And word reached the king of Nineveh, and he got
     up from his throne, and doffed and laid aside his
     splendid robe, and clothed himself in a gunnysack, and
     sat in the dirt.

7   And he had heralds proclaiming his words throughout
     Nineveh, to wit: "From the mouth of the king and his
     grandees: neither any human being nor farm animal,
     neither any creature in a herd of cattle or flock of sheep
     may put a thing in his/her/its mouth: that means no
     grazing, and no drinking of water either.

8   "People and animals must clothe themselves in produce
     sacks and cry to God with everything that's in them;
     and each one of them must turn aside from his/her/its
     path of evil, and from the violent wrongdoing they have
     in hand/hoof.

9 "Who knows whether this God (or gods?) will turn around and relent, turning away from his (or their?) blazing, snorting rage,* so that we don't have to be annihilated."

10 And God saw what they were doing, namely that they turned away from their evil ways; and God relented, deciding against the evil he'd said he was going to do to them, and didn't actually do it.

Paul on Circumcision (Galatians 5:1–12)

The King James Version

1 Stand fast therefore in the liberty wherewith Christ hath made us free, and be not entangled again with the yoke of bondage.

2 Behold, I Paul say unto you, that if ye be circumcised, Christ shall profit you nothing.

3 For I testify again to every man that is circumcised, that he is a debtor to do the whole law.

4 Christ is become of no effect unto you, whosoever of you are justified by the law; ye are fallen from grace.

5 For we through the Spirit wait for the hope of righteousness by faith.

6 For in Jesus Christ neither circumcision availeth any thing, nor uncircumcision; but faith which worketh by love.

7 Ye did run well; who did hinder you that ye should not obey the truth?

8 This persuasion cometh not of him that calleth you.

9 A little leaven leaveneth the whole lump.

10 I have confidence in you through the Lord, that ye will be none otherwise minded: but he that troubleth you shall bear his judgment, whosoever he be.

---

*Classical Hebrew normally associates anger with heat of the nose, as if of a snorting bull, but here the image may connect comically to the danger of heatstroke (Jonah, chapter 4).

11 And I, brethren, if I yet preach circumcision, why do I
yet suffer persecution? then is the offence of the cross ceased.

12 I would they were even cut off which trouble you.

My translation

1 It was *for freedom* that the Anointed One *freed* all of
you. Stand your ground, then, in this new battle, and
don't take the harness of slavery on your shoulders
again.

2 Look, it's me, Paul, telling you that if you get
circumcised, the Anointed One will be a wash for you.

3 I give my solemn word one more time to every man
who gets himself circumcised that he will be on the
hook for performing the entire Jewish law.

4 You've nullified your bond with the Anointed One,
those of you who are being so upright and righteous
according to the law—you've forfeited his free gift!

5 In the Spirit, I'm telling you, and through faith: we
have already welcomed the hope for what is truly right.

6 This is because in Jesus the Anointed neither being
circumcised nor having a foreskin has any power; the
power is in faith doing its work through love.

7 You were running such a good race! Who cut you off,
so that you stopped believing the truth?

8 This new thing you've been made to believe doesn't
come from the one who calls you.

9 A little yeast lifts the whole lump.

10 I myself believe, through the Lord, in your having
nothing extraneous in your minds; and the person,
whoever he is, who's getting you all excited will be the
one to take the punishment.

11 As for me, brothers and sisters, if I were still preaching
circumcision (as they claim), why am I still being
hounded? So: this obstacle to the cross has been
nullified.

12 I wish that the person who's arousing—sorry, rousing
you up—this way would get his own pair cut off.

PART THREE

AN ACCOUNT OF THE FULLER FACTS

My Scholarly Resources
and Methods—As If

My writing depends less on any knowledge or expertise I have (though I *can* decipher various things) than on remembering, with almost the same helpless pain I felt at the time, my barely successful stint as a PhD student in Harvard's Classics Department.

The first week I was there, I saw in a book the abbreviation "loc. cit." (for the Latin *locō citatō* ["in the place cited"], to indicate, "I've already made that citation: go look under the proper heading"), and I didn't know what it meant, so I crossed Smyth Classical Library to ask a senior graduate student. He snarled at me that I should know the answer already, and that I shouldn't be asking him. My scholarly career went pretty much downhill from there, though I did have plenty of time on my own to read ancient literature that interested me.

I'm sorry to have inserted personal reminiscence where I'm supposed to be just listing the main scholarly works I've used, the assumptions behind their use, my methods of presenting information, and related matters. But I wanted to show how strongly I feel about the duty to share what I know (such as it is), and at the same time how much I sympathize with suspicion of academics, of whom I'm one, kind of. When I burble, "Let me tell you about the Bible in its earliest known forms," I do expect to have to back that up—and I hope I'm doing that in terms that don't echo a certain tenured Harvard professor who, when asked at a public lecture what his authority was for a statement, snapped, "I don't need to cite any authority; I *am* an authority."

One important question of readers must be "How do we know

that what you write about the Bible in this book is really the case? Why should we believe you, when much of what you write contradicts established assertions, and we can't check for ourselves directly?" I'd like, first of all, to go over the basics of what's conventionally regarded as evidence in the study of ancient documents.

Early Hebrew writing survives in inscriptions in stone and other durable material, which date as early as the tenth century B.C.E.— *if* not only inscriptions in actual Hebrew count (but also those in Paleo-Hebrew and related Semitic languages); the oldest surviving Hebrew literary manuscripts are from hundreds of years later. Yet the kingdom of Saul, David, and Solomon, about 1000–900 B.C.E., would have represented a strange concentration of temporal power (however great or small, and that's disputed) if there had been no literature of any kind in it, so it's not absurd to link the origins of stories *about* that kingdom *to* that kingdom; and it's a no-brainer to speculate back far earlier, as long as there's no insistence that the stories then belonged, or belonged exclusively, to people known as Israelites or Hebrews.

Ancient Greek evidence yields roughly the same pattern: inscriptions from a "dark age," at which time a great deal of (probably mostly oral) literature existed; oldest literary manuscripts very nearly only within the Hellenistic period, which started in the late fourth century B.C.E.—most of them *well* within that period.

But ordinary readers of ancient literature like myself have little or no experience of the oldest physical versions (or exact copies of them). We work from extensively restored and spiffed-up versions. These use standardized, easily legible printed letters, and reading aids of many kinds—more on these below.

Modern scholarly editions of the texts are essential basically because almost every important piece of writing to survive from the ancient world has undergone repetitive copying and constant editing. For the Bible, I'll start to explain the conditions from the New Testament Greek side,* in which the "text tradition" is more similar to the one for pagan literature.

Typically in both cases, a revered but not super-revered text from

---

*In Western Europe, this became the Latin side. The Old Testament was also covered in the Vulgate (= "Made Available to the Public") Latin translation. In Eastern Orthodox Christianity, the Septuagint Greek translation of the Old Testament was adopted along with the Greek New Testament to make up the full Bible.

antiquity was passed around late-antique and early-modern communities a little like a popular hereditary recipe. Quite different versions developed, chiefly due to accumulated mistakes, because all copying was done by hand until the advent of printing technology. A graduate-school classmate of mine emerged chagrined from an experiment a young professor had suggested: trying to transcribe just a few lines of Greek poetry without any errors. Imagine the effect on a text of hundreds of such people copying and recopying in a sort of endless relay event.

In the Christian world, moreover, the clever scribe lurked, a man who felt authorized to "correct" the text and not obligated to question his own prejudices. In an era without scientific principles (from the field of linguistics, for example) to assist him in his decisions, the text was likely to become more inauthentic the more comfortable he made it for himself. Greek Bibles, and especially the Latin ones that branched off from them early on, are therefore pretty soupy.

The modern process of sorting out inauthenticity is necessarily a tentative and fraught one. Even in the oldest and most generally reliable manuscripts (whole classes of the newer ones can be more or less ignored, as derivative), some words and forms of words are clearly unlikely to be right and can be readily corrected; but experts can reasonably disagree about many others. The grounds for reasonable disagreement are shown in the *apparatus criticus* (Latin for "critical apparatus"—like that clears it up) in modern original-language scholarly editions, at the bottom of each page. There, the editor indicates, in a highly abbreviated form, "Though I chose the reading printed above in the text, you should know what my range of nonabsurd options was: here it is, and here are the manuscripts or groups of manuscripts in which it is found." The Nestle-Aland Greek New Testament has an *apparatus criticus* that often covers a third of a page: that's how much doubt about the text survives the most skilled and objective scrutiny available today.

Why am I going into all this, when in my book I generally just rely on this best modern text of the Greek (and occasionally refer to the Latin) and don't second-guess the editors? Well—alas for present-day translators—punctilious academic vetting took place long after the standardization and printing of the Bible in Greek during the Renaissance, when Greek scholarship had been reintroduced to Western Europe; and long after the foundational modern translations, too. Erasmus of Rotterdam did produce purportedly superior Greek versions of the New Testament in the early sixteenth century, but his building blocks were just a few Greek manuscripts, backed up by Latin translations. Martin Luther's German Scripture, the Tyndale corpus, the Geneva Bible, and the King James Version were all heavily influenced by this inferior product.

Confronted with this long, flowing, regalia-like but quite holey tradition of what the Bible "says," a translator deeply concerned with the exact meanings and effects of the original texts (or the earliest available versions of them) has a lot of extra explaining to do. I have to tell people that some of what they've heard or learned, and what in some cases they're deeply attached to, isn't the case: not only are they used to translations that are far from precise, but in some places the Bible's actual authors probably gave no basis whatsoever for the standing English translations, precise or not.

Paul very likely didn't write about willingness to "give my body to be burned" (1 Corinthians 13:3). It's really "give up my body so that I can boast about it." That's not what people imbibed as children. That's not what came from the pulpit. The correction of the Greek has in fact found vindication in many new translations; but people will naturally be slow to accept the change, and it's priggish and condescending to blame them.

But when, in the course of discussing the original Bible's aesthetics and significance, I indicate that a word *is there,* I'm looking at it and have generations of scholars barking in my ears about what it is—not that anybody can say she *knows for sure,* as if through a math equation completed and checked. Nevertheless, I'm never drawing a conclusion off my own bat but rather on the best available data. Though some people get away with making stuff up about the Bible for fun and profit, I'm not in their category. Holding no regular academic post but using the academy's research to write popularizing books, I'd be ground to hamburger if I capered around frivolously.

The same, of course, goes for the Hebrew side of the evidence— and my relative newness to Hebrew only increases my paranoid propensity to *check* and *recheck* everything before it goes to print. But at least Classical Hebrew, though historically a much more shadowy language than ancient Greek, comes out in a more cohesive version of a scholarly Bible. The so-called Leningrad Codex, dating from the early eleventh century c.e., is the oldest complete canonical Hebrew

Bible and has few serious rivals as the best text. It is a sweet mix of preservation and elaboration. In addition to the original consonant letters, it contains not only vowel markings, accents, cantillation (a musical score of a sort, for chanting the text liturgically), but also the marginal notes of the learned Masoretes, to whose devotion this very codex is the greatest surviving monument.

These notes show the super-reverent, arms-length Jewish attitude toward the traditional text. Much unlike copyists of Greek and Latin Bible manuscripts, the late-antique and early medieval Masoretes did not feel entitled to change a single letter—and they transcribed with elaborate ritual care, to back up their pious intentions. They would note alongside a line any word or form of a word that they believed should be read out loud instead of what was written—and retained—in the text. For the Hebrew Bible, therefore, there is a visible and fairly explicit distinction between the Scriptural inheritance itself and what the inheritors did in order to make it comply with changes in their culture. Christians went ahead and simply rewrote their Greek and Latin. Jews didn't do that to their Hebrew; hence more of the oldest version is intact.

The Stuttgart Bible, the standard modern edited version of the Leningrad Codex, is thus—astonishingly—a presentation of the Hebrew from one manuscript, not a cobbling together from many. Its *apparatus criticus* is relatively modest in size because there isn't as much basis for correction and controversy to be found in this or other manuscripts of Hebrew, even when scholars consider the Greek Septuagint and the Targum (the Aramaic explications of the Hebrew), both dating from antiquity, and other factors (that emerge from, say, modern linguistics research). You have to worry even less about my wandering off track in reporting what is or might have been in the Hebrew. There are fewer places to go.

But as for interpretation, the situation was flipped, with Christianity tending toward the monolithic and Judaism toward pluralism. Yet neither tendency, alas, is particularly helpful to a translator, because of the piety and didacticism of both. Rabbis ("Great Ones") have commented to beat the band, most famously in late-antique literature collectively called the Talmud, but most of their contributions are ingenious aids to the religious life. Legal opinion figures prominently. A favorite of many Jews is the debate, recited at Passover, concerning just how many plagues God visited on Egypt. The number rises from the Scripturally attested ten into the thousands, like a math problem getting joyfully drunk.

This is *not,* of course, the succinct-footnote type of interpretation a student longs for when seeing a phrase and wondering, "Huh?"—and it's not the type of interpretation a translator needs, especially in the poetic passages, those most crammed with imagery as they consider the material world with all of its intricate specifics. Where considerations like "That word looks borrowed from a heathen literature, where it signified such and such" weren't permitted, piety could go its own way and leave a great deal of confident interpretation that merely clouds over original meanings.

Similarly, pious Christians, such as the medieval glossators (or annotators), tended to have priorities far different from knowing and making known exactly what Biblical texts meant. Open-minded engagement with potentially useful materials in the cause of objective interpretation? (Here, resources included works on language produced by pedants of pagan antiquity, literary-critical treatises, and guides to rhetoric, plus a canon of fraternal pagan literature that would fill a Walmart truck.) Or at least an engagement that, though religious, wasn't beholden to self-interested institutions and their doctrine? Until the Enlightenment, forget it. And as I complain in my previous book on the Bible, *Paul Among the People,* modern Biblical scholars themselves don't appear to have even inventoried the more popular and smutty parts of that vast antiquarian literary stock.

But there is no possibility that, with my existing knowledge and the time I have, I could make any original, specialized, academic "research contribution" myself, even if I wanted to. All I can be is a reader sharing my reading. I've therefore stuck mainly to the most straightforward and reliable sources, the reference books. The word "dictionary" might invoke the image of a one- or two-line definition of a word following a boldface heading, but the major scholarly dictionaries of the ancient languages are intricate and pretty exhaustive. One or two volumes can cover every word of Classical Hebrew (or both Classical Hebrew and its lingua franca version and successor, Aramaic) very thoroughly, recording each existing form and each existing use of all but the most common words and offering the scholarly consensus on translation. A Greek dictionary has to run to multiple volumes to do the same, but a liftable (if not exactly portable) version contains summaries adequate for all normal needs: it lists chronologically the authors (or classes of authors) in which a word occurs, and all of the apparent meanings by example. The main cause of my success as a translator so far is that I look words up.

I can read on my own up to the prevailing standard—anybody who's put enough years in can do that—but the prevailing standard is, well . . . let me put it this way: in thirty years as a reader of pagan literature, I've had to face down, again and again and again, my natural tendency to translate *comfortably for myself*, and I've had to recognize such a tendency as prevailing throughout the scholarly world. The good fight I must fight is against received wisdom, personal prejudice, and collegial back-scratching. My model is my late father, an environmental biologist who didn't give a flip what anybody self-interestedly called anything—once, for example, a state legislature reclassified toxic waste as "beneficial" waste that could be sprayed straight onto floodplains. Chemicals and physical forces are what they are, and they do what they do. Likewise the words in ancient documents.

But—sorry—back to the reference books I use. Concordances to the Bible, showing (either in the original language or in translation) every instance of every word in context, tighten the semantic net. Much of a word's significance can be inferred from how rare it is, or in which parts of the Bible it occurs, or in which forms. A glance at a concordance summarizes such data, though it may be necessary to chase down a number of the relevant passages in order to explore nuances.

A good line-by-line commentary on an original text does marvels for sparing tedious recourse to dictionaries and concordances, but a good commentary can be marvelously hard to find. Particularly where the Bible is concerned, there seems to be an accordion-like set of definitions for "commentary." A volume may turn out to be full of summaries ("Isaiah mourns the fate of Israel in this touching passage") or sermonizing ("From this prayer we learn the importance of always calling on God when we are in trouble"). Conversely, the exposition may be so dense and technical that its writer's own expert opinion drowns amid innumerable citations and intricate qualifications.* Hardly any books really help a translator like myself in interpreting the text word by word, so in listing only one or two commentaries for each passage I dealt with, and just a few commentaries on the Bible overall, I'm just being honest: I used the best I could find, but the best wasn't a broad, crowded assemblage. I don't know what I would have done without the Anchor Bible series. But I must stipulate that, out of the series' admittedly interesting accounts of passages' remote backgrounds, I haven't represented much at all, especially regarding indebtedness to the non-Jewish literature of the Middle East (in the case of the Hebrew Bible) and Jewish sectarian literature (in the case of the New Testament). I really doubt that the average original reader or hearer of Scripture—if not also the average "author" of it—would have been au fait with such influences.

When we talk about Scripture in its early flowering and try to imagine its essence, we're talking about functionally stand-alone documents: the Hebrew Bible as the incomparable treasure of a unique nation and religion; and the New Testament as the guide to a new religion to which cosmopolitan subjects of the Roman Empire were laying claim—soon with no one to challenge them about the details of its origins, as the parent religion, Judaism was, after the destruction of the Second Temple in 70 C.E., cataclysmically torn away from the politically dynamic, outward-looking form in which Jesus and his immediate followers knew it. These readers and listeners were like their Jewish predecessors—and like us—in that they mainly just took in the text and shared it, concentrating on the words before them—though with far more attention to form than we're used to. Pagan literary tropes (if only by contrast to the new religious ideas) may be the best map of what the early Christians felt and understood to start with—but these are for the most part neglected in Bible commentaries. In trying to imagine the experience of ancient Jewish readers and listeners, for their part, before the Rabbinic age of multifaceted learned dispute, I'm thrown even more

---

*The Internet, on balance, seems to me to have been no friend of scholarship. When you had to tramp to the library for books and articles, you tramped only when well motivated, and you studied and evaluated whatever you hauled home so as not to feel like a total chump. The current capacity to pull up an article a minute on a screen creates an apparently powerful temptation to staple together a nonargument from five hundred sources and to stuff a bibliography with crap.

strongly back on impressions of what the texts were internally—and here, as elsewhere in the Bible, aesthetics seems to be the great factor disregarded by the modern mind.

Well, okay, so much for commentaries; my plea in short is that I respect and study certain ones but can't fit their content or methodology into a book of this kind. What you will not find any evidence of in my bibliography, kind readers, is interest in "gendered perspectives" or other pseudo-political folderol; or in rehash (with quibbles) or frivolous challenge of any classic work of history or criticism; or in anything concerned with matters so minute that nobody distant from the tenure track would agree that the exploration is worthwhile. The "secondary literature" (a term that applies mainly to journal articles and monographs) I did consult, I consulted only to pursue obvious questions that arose from my classroom study of Greek and Hebrew.

On the other hand, a Tea Party sort of approach to explicating and celebrating the Bible isn't helpful either. Like a claimed passion for the Constitution and claimed hatred of Washington bureaucrats, a claim to be rescuing holy writ from the evil manipulations of liberal academics hardly ever washes. If Scripture (the term I prefer, because the Latin word from which it comes started out meaning simply "writing") gets rescued from the hands of one faction only to serve another faction, then what's the point?

More practically, the power of academic frivolity, even tendentious frivolity, is limited. Academics do compete with one another; if one makes a *factual* claim that's clearly wrong, that's fancy hogwash (*porc laver,* as my friend the religious writer and anthologist Leslie Williams puts it), others quickly gang up. When I tried (and thank goodness, I tried quite late) to use popular sources to get objective data on the Bible, I was sometimes alarmed. Not only might online, self-publishing, and broadcast fora contain basic errors; but also, certain bestselling authors appeared to be just making things up.

Happily, though I myself am quite ignorant, I know and confess it. Whenever I light on a passage, I'm aware I need all the help I can get with it. I can't afford to reject anyone's plausible information because of what she does or doesn't believe or practice as religion, or where she works, or where she publishes. If there's anything I need to keep an eye on, it's my own inadequacies. As George Herbert put it,

> Though I fail, I weep;
> Though I halt in pace,
> Yet I creep
> To the throne of grace.

For most passages I discuss in detail, I've provided a literal translation as well as a transliteration below it, in the rest of this third
part of my book. I hope this helps readers check my claims and
explore further if they like. In "translating literally," I always wilted
within while trying to strike a balance in English between gibberish
and same-old same-old, and between showing readers a mendacious
English "equivalent" and showing them something so weird that
they might as well go buy textbooks, grammars, and dictionaries
and start puzzling out the text for themselves, or sign up for a language course. (Those are the better routes, I know; I wrote this book
because most people don't have the time.)

Here, anyway, is an outline of what I did. Everywhere in my
literal translation, I placed hyphens between multiple words in
English that are "representing" a single Hebrew or Greek word or
word cluster. For instance, the ideas for subject pronouns (I, we,
you, he, she, it, they) in both Greek and Hebrew are folded into
finite verb forms: authors did not have to, but sometimes did, add
subject pronouns as distinct words, separate from the verbs; this
means that basic characteristics of the subject, such as gender, may
be expressed twice in a sentence, a potentially interesting emphasis
(though other factors, such as the development of the Koinē dialect
of Greek toward the ordinary use of more subject pronouns, must
be considered).

Possessives (my, our, your, his, her, its, their) may be built into
Hebrew nouns; in Greek, in contrast, they are often absent and
implied but must be separate words if they are explicit. As for pronoun direct objects (me, us, you, him, her, it, them), Hebrew routinely absorbs them into the verbs that govern them, whereas Greek
never does; there, they *must* be separate words if they are expressed.
All of these phenomena are visible in my "literal" text.

Also everywhere, I placed in square brackets English words representing ideas that aren't explicit anywhere in the original text but are
necessary for the sense in English—such as "I saw [it]" or "life [of]

vanity." Conversely, I place in ordinary parentheses (that is, round brackets) words and parts of words that represent what's there in the Hebrew or Greek but can't be translated directly—or properly, at any rate—into English. An example is the plural ending of one common Hebrew word for "God," *Elohim* (pronounced *elōheem*). It *is* a plural, but by the time the Scriptures were written down, it didn't normally *mean* "gods." I want to show what it looks like, because that has some fascinating historical implications—and in the Book of Jonah, some humorous ones—but it would be confusing and deceptive to suggest that early readers understood the word, in its typical context, the way it looks and sounds.

Some elements can't be translated at all, such as the word notifying you that the noun that follows is a certain kind of direct object; trying not to be too wordy, I identify in English (again, in parentheses) these elements as what they are.

Apparent inconsistencies spotted in my literal translation may be due to inconsistencies *within* languages. Don't be like me, sitting in beginning Hebrew class during the fourth week of the term and becoming convinced that this was all a practical joke, and that at any moment the teacher would whip out the real, logical rules, exclaiming, "Fooled ya!" As it is, elements as simple (you'd think) as prepositional phrases may be quite different from verse to verse, depending on such variables as their placement in a clause, and sometimes for no apparent reason. In summary, I'm not pulling your leg. Luckily, ancient Greek, in contrast to Hebrew, inhabits the Stoic empyrean of rationality and consistency. Yeah.

In composing my "literal translations," I've been harassed by the question "*How* literal?" Any possible answer comes down to certain issues of linguistics and psychology, and these in turn come down, darn it, to the unknowability of ancient people's vision of their own words and world. But I came to favor unpacking words to the greatest extent possible—their suggested imagery, their visible origins, even their internal structure—and including all of this to the fullest degree practical.

For instance, the Hebrew word usually translated as "holy" or "sanctified" is visibly "set apart." Would I be justified in writing "set apart" as a "literal translation"? Not according to today's modes of language use. When I catch my husband feeding prime rib to the dog, and he (the husband) exclaims, "I'm busted!" neither of us (but I don't know about the dog) pictures that he has mechanically malfunctioned or physically fallen to pieces.

But in the ancient Near East (and southeastern Europe, too), there probably wasn't as firm a division between the concrete and the abstract, the real and the symbolic, as with us, to encourage such forgetting. Holy things, like sacrifices and sanctuaries, literally *were* set apart. And society didn't revamp itself every single generation, so as always to be distancing the language from everyday experience, and making an ongoing awareness of, say, the *setting apart* of sacrifices seem like a sickly piece of pedantry. And finally, all the evidence (such as the migration of our school systems away from languages and toward technology) tells us that *our* toys, *our* treasures, *our* abiding preoccupations are more material; they are not words anymore. This is a huge change, so to suppose that the ancients ordinarily heard or read more in their words than we do in ours doesn't seem all that outrageous.

Granted, there is what linguists call "diachronic [= through time] change" to consider. What the priestly authors or compilers, on the one hand, and the Rabbis, on the other, pictured when they saw or heard the word "holy" would have been quite different, so fundamental were the changes in Jewish ritual. However, as a literary translator, I'm naturally most interested in pushing toward the original inspiration and impressions of a text. But in many cases, I've got no more confidence in being right than the boxing writer Bert Sugar used to express in remarking, "Don't listen to me: I picked the Japs in the Big One." To avoid heavy-handedness or just the appearance of being stupid, I frequently give two English versions of a term, separated by a forward slash.

Again, in this part of the book, I've added a version of the original text's sounds under each literal translation. I need to stress, however, that this is my own system, and isn't real transliteration, which is a consistent, letter-by-letter rendering. Existing systems of representing Hebrew this way are technically useful but would be wildly unsuitable here. The first letter of the Hebrew alphabet, aleph (א), for example, can be represented sonically by a figure sort of like an apostrophe. What are my readers supposed to do with that? Granted, the letter aleph on its own is silent, but it usually has a vowel sound added to it, so that there it functions phonetically as one vowel or another. It's the vowel sound, but otherwise nothing, that I show.

English spelling is, of course, a wilderness, so I've come up with an eclectic, rather dorky-looking "transliteration" system—strictly in the hope of making it self-explanatory. The only two English vowels that are not at all confusing with long marks on them are o and u, so only those (when long) get long marks, appearing as ō and ū. The most reliable English diphthongs and the digraph ee have to serve for the other long vowels, but I still have to stipulate that my ai is the way it sounds in "mai tai," not in "wait"; for that sound, I use ei, as in "freight."

With eh, I try to make sure that in certain cases an e intended to be short is not understood as being either silent or like the e in "he"; "ah" is similarly used to pin down one pronunciation of the English "a." When I write to, the neuter Greek definite article ("the"), I have to expect that readers will see and pronounce the English "to," so this is one of the few places where I've employed a mark for a short o (ŏ).

I put hyphens between letters wherever I think the correct syllable division isn't likely to jump out at a reader—so that the h won't be pronounced in the combination ah-ō, for instance. Otherwise, I visibly set off syllables only to track meanings that, in English, are shown by separate words, such as "his head," which in Hebrew is structured as "head-his." I've thus put hyphens in the corresponding places in the literal English translation, and coordinated the transliteration line vertically as far as possible, so that it's easier to see what's going on. Sometimes two semantic units, like the Hebrew lahk or "to-you," form a single syllable and so can't be divided in the transliteration. Sometimes, the correct syllabic division in Hebrew is at war with the literal translation; I've always privileged the sounds, which I can roughly replicate on the page, to the grammar, which I can't. In Psalm 23:2, for example, I hear the word commonly translated "in . . . pastures" as bin-ōt, but that cuts the noun in two and suggests that the Hebrew for "in" is bin and that "pastures" are ōt. Not so; too bad. Experts who feel agitated about my choices can deliver an effective punishment by never including me in another call for papers for a conference on the modalities of desire or the geography of indifference.

I'm constrained to add that scholars differ on the sounds of

ancient Hebrew and Greek, and that I'm just passing on the pronunciations I've learned. I happen to have learned them at four
American universities, and anyone who thinks I should have studied
at Oxford or Heidelberg or Jerusalem instead can go fill out a form.

But important to note concerning my transliteration of the Koinē
dialect of Greek used in the original New Testament is that the
everyday pronunciation had probably changed a lot from the standard, elite, dialect of Athens, home of the best-known pagan Greek
literature. The trouble is, first, that this change took place over a
period of several hundred years, and over bewildering distances, so
that it's very hard to tell exactly what the differences would have
been to the ears of the New Testament authors—about whose ethnicity, class, and education we can know little. I can't concur with
papyrologists who, on discovering evidence of what may be simply mishearings, misspellings, or local variations in pronunciation,
conclude, for example, that the sound of a certain diphthong had
decisively merged with the sound of a certain short vowel—so that
a very early stage of Modern Greek "iotacization" (through which
a bunch of differently written vowels and diphthongs came to be
pronounced alike) can be inferred. You only have to contemplate
aristocratic English mispronunciations and misspellings of French
during the past few centuries to grasp the distinction between a
powerful language's basic, persistent integrity and the ways people
on the margins adapt that language.

With this in mind, I favor the Attic or Athenian pronunciations with their maximum differentiation among sounds. Scripture
was authoritative performative literature, and thus very probably
enjoyed strict conservative care not evident in the language of the
street (sometimes exemplified by graffiti), of business documents
and private letters, and of Scriptural spin-offs that never entered
corporate worship and teaching. The substantially preserved old
spellings in ancient Scriptural manuscripts suggest this cultural gap.
We keep the Chaucerian spellings because we choose to preserve the
Chaucerian pronunciation; we extensively change the Shakespear-
ean spellings because we impose our own pronunciation.

In a similar vein, when I attend an American Jewish worship
service and hear substantially the same pronunciations I heard in
the classroom, I feel confident in not worrying about the immense
changes in Jewish languages since the time of Jewish literature that

is called "Classical." And in any case, I'd rather accept a broad consensus and an established standardization than spend a lifetime in
research and still not be positive I could accurately pronounce a
single word.

Inherited texts of Classical Hebrew show quite a complicated
system of accents related to grammar, syntax, and verse structure;
Koinē Greek has quite simple accentuation. I don't write accent
marks anywhere in my transliteration for the simple reason that I'm
not sure that the accents in themselves originally conveyed much
literary effect; for both languages, patterns of consonant and vowel
sounds probably meant a lot more. I think I've found an occasional
exception, which I point out. But since in researching this book I
often went down the garden path myself—thinking, "This rhythm
is special," where it wasn't—I decided that it wouldn't be helpful
to include accents in the transliterations. I'm reliably told these are
busy-looking enough as they are.

I

The Translation of Vai-hee *("And It Was/
Became/Happened") in the Story of David
and Bathsheba (2 Samuel 11–12:7),
According to Various Important Bibles*

I don't see where I would get off—actually, where anyone would
get off—as a Bible pedant; and that's to say nothing of the Bible
snobs on the cultural right or the bulldozers of the Bible on the
political left. Despite considerable ingrained orneriness, I accept
that whenever translations fail to satisfy my yearning for perfection,
this should be first of all a useful reminder that I'm looking for perfection in the wrong place. (Hint as to the nature of my mistake:
"[T]here is none good but one . . ." [Matthew 19:17].)

When someone gives me a Bible on the street, I take it and use
it. Once, someone from the United Bible Societies gave me a Greek
New Testament to which the celebrated scholars Kurt Aland and
Bruce Metzger had contributed. Only those weird hippie Bibles I
ran into once or twice in my childhood don't seem to have anything to teach me. Therefore, it's natural for me now to just reach
onto the shelf when asking what some ways are of dealing with
vai-hee—other than the King James's "and it came to pass," which I
discuss in Part One, Chapter 1 (pp. 11–13), in connection to the story
of David and Bathsheba in 2 Samuel, chapters 11 and 12. Here is the
King James translation of the verses in question:

> **11:1**   And it came to pass, after the year was expired, at the
> time when kings go forth to battle, that David sent Joab, and
> his servants with him, and all Israel; and they destroyed the
> children of Ammon, and besieged Rabbah. But David tarried
> still at Jerusalem.

2   And it came to pass in an eveningtide, that David arose from off his bed, and walked upon the roof of the king's house: and from the roof he saw a woman washing herself; and the woman was very beautiful to look upon.

. . .

14   And it came to pass in the morning, that David wrote a letter to Joab, and sent it by the hand of Uriah.

. . .

16   And it came to pass, when Joab observed the city, that he assigned Uriah unto a place where he knew that valiant men were.

I'll start with the first known translation of the Old Testament, the Greek Septuagint. The ho-hum rendering of the first three instances of the Hebrew *vai-hee* in this story (verses 1, 2, and 14) is *kai egenetŏ*, "and it became/happened." But the fourth instance (verse 16), using that same Greek verb for the identical Hebrew phrase, uses a different, rarer form of the verb, though there is no obviously overriding contextual difference. Is that supposed to *mean* something different, or are the much heavier sounds of the second verb, *egeneithei*, just more ominous as the story veers toward the effective murder of Uriah—or is the variation merely about carelessness or randomness? The Talking Heads lyrics sound in my brain: "This is not my beautiful house!"

In contrast to the Septuagint, the Vulgate Latin Bible seems to interpret up a storm, using two different verbs for happening, and even adding adverbs. The first verb, occurring in verse 1, is *fio*, which is (here, anyway) a quite neutral indication of something taking place, and it's used with the word *autem*, "however": now we're turning a narrative corner. But in verse 2, the verb is *accidit*, which emphasizes chance: literally, "it fell to." Here the woman's world and the king's world collide. Perhaps even more strikingly, there is added, out of nowhere in the Hebrew, a little historiographic sort of riff, *Dum haec agerentur,* most literally "while these things [= the war, and David's staying home] were being driven forward"; it's a very common way to write "meanwhile" but does serve to stress the action elsewhere, which is David's shirked responsibility.

In the Vulgate, verses 14 and 16 deploy adverbs as pretty obtrusive comments (with no basis in the Hebrew) on the logic of the events: respectively, "It happened [from *fio*] *therefore* on the next day," and *only* "Therefore" start the sentences. In this latter case, there is no verb of happening in the verse at all, as opposed to the two verbs in the Latin of verse 2 (*agerentur* and *accidit*). In its very form, the story is speeding up. In verses 14 and 16, this Latin translation uses two *different* verbs for "therefore," *ergo* and *itaque*. (I can't tell their meanings in this context apart, so I don't know how much to read into the difference between them; or I doubly don't know, because in Vulgar Latin such adverbs may be thrown around rather carelessly and sometimes even combined; *ergo igitur* reminds me of the "How-somever" of my rural Ohio childhood.)

Now, ah, a few of the modern Bibles! The Jewish Study Bible just elides the phrase *vai-hee* in English translation, except for a "So . . ." in verse 16, a logical nudge toward further events. Doesn't this just make me want to hop on the current anti-Semitic bus?

Oh, but wait: the Catholic Study Bible commits the same sin of elision. The HarperCollins Study Bible even omits verse 16's "So . . ."; but the beginning of verse 2 is packed with drama: "It happened, late one afternoon . . ."—that's an edition of the New Revised Standard Version, my go-to Modern Bible. A certain suspicion that these people are cribbing from one another grows in me.

But I would be in a peck of trouble as a hypocrite for calling such interpretation (and particularly such shared interpretation of a communal book) heinous. Look (for example) how beautifully David Rosenberg takes the process just a couple of steps further in *A Literary Bible:*

> Verse 1: "Here we are: a year was passing . . ."
> Verse 2: "It happens late one afternoon . . ."
> Verse 14: "Here we are: in the morning . . ."
> Verse 16: "So it happens: Joab explores his siege of the city . . ."

I love this! The English present tense, especially "Here we are," captures the fact that *vai-hee* contains no true past tense and thus can refer to a timeless present. The slightly varying uses of "happens" suggest first chance and then forward propulsion, too.

The Two Lord's Prayers

MATTHEW 6:9–13

9 . . . Our Father which art in heaven, Hallowed be thy name.

father	*of-us*	*the [one] in*	*the*	*skies/heavens*
pahter	heimōn hŏ	en	tois	ūrahnois

let-be-made-holy	*the*	*name*	*of-you*
hahgiahstheitō	tŏ	onoma	sū

10 Thy kingdom come, Thy will be done in earth, as it is in heaven.

let-come	*the kingdom*	*of-you*
elthetō	hei bahsileia	sū

let-come-into-being	*the wanting*	*of-you*
geneitheitō	tŏ theleima	sū

as	*in [the]*	*sky*	*also/even*	*on*	*land/earth*
hōs	en	ūrahnō	kai	epi	geis

11 Give us this day our daily bread.

the loaf/bread	*of-us*	*the [one]*	*coming-on*	*give*	*to-us*	*today*
tŏn artŏn	heimōn	tŏn	epiūsion	dos	heimin	seimeron

12 And forgive us our debts, as we forget our debtors.

and	*let-go*	*to-us*	*the*	*debts*	*of-us*
kai	ahfes	heimin	ta	ŏfeileimahta	heimōn

as	also/even	we	[have?]-let-go	to-the	debtors	of-us
hōs	kai	heimeis	ahfeikamen	tois	ofeiletais	heimōn

13   And lead us not into temptation, but deliver us from evil:
For thine is the kingdom, and the power, and the glory, for ever.
Amen.

and	do-not [please]	into-bring	us	into	testing
kai	mei	eisenengkeis	heimahs eis	peirahsmon	

but	save us	from the	evil [one]
ahlla	rūsai heimahs	ahpŏ tū	poneirū

LUKE 11:2–4

2   . . . Our father which art in heaven, Hallowed be thy name.
Thy kingdom come. Thy will be done, as in heaven, so in earth.

. . . *father,*
. . . pahter

let-be-made-holy	the	name	of-you;
hahgiastheitō	tŏ	onoma	sū

let-come the	kingdom	of-you
elthetō hei	bahsileia	sū

3   Give us day by day our daily bread.

the	bread/loaf	of-us	the [one]	coming-on	give	to-us	the
tŏn	artŏn	heimōn tŏn		epiūsion	didū	heimin	tŏ

[day] by day
kahth'heimerahn

4 And forgive us our sins; for we also forgive every one that
is indebted to us. And lead us not into temptation; but deliver us
from evil.

and	*let-go*	*to-us*	*the*	*sins*	*of-us*
kai	ahfes	heimin	tahs	hahmartiahs	heimōn

for	*even/and-indeed*	*[we] ourselves*	*let-go*	*to-everyone indebted*
kai	gar	owtoi	ahfiomen	pahnti ŏfeilonti

to-us
heimin

and	*do-not [please]*	*into-bring*	*us*	*into*	*testing*
kai	mei	eisenengkais	heimahs	eis	peirahsmon

2

Genesis 1:1–5

1   In the beginning God created the heaven and the earth.

in-beginning   made   god(s)   (direct object marker)
beh-reisheet   bara   elōheem   eit

the-heaven/sky   and-(direct object marker) the-earth/land
hahsh-shahma-yim veh-eit   ha-aretz

2   And the earth was without form, and void; and darkness was upon the face of the deep. And the Spirit of God moved upon the face of the waters.

and-the-earth/land   was-in-a-state-of formlessness/confusion/unreality
veh-ha-aretz   hahyeta   tōhū

and-emptiness and-darkness [was]   on/above [the] face [of the]
va-bōhū   veh-chōshek   ahl   penei

subterranean-water/abyss   and-[the]-spirit/breath/wind [of]
tehōm   veh-rūach

god(s) [was]   hovering/brooding   on [the] face [of] the-water
elōheem   mehrachefet   ahl   penei   hahm-ma-yim

3 And God said, Let there be light: and there was light.

and-said   god(s)   let-exist light and-existed light
vai-yōmer elōheem yehee   ōr   vai-hee   ōr

4 And God saw the light, that it was good: and God divided the light from the darkness.

and-saw god(s)   (direct object marker)   the-light that [it was]
vai-yar   elōheem   et   ha-ōr   kee

good and-divided god(s)   between the-light and-between
tōv   vai-yavdeil elōheem   bein   ha-ōr   ū-vein

the-darkness
ha-chōshek

5 And God called the light Day, and the darkness he called Night. And the evening and the morning were the first day.

and-called god(s)   (to)-the-light day   and-(to)-the-darkness
vai-yikra   elōheem   la-ōr   yōm   veh-la-chōshek

he-called night   and-existed evening and-existed morning
kara   la-yeh-ta vai-hee   erev   vai-hee   bōker

day one
yōm echahd

John 1:1–14
———

1 In the beginning was the Word, and the Word was with God, and the Word was God.

in	*beginning*	*was*	*the*	*idea*	*and*	*the*	*idea*	*was*
en	archei	ein	hŏ	logos	kai	hŏ	logos	ein

toward/in-relation-to	*the*	*god*	*and*	*god*	*was*	*the*	*idea*
prŏs		tŏn theh-on	kai	theh-os	ein	hŏ	logos

2   The same was in the beginning with God.

this	*was*	*in*	*beginning*	*toward/in-relation-to*	*the*	*god*
hūtos	ein	en	archei	prŏs	tŏn	theh-on

3   All things were made by him; and without him was not made any thing that was made.

everything	*through*	*it/him*	*came-into-existence/was-born*	*and*	*apart-from*
pahnta	di'owtū		egenetŏ		kai chōris

it/him	*came-into-existence/was-born*	*not-even*	*one [thing]*	*that*
owtū	egenetŏ		ūdeh	hen	hŏ

has-come-into-existence/has-been-born
gegonen

4   In him was life; and the life was the light of men.

in	*it/him*	*life*	*was*	*and*	*the*	*life*	*was*	*the*	*light*	*of-the*
en	owtō	zōei	ein	kai	hei	zōei	ein	tŏ	fōs	tōn

human-beings
ahnthrōpōn

5   And the light shineth in darkness; and the darkness comprehended it not.

and	*the*	*light*	*in the darkness*	*shone and*	*the*	*darkness it*	*not*
kai	tŏ	fōs	en tei skotia	fainei kai	hei	skotia	owtŏ ū

caught/understood
kahtelahben

6 There was a man sent from God, whose name was John.

came-into-existence/was-born [a] human-being	*dispatched*	*from*
egenetŏ ahnthrōpos	ahpestahlmenos	para

god,	*[the] name*	*to-him*	*John*
theh-ū,	onoma	owtō	yōahnneis

7 The same came for a witness, to bear witness of the Light, that all men through him might believe.

this [one]	*came*	*into*	*testimony*	*in-order-that*	*he-testify*
hūtos	eilthen	eis	marturiahn	hina	martureisei

about the	*light*	*in-order-that*	*all [people]*	*would-believe*	*through him*
peri	tū	fōtos hina	pahntehs	pisteusōsin	di'owtū

8 He was not that Light, but was sent to bear witness of that Light.

not	*was that [one] the*	*light*	*but in-order-that*	*he-testify*	*about*
ūk	ein ekeinos tŏ	fōs	ahll'hina	martureisei	peri

the	*light*
tū	fōtos

9 That was the true Light, which lighteth every man that cometh into the world.

was	*the*	*light the*		*true [one]*	*which*	*lights*	*every*
ein	tŏ	fōs	tŏ	ahleithinon	hŏ	fōtidzei	pahnta

human-being	*coming*		*into*	*the world*
ahnthrōpon	erchomenon	eis	tŏn kosmon	

10   He was in the world, and the world was made by him, and
the world knew him not.

in the world	*he-was*	*and*	*the*	*world*	*through him*
en tō kosmō	ein	kai	hŏ	kosmos	di'owtū

came-into-existence/was-born	*and/but*	*the*	*world*	*him*	*not*
egenetŏ	kai	hŏ	kosmos	owtŏn	ūk

recognized
egnō

11   He came unto his own, and his own received him not.

into	*the*	*own [things]*	*he-came*	*and/but*	*the own [people]*	*him*
eis	ta	idia	eilthen	kai	hoi idioi	owtŏn

not	*accepted*
ū	parelahbon

12   But as many as received him, to them gave he power to
become the sons of God, even to them that believe on his name:

as-many	*on-the-other-hand*	*received*	*him*	*he-gave*	*to-them*
hosoi	deh	elahbon	owtŏn	edōken	owtois

[the]	*right [as]*	*children*	*of-God*	*to-come-into-being/to-be-born*
	eksūsiahn	tekna	theh-ū	genesthai

to-the [ones]	*believing/trusting*	*into*	*the*	*name*	*of-him*
tois	pisteuūsin	eis	tŏ	onoma	owtū

13   Which were born, not of blood, nor of the will of the flesh, nor of the will of man, but of God.

who	*not*	*out-of*	*bloods*	*neither*	*out-of*	*wanting*
hoi	ūk	eks	haimahtōn	ūdeh	ek	theleimahtos

of-flesh	*neither*	*out-of*	*wanting*	*of-[a]-husband/man*	*but*
sarkos	ūdeh	ek	theleimahtos	ahndros	ahll'

out-of	*god*	*came-into-being/were-born*
ek	theh-ū	egenneitheisahn

14   And the Word was made flesh, and dwelt among us, (and we beheld his glory, the glory as of the only begotten of the Father,) full of grace and truth.

and	*the*	*idea [as]*	*flesh*	*came-into-being/was-born*	*and*	*camped*
kai	hŏ	logos	sarks	egenetŏ	kai	eskeinōsen

among	*us*	*and*	*we-were-the-audience-of*	*the*	*glory*
en	heimin	kai	etheh-ahsahmetha	tein	doksahn

of-him	*glory*	*as*	*of-[the]-only-born*	*from [a]*	*father*
owtū	doksahn	hōs	monogenūs	para	pahtros

full	*of-goodwill/kindness/a-free-gift*	*and*	*of-truth*
pleireis	charitos	kai	ahleitheiahs

3

Ezekiel's Dry Bones (Ezekiel 37:1–14)

1   The hand of the Lord was upon me, and carried me out in the spirit of the Lord, and set me down in the midst of the valley which was full of bones,

was   on-me [the] hand [of]   yahweh/[the] lord
ha-yeta ahl-ai   yahd   yahweh/ahdōnai

and-he-caused-to-go-out-me   with-[the]-spirit/breath [of]
vai-yōtsee-ei-nee   beh-rūach

yahweh/[the] lord   and-he-set-down-me   in-the-middle-of
yahweh/ahdōnai   vai-neechei-nee   beh-tōk

the-valley   and-it-was full [of] bones
hahb-bika veh-hee   meleia ahtsahmōt

2   And caused me to pass by them round about: and, behold, there were very many in the open valley; and, lo, they were very dry.

and-he-caused-to-pass-me beside-them round   round   and-look
veh-heh-eh-veera-nee   ahlei-hem sahveev   sahveev veh-hinnei

many   very   on-[the]-face [of] the-valley   and-look [they were]
rahbbōt meh-ōd ahl-penei   hahb-bika veh-hinnei

dry   very
yeveishōt   meh-ōd

3   And he said unto me, Son of man, can these bones live? And
I answered, O Lord God, thou knowest.

and-he-said   to-me   son [of] man   (question indicator)-will-live
vai-yōmer   eil-ai   ben   ahdahm ha-tichyena

the-bones   the-these and-I-said   lord   yahweh/lord   you
ha-ahtsahmōt   ha-eilleh va-ōmar   ahdōnai yahweh/ahdōnai ahtta

know
yahda-ehta

4   Again he said unto me, Prophesy upon these bones, and say
unto them, O ye dry bones, hear the word of the Lord.

and-he-said   to-me prophesy   to   the-bones   the-these
vai-yōmer   eil-ai hinnahvei ahl   ha-ahtsahmōt   ha-eileh

and-you-will-say to-them   the-bones   the-dry   hear
veh-ahmarta   ahl-eihem   ha-ahtsahmōt hai-veishōt shimū

[the] word [of]   yahweh/[the] lord
        dehvar   yahweh/ahdōnai

5   Thus saith the Lord God unto these bones; Behold, I will
cause breath to enter into you, and ye shall live:

thus spoke lord   yahweh/lord   to-the-bones   the-these look
kō   ahmar ahdōnai yahweh/ahdōnai la-ahtsahmōt ha-eileh hinnei

I [am]   causing-to-come in-you   breath   and-you-will-live
ahnee   meivee   va-kem rūach   vich-yeetem

6   And I will lay sinews upon you, and will bring up flesh upon
you, and cover you with skin, and put breath in you, and ye shall
live; and ye shall know that I am the Lord.

and-I-will-give   on-you   muscles and-I-will-cause-to-come-up
veh-nahtahtee   ahlei-kem gideem veh-ha-ahleitee

on-you   flesh   and-I-will-cover on-you   skin and-I-will-give
ahlei-kem bahsar veh-karahmtee   ahlei-kem ōr   veh-nahtahtee

in-you   breath   and-you-will-live   and-you-will-know that I [am]
va-kem rūach   vich-yeetem   vee-dahtem   kee ahnee

yahweh/[the] lord
yahweh/ahdōnai

7   So I prophesied as I was commanded: and as I prophesied,
there was a noise, and behold a shaking, and the bones came
together, bone to his bone.

and-I-prophesied as-that   I-was-commanded and-was   [a] noise
veh-nibbeitee   ka-ahsher tsuvveitee   vai-hee   kōl

as-prophesying-my   and-look [there was] shaking   and-came-together
keh-hinnahveh-ee veh-hinnei   rah-ahsh   vaht-tikrevū

bones   bone   to bone-his
ahtsahmōt etsem   el ahts-mō

8   And when I beheld, lo, the sinews and the flesh came up
upon them, and the skin covered them above: but there was no
breath in them.

and-I-saw   and-look   on-them   muscles and-flesh   rose
veh-rah-eetee veh-hinnei ahlei-hem gideem ū-vahsar   ahla

and-covered	on-them	skin	on-top-of	and-breath
vai-yikrahm	ahlei-hem	ōr	mil-ma-ela	veh-rūach

there-was-not	in-them
ein	ba-hem

9 Then said he unto me, Prophesy unto the wind, prophesy, son of man, and say to the wind, Thus saith the Lord God; Come from the four winds, O breath, and breathe upon these slain, that they may live.

and-he-said	to-me	prophesy	to the-wind	prophesy	son [of]
vai-yōmer	eil-ai	hinnahvei	el ha-rūach	hinnahvei	ven

man	and-you-will-say	to the-wind	thus	said	lord
ahdahm	veh-ahmarta	el ha-rūach	kō	ahmar	ahdōnai

yahweh/[the] lord	from four	winds	come the-wind/breath
yahweh/ahdōnai	mei-arba	rūchōt	bōee ha-rūach

and-blow/breathe	on-the-killed	the-these	and-they-will-live
ū-fechee	ba-ha-rūgeem	ha-eilleh	veh-yichyū

10 So I prophesied as he commanded me, and the breath came into them, and they lived, and stood up upon their feet, an exceeding great army.

and-I-prophesied	as-that	he-ordered-me	and-came	in-them
veh-hinnahbbeitee	ka-ahsher	tsivva-nee	vaht-tahvō	va-hem

the-wind	and-they-lived	and-they-stood-up	on feet-their
ha-rūach	vai-yichyū	vai-ya-ahmdū	ahl rahglei-hem

army	large	very	very
chahyil	gahdōl	meh-ōd	meh-ōd

11　Then he said unto me, Son of man, these bones are the whole house of Israel: behold, they say, Our bones are dried, and our hope is lost: we are cut off for our parts.

and-he-said	*to-me*	*son [of]*	*man*	*the-bones*	*the-these [are]*
vai-yōmer	eil-ai	ben	ahdahm	ha-ahtsahmōt	ha-eilleh

all [the]	*house [of]*	*israel*	*these*	*look [they are]*	*saying*
col	beit	yisra-eil	heimma	hinnei	ōmereem

are-dried-out	*bones-our*	*and-has-perished*	*hope-our*
yahbeshū	ahtsmōtei-nū	veh-ahveda	tikvahtei-nū

we-are-cut-off	*to/from-ourselves*
nigzarnū	la-nū

12　Therefore prophesy and say unto them, Thus saith the Lord God; Behold, O my people, I will open your graves, and cause you to come up out of your graves, and bring you into the land of Israel.

therefore	*prophesy*	*and-you-will-say*	*to-them*	*thus*	*has-spoken*
lahkein	hinnahvei	veh-ahmarta	ahlei-hem	kō	ahmar

[the] lord	*yahweh/[the] lord*	*look*	*I [am]*	*opening*
ahdōnai	yahweh/ahdōnai	hinnei	ahnee	fōteiach

(direct object marker)	*graves-your*	*and-I-will-cause-to-come-up*
et	kivrōtei-kem	veh-ha-ahleitee

you	*from-graves-your*	*people-my*	*and-I-will-cause-to-come*
etkem	mik-kivrōtei-kem	ahm-mee	veh-heiveitee

you	*to*	*[the] land [of]*	*israel*
etkem	el	ahdmaht	yisra-eil

13　And ye shall know that I am the Lord, when I have opened your graves, O my people, and brought you up out of your graves,

and-you-will-know *that I [am] yahweh/[the] lord*   *in-opening-my*
vee-dahtem   kee ahnee yahweh/ahdōnai   beh-fit-chee

(direct object marker) *graves-your*   *and-in-causing-to-rise-my* *you*
et   kivrōtei-kem ū-beh-ha-ahlō-tee   etkem

from-graves-your   *people-my*
mik-kivrōtei-kem   ahm-mee

14 And shall put my spirit in you, and ye shall live, and I shall place you in your own land: then shall ye know that I the Lord have spoken it, and performed it, saith the Lord.

and-I-will-put   *spirit/breath-my* *in-you*   *and-you-will-live*
veh-nahtahttee   rū-chee   va-kem   vich-yeetem

and-I-will-cause-to-settle *you*   *in*   *land-your*
veh-hinnachtee   etkem   ahl   ahdmaht-kem

and-you-will-know *that I*   *yahweh/[the] lord*   *have-spoken*
vee-dahtem   kee ahnee yahweh/ahdōnai   dibbartee

and-I-will-do [it this is the]   *spoken [thing] [of]* *yahweh/[the] lord*
veh-ahseetee   neh-ūm   yahweh/ahdōnai

Revelation's Martyrs in Paradise (Revelation 7:9–17)

———

9 After this I beheld, and, lo, a great multitude, which no man could number, of all nations, and kindreds, and people, and tongues, stood before the throne, and before the Lamb, clothed with white robes, and palms in their hands;

after these [things] *I-looked/saw* *and* *look* *[a] crowd* *large*
meta towta   eidon   kai   idū   ochlos   polus

which   to-count   it   no-one   was-able   out-of   every
hŏn   arithmeisai owtŏn   ūdeis   edunahtŏ   ek   pahntŏs

race   and   of-tribes and   of-peoples   and   of-tongues/languages
ethnūs   kai   fūlōn   kai   la-ōn   kai   glōssōn

standing   in-face   of-the   throne   and   in-face   of-the
estōtehs   enōpion   tū   thronū   kai   enōpion   tū

little-lamb   wrapped-around [as to] robes/clothes   white [ones]   and
arniū   peribebleimenūs   stolahs   leukahs   kai

palm-branches in the   hands   of-them
foinikehs   en tais chersin owtōn

10   And cried with a loud voice, saying, Salvation to our God
which sitteth upon the throne, and unto the Lamb.

and   they-shout [with a]   voice   loud/big   saying   the
kai   kradzūsin   fōnei   megahlei   legontes hei

rescue/salvation   to-the   god   of-us   to-the [one]   sitting
sōteiria   tō   theh-ō   heimōn tō   kahtheimenō

on   the   throne   and   to-the   little-lamb
epi   tō   thronō   kai   tō   arniō

11   And all the angels stood round about the throne, and about
the elders and the four beasts, and fell before the throne on their
faces, and worshipped God,

and   all   the   angels/messengers   stood   in-[a]-circle
kai   pahntehs hoi ahnggeloi   heisteikeisahn   kuklō

[around]   the   throne   and   the elders   and   the   four
            tū   thronū   kai   tōn presbuterōn   kai   tōn   tessarōn

animals	*and*	*[they]*	*fell*	*in-face*	*of-the*	*throne*	*on*	*the*
zō-ōn	kai		epesahn	enōpion	tū	thronū	epi	ta

faces	*of-themselves*	*and*	*prostrated-themselves/worshipped*
prosōpa	owtōn	kai	prosekuneisahn

to-the	*God*
tō	theh-ō

12   Saying, Amen: Blessing, and glory, and wisdom, and thanks-giving, and honour, and power, and might, be unto our God for ever and ever. Amen.

saying	*truly*	*the*	*blessing*	*and*	*the*	*glory*	*and*	*the wisdom*
legontes	ahmein	hei	eulogia	kai	hei	doksa	kai	hei sofia

and	*the*	*gratitude*	*and*	*the*	*honor*	*and*	*the*	*power*
kai	hei	eucharistia	kai	hei	teemei	kai	hei	dunahmis

and	*the*	*strength*	*to-the*	*god*	*of-us*	*into*	*the ages*
kai	hei	ischus	tō	theh-ō	heimōn	eis	tūs aiōnahs

of-the	*ages*	*truly*
tōn	aiōnōn	ahmein

13   And one of the elders answered, saying unto me, What are these which are arrayed in white robes? and whence came they?

and	*answered*	*one*	*out*	*of-the elders*	*saying*	*to-me*
kai	ahpekreethei	heis	ek	tōn presbuterōn	legōn	moi

these	*the*	*wrapped-around [as to]*	*the*	*robes/clothes*	*the*
hūtoi	hoi	peribebleimenoi		tahs stolahs	tahs

white [ones]	*who*	*are-they*	*and*	*from-where*	*did-they-come*
leukahs	tines	eisin	kai	pothen	eilthon

14   And I said unto him, Sir, thou knowest. And he said to
me, These are they which came out of great tribulation, and have
washed their robes, and made them white in the blood of the Lamb.

and	*I-said*	*to-him*	*lord*	*of-me*	*you*	*know*	*and*	*he-said*
kai	eireika	owtō	kūrieh	mū	su	oidahs	kai	eipen

to-me
moi

these are	*the [ones]*	*coming*	*out*	*of-the*	*crushing/disaster*	*the*
hūtoi eisin	hoi	erchomenoi	ek	teis	thlipseh-ōs	teis

large [one]
megahleis

and	*they-washed*	*the*	*robes/clothes*	*of-themselves*
kai	eplūnahn	tahs	stolahs	owtōn

and [they]	*whitened*	*them*	*in the blood*	*of-the*	*little-lamb*
kai	eleukahnahn	owtahs	en tō haimahti	tū	arniū

15   Therefore are they before the throne of God, and serve him
day and night in his temple: and he that sitteth on the throne shall
dwell among them.

through	*this [thing]*	*they-are*	*in-face*	*of-the*	*throne*	*of-the*
dia	tūtŏ	eisin	enōpion	tū	thronū	tū

god
theh-ū

and	*serve*	*to-him*	*[entire] days*	*and*	*by-night*	*in the*
kai	latreuūsin	owtō	heimerahs	kai	nuktos	en tō

shrine	*of-him,*
nah-ō	owtū

and	*the [one]sitting*		*on*	*the*	*throne*	*will-put-a-tent*
kai	hŏ	kahtheimenos	epi	tū	thronū	skeinōsei

over them
ep'owtūs

16 They shall hunger no more, neither thirst any more; neither shall the sun light on them, nor any heat.

not	*they-will-hunger*	*still*	*neither*	*they-will-thirst*	*still*
ū	peinahsūsin	eti	ūdeh	dipseisūsin	eti

neither	*not*	*will/should-fall*	*onto them*	*the*	*sun*	*neither*
ūdeh	mei	pesei	ep'owtūs	hŏ	heilios	ūdeh

any heat/burning
pahn kowma

17 For the Lamb which is in the midst of the throne shall feed them, and shall lead them unto living fountains of waters: and God shall wipe away all tears from their eyes.

because	*the*	*little-lamb*	*the [one]up*	*middle*	*of-the throne*
hŏti	tŏ	arnion	tŏ	ahna meson	tū	thronū

will-shepherd them
poimahnei   owtūs

and	*will-lead-on-road them*	*to/into*	*of-life*	*streams/springs*
kai	hodeigeisei	owtūs	epi	zōeis	peigahs

of-waters
hudahtōn

and	*will-wipe*	*the*	*god*	*every tear*	*out*	*of-the*
kai	eksahleipsei	hŏ	theh-os	pahn dahkruon	ek	tōn

eyes   *of-them*
ŏfthahlmōn owtōn

4

The Twenty-Third Psalm

1   The Lord is my shepherd; I shall not want.

yahweh/[the] lord [is] pasturing-me		*not*	*I-will-go-without*
yahweh/ahdōnai	rōee	lō	echsar

2   He maketh me to lie down in green pastures: he leadeth me beside the still waters.

in-grazing-places [of]	*fresh-shoots*	*he-will-cause-to-stretch-out-me*
bin-ōt	desheh	yarbeetsei-nee

to	*water [of]*	*rest*	*he-will-guide-me*
ahl	mei	menuchōt	yenahahlei-nee

3   He restoreth my soul: he leadeth me in the paths of righteousness for his name's sake.

life-force-my	*he-will-cause-to-return*
nahf-shee	yeshōveiv

he-will-lead-me	*in-wagon-tracks [of]*	*righteousness*	*because-of*
yahnchei-nee	veh-mahgelei	tsedek	lema-ahn

name-his
shemō

4   Yea, though I walk through the valley of the shadow of death,
I will fear no evil: for thou art with me; thy rod and thy staff they
comfort me.

also	*though*	*I-will-walk*	*in-[the]-valley [of]*	*darkness-death*
gahm	kee	eileik	beh-gei	tsahl-mahvet

not	*I-will-fear*	*evil*
lō	eera	ra

since	*you [are] with-me*	*rod-your*	*and-staff-your*	*these*
kee	ahtta	imma-dee	shivteh-ka	ū-mishahnteh-ka	heimma

will-comfort-me
yenachahmū-nee

5   Thou preparest a table before me in the presence of mine
enemies: thou anointest my head with oil; my cup runneth over.

you-will-arrange	*before-face-my table*		*opposite [those]-harassing-me*
ta-arōk	lefa-nai	shulchahn	neged	tsōreh-rai

you-have-anointed	*with-oil*	*head-my*	*cup-my*
dishshahnta	vahsh-shemen	rō-shee	kō-see

has-abounded
revahya

6   Surely goodness and mercy shall follow me all the days of my
life: and I will dwell in the house of the Lord for ever.

surely goodness and-care   will-pursue-me   all [the] days [of]
ahk   tōv   va-chesed   yirdefū-nee   kol   yemei

my-life
hai-yai

and-I-will-live in-[the]-house [of]   yahweh/[the] lord   to-length [of]
veh-shahvtee   beh-beit   yahweh/ahdōnai   leh-ōrek

days
yahmeem

The Beatitudes (Matthew 5:3–12)

3   Blessed are the poor in spirit: for theirs is the kingdom of heaven.

blessed   the   beggars [?]   as-to-the   spirit/disposition/breath
mahkarioi   hoi   ptōchtoi   tō   pneumahti

because of-them is   the kingdom of-the   skies/heaven
hŏti   owtōn   estin hei bahsileia tōn   ūrahnōn

4   Blessed are they that mourn: for they shall be comforted.

blessed   the   mourning [ones]
mahkarioi   hoi   penthūntes

because they   will-be-consoled
hŏti   owtoi   parahkleitheisontai

5   Blessed are the meek: for they shall inherit the earth.

blessed   the   gentle [?]
mahkarioi hoi   prah-eis

because they   will-inherit   the   earth/land
hŏti   owtoi   kleironomeisūsin tein gein

6   Blessed are they which do hunger and thirst after righteousness: for they shall be filled.

blessed   those going-hungry and going-thirsty as-to-the
mahkarioi hoi   peinōntes   kai   dipsōntes   tein

   righteousness/justice
   dikaiosunein

because they   will-be-[stuffed?]-full
hŏti   owtoi   chortahstheisontai

7   Blessed are the merciful: for they shall obtain mercy.

blessed   the   merciful
mahkarioi hoi   eleh-eimones

because they   will-be-shown-mercy
hŏti   owtoi   eleh-eitheisontai

8   Blessed are the pure in heart: for they shall see God.

blessed   the   pure/clean as-to-the   heart
mahkarioi hoi   kahtharoi tei   kardia

because they   the   god   will see
hŏti   owtoi   tŏn   theh-on   opsontai

9   Blessed are the peacemakers: for they shall be called the children of God.

blessed   the   peacemakers
mahkarioi hoi   eireinopoioi

because they   sons   of-god   will-be-named
hŏti   owtoi   hwi-oi   theh-ū   kleitheisontai

10   Blessed are they which are persecuted for righteousness'
sake: for theirs is the kingdom of heaven.

blessed   the   prosecuted   because-of righteousness/justice
mahkarioi hoi   dediōgmenoi heneken   dikaiosuneis

because of-them is   the   kingdom   of-the   skies/heaven
hŏti   owtōn   estin hei   bahsileia   tōn   ūrahnōn

11   Blessed are ye, when men shall revile you, and persecute you,
and shall say all manner of evil against you falsely, for my sake.

blessed   are-you when   they-insult you   and   prosecute
mahkarioi este   hŏtahn oneidisōsin hūmahs   kai   diōksōsin

and   say   every   evil [thing] against you   lying
kai   eipōsin pahn   poneiron   kath'hūmōn pseudomenoi

because-of me
heneken   ehmū

12   Rejoice, and be exceeding glad: for great is your reward in
heaven: for so persecuted they the prophets which were before you.

be-joyful   and be-very-gleeful   because the   wage   of-you
chaireteh   kai   ahgahlliahstheh hŏti   hŏ   misthos hūmōn

much	*in*	*the*	*skies/heaven*	*thus*	*for*	*they-prosecuted*	*the*
polus	en	tois	ūranois	hūtōs	gar	ediōksahn	tūs

prophets	*those*	*before*	*you*
profeitahs	tūs	prŏ	hūmōn

5

Ecclesiastes on the Fragile Joys of Life
(Ecclesiastes 9:7–11)

7   Go thy way, eat thy bread with joy, and drink thy wine with a merry heart; for God now accepteth thy works.

walk/go	*eat*	*with-joy*	*bread-your*	*and-drink*	*with-[a]-heart*
leik	ekōl	beh-simcha	lachmeh-ka	ū-shahtei	beh-lev

good [= cheerful]	*wine-your*
tōv	yeineh-ka

because	*already*	*is-pleased-with*	*the god(s)*	*(direct object marker)*
kee	kevar	rahtsa	ha-elōheem	et

works-your
ma-ahseh-ka

8   Let thy garments be always white; and let thy head lack no ointment.

at-every	*time*	*let-be*	*clothes-your*	*white*	*and-oil*	*on*
beh-kol	eit	yiyū	begahdeh-ka	levahneem	veh-shemen	ahl

head-your	*not*	*let-it-lack*
rōsheh-ka	ahl	yechsar

9   Live joyfully with the wife whom thou lovest all the days of
the life of thy vanity, which he hath given thee under the sun, all
the days of thy vanity: for that is thy portion in this life, and in thy
labour which thou takest under the sun.

see [= enjoy]	*life*		*with [a] wife*	*whom*	*you-have-loved*
reh-ei	haiyeem	im	ishsha	ahsher	ahahvta

all	*[the] days [of the]*	*life [of]*	*evanescence-your*
kol	yemei	haiyei	hevleh-ka

which	*he-gave*	*to-you*	*under*	*the-sun*	*all [the]*
ahsher	nahtahn	leh-ka	tahchaht	hahsh-shemesh	kōl

days [of]	*evanescence-your*
yemei	hevleh-ka

because	*this [is]*	*share/award-your in-life*		*and-in-trouble-your*
kee	hū	helkeh-ka	ba-haiyeem	ū-ba-ahmahleh-ka

which	*you [are]*	*troubled-with*	*under*	*the-sun*
ahsher	ahtta	ahmeil	tahchaht	hahsh-shemesh

10   Whatsoever thy hand findeth to do, do it with thy might;
for there is no work, nor device, nor knowledge, nor wisdom, in the
grave, whither thou goest.

all	*that*	*will-find*	*hand-your*	*to-do*	*with-strength-your*	*do [it]*
kōl	ahsher	timtsa	yahdeh-ka	la-ahsōt	beh-kōcha-ka	ahsei

because	*there-is-not*	*work*	*or-ingeniousness*
kee	ein	ma-ahseh	veh-cheshbōn

or-knowledge	*or-shrewdness*	*in-sheol/[the]-pit/[the]-grave*
veh-da-aht	veh-chahkema	bish-ōl

which [= where]	*you [are]*	*going/walking*	*there-toward*
ahsher	ahtta	hōleik	shahm-ma

11   I returned, and saw under the sun, that the race is not to the
swift, nor the battle to the strong, neither yet bread to the wise, nor
yet riches to men of understanding, nor yet favour to men of skill;
but time and chance happeneth to them all.

I-returned   and-I-saw   under   the sun   that
shahvtee   veh-ra-ō   tahchaht   hahsh-shemesh   kee

not   to-nimble [people] [is]   the-race   and-not to-heroic [men]
lō   lahk-kahlleem   hahm-meirōts veh-lō   lahg-gibbōreem

   the-battle
   hahm-milchahma

and-also   not   to-shrewd [people]   bread   and-also   not
veh-gahm lō   la-chahkahmeem   lechem   veh-gahm lō

   to-discerning [people]   wealth
   lahn-nevōneem   ōsher

and-also   not   to-knowledgeable [people] popularity because
veh-gahm lō   lai-yōdeh-eem   chein   kee

   time   and-chance   will-meet/continually-meet
   eit   va-fega   yikreh

   (direct object marker)   all-of-them
   et   kul-lahm

Paul on the Love of God Through Jesus (Romans 8:31–39)

———

31   What shall we then say to these things? If God be for us, who
can be against us?

what therefore will-we-say regarding   these [things]   if the god [is]
ti   ūn   erūmen   prŏs   towta   ei hŏ theh-os

on-behalf-of   us   who [is] against us
huper   heimōn tis   kahth'heimōn

32   He that spared not his own Son, but delivered him up for us all, how shall he not with him also freely give us all things?

who indeed of-[his] own son   not   begrudged but on-behalf-of
hŏs geh   tū   idiū hwiū ūk   efeisahtŏ ahlla huper

us   all   handed-over him   how not also/even
heimōn pahntōn   paredōken   owtŏn pōs ūchi kai

along-with him   the all [things]   to-us   he-will-give-for-free
sŭn   owtō   ta pahnta   heimin charisetai

33   Who shall lay any thing to the charge of God's elect? It is God that justifieth.

who will-bring-charges   against chosen [ones] of-god   god [is]
tis   engkahlesei   kahta eklektōn   theh-ū theh-os

the [one] judging
hŏ   dikaiōn

34   Who is he that condemneth? It is Christ that died, yea rather, that is risen again, who is even at the right hand of God, who also maketh intercession for us.

who [is] the [one]   condemning   [the] anointed [one]
tis   hŏ   kahtahkrīnōn   christos

Jesus [is]   the [one]   having-died   rather   on-the-contrary
yeisūs   hŏ   ahpŏthanōn mahllon   deh

having-been-awakened who   even/also   is   on [the] right [hand]
egertheis   hŏs kai   estin en   deksia

of-the god   *who* *even/also* *makes-an-appeal*   *on-behalf-of* *us*
tū   theh-ū hŏs kai   entungchahnei   huper   heimōn

35   Who shall separate us from the love of Christ? shall tribulation, or distress, or persecution, or famine, or nakedness, or peril,
or sword?

who *us*   *will-separate* *from the* *love*
tis   heimahs   chōrisei   ahpŏ teis ahgahpeis

of-the anointed [one]   *pressure/oppression*   *or narrowness/hardship*
tū   christū   thleepsis   ei stenochōria

or pursuit/persecution *or hunger or* *nakedness* *or danger*
ei diōgmos   ei leemos ei   gumnŏteis ei kindūnos

or [a] sword
ei   mahchaira

36   As it is written, For thy sake we are killed all the day long;
we are accounted as sheep for the slaughter.

accordingly *it-has-been-written* *that*
kahthōs   gegrahptai   hŏti

because *of-you* *we-are-being-killed* *whole* *the* *day*
heneken   sū   thahnahtūmetha   hŏlein tein heimerahn

we-are-reckoned-up *as*   *herd-animals* *of-slaughter*
elogistheimen   hōs   prŏbahta   sfahgeis

37   Nay, in all these things we are more than conquerors through
him that loved us.

but in   *these [things]* *all*   *we-prevail-completely* *through* *the*
ahll'en tūtois   pahsin huperneekōmen   dia   tū

one-who-loved   us
ahgahpeisahntos heimahs

38   For I am persuaded, that neither death, nor life, nor angels, nor principalities, nor powers, nor things present, nor things to come,

I-have-been-persuaded in-fact that neither death   nor   life
pepeismai   gar   hŏti ūteh   thahnahtos ūteh zōei

nor   angels   nor   governments nor   present [things]
ūteh ahnggeloi ūteh archai   ūteh enestōta

nor   about-to-be [things]   nor   powers
ūteh mellonta   ūteh dunahmeis

39   Nor height, nor depth, nor any other creature, shall be able to separate us from the love of God, which is in Christ Jesus our Lord.

nor   height   nor   depth   nor   any created-thing else
ūteh hupsōma   ūteh bahthos   ūteh tis ktisis   hetera

will-be-able   us   to-separate from the love   of-the
duneisetai   heimahs   chōrisai   ahpŏ teis ahgahpeis tū

god   the [love]   in   [the] anointed Jesus   the   lord
theh-ū teis   en   christō   yeisū tō   kūriō

of-us
heimōn

6

The Hebrew Lexicons on the Word Rei-a *in the Ten Commandments and the Great Commandment (Deuteronomy 5:6–21 and Leviticus 19:18)*

Here's a humiliating juncture in my book. I must admit that to gather data on this word from Hebrew dictionaries, first I have to *find* it in Hebrew dictionaries.

The various forms of single words in this language are so numerous that it wouldn't be practical just to list them all alphabetically—the resulting book would be five feet wide and weigh more than I do. And I have to agree with the professors that this kind of presentation would be ruinous to training in the language. You can't read Hebrew, except in a rote, extremely restricted way, without understanding the grammar, and that means understanding grammatical rules and exceptions and being able to work back to the three-letter verbal root that is the basic form of most words (not just verbs, but other parts of speech as well), and comprises their main dictionary headings. I studied the rules diligently (when I wasn't rejoicing along with Yale Divinity School's ministerial candidates—and there was admittedly much rejoicing, because they were henceforward going to have to rejoice with a lot less noise and booze and drag clothing), but the use of a Hebrew dictionary still isn't straightforward for me.

Worse in the case of *rei-a* is that it's part of a weed patch of common words, identical or nearly identical (sometimes in actual spelling and not just in sound), choking up the resh (= r) section. There's the *ra-a* for pasturing, the *ra* of evil and the *ra* of misery, and also the *ra-a* of misery, and don't forget the *ra-a* of breaking. Then, there's the *ra-a* of seeing. That's not even getting into any *rei-* stuff. As usual in a language, the fact that one word sounds or looks like another doesn't in itself mean much of anything, but the semantic variety around *rei-a* seems ridiculous.

Once again: the place to look for guidance as to the basic meaning of a word is at the verbal root entry. In the Brown-Driver-Briggs lexicon, the root *ra-a*, related to *rei-a*, has the definition heading (though it includes the ominous abbreviation "prob." for "probably") "associate with." There follows, in parentheses, a six-line, densely abbreviated, tiny-print backup of this definition, with references to eminent authorities citing possible parallels in languages older and newer than Hebrew. The verb does seem to have actual Hebrew Bible connections to tender companionship, but some of the statements cited about "association" suggest a much looser fundamental definition of the word, to fit ideas like "It's bad to be around bad people." The key poetic requirement, the image, is lacking: is the idea behind this word spatial, or ethical, or emotional, or interpersonal, or what? Critically, how restrictive to the Hebrew community is the word?

One thing is certain: neither the authors of Jewish Scripture, nor its early readers, nor Jesus, nor the lawyer who confronted him had this lexicon. They had to feel and debate their way along, as Jesus and his interlocutor do in chapter 10 of Luke. Maybe a literary relationship with them—that is, a relationship with them as clever and imaginative people—can do as much to advance translation as a lexicon can do.

The Greek Lexicon and the Word Pleision *in the Parable of the Good Samaritan (Luke 10:25–37)*

———

There's only one standard dictionary of ancient Greek that an ordinary scholar would own or routinely consult, the Liddell and Scott. It was sometimes described by us undergraduates via a limerick:

There once was a lexicon, Liddell and Scott.
One part was riddle, and one part was rot.
The part that was riddle

Was written by Liddell,
And the part that was rot by Scott.

This puerile, British-public-school sort of mockery did suit the tome to a degree. One classmate of mine told of his lexical search for an obscene word he'd come across in an assigned author. He went to Liddell and Scott, where the word was not defined but only translated into Latin; in a standard Latin dictionary, the Lewis and Short, the Latin word was merely translated into Greek.

The major Hebrew dictionaries are about wonkish joy, the fresh and increasingly scientific European exploration of Hebrew from the Renaissance on. The major Greek and Latin dictionaries are about pedagogy, the continuity of Classical studies in Europe (Greek based in the East, Latin in the West). The advantage: there was a heck of a lot there for you to learn, and plenty of people to teach it to you. The disadvantage: like Mark Twain's Adam (in the view of Eve), though they knew a great many things, these were not so. They had just adapted the ancient languages to their own thinking and were translating them backward, especially in relation to the religion around which their education and culture centered.

Classical-language dictionaries preserve this state of affairs insouciantly. Take the treatment of *apostolos* (literally, "a man dispatched away") in Liddell and Scott. Entries are chronological, so it's clear that up to its use in sacred literature, the word meant "messenger, ambassador, envoy," or someone else sent on or leading a mission. But then definition "2" is "messenger from God." The first citation is of 1 Kings 14:6, concerning the prophet Ahijah as a messenger from God to King Jeroboam's wife. Then the lexicon says that the meaning "messenger from God" is especially applicable to the "Apostles" of the New Testament, and cites only Matthew 10:2 as an example. In this verse, however, the twelve men Jesus is entrusting with healing and exorcism are simply listed under the heading of his *apostoloi*, something like "agents." There is no necessary numinous infusion in this use of the word.

I consider it unlikely that the original translator of Kings (or of any other Hebrew Bible book), or the author of Matthew (or of any other New Testament book) said to himself, "Here and henceforward, *apostolos* is not an ordinary, multivalent word; just because I'm using it in sacred literature, it has and must continue to have a holy aura, so that an *apostolos* is *only* God's *special* messenger or agent. By the way, the 'donkey' ridden by Jesus is also a divine donkey, and any donkey in Scripture shall be known in English not as a 'donkey' but an onos. The whole point of the Gospels is to show the son of God negotiating the ordinary social and material world until his miraculous resurrection, but phooey. I am creating a language with words that can be 'translated' merely by sounding them out, and that will form a sort of secret code to make adherents of this religion smug and outsiders irritated. Just hope everybody gets what I'm up to!"

Therefore, I was ready to take with a grain of salt whatever Liddell and Scott said about *pleision* in the Old or New Testament. But the only citations from Scripture were of the comparative adverb, *pleisesteron*.

7

The Book of Jonah (Chapter 3)

1   And the word of the Lord came unto Jonah the second time, saying,

and-was/happened [the]	*word [of]*	*yahweh/[the] lord*	*to dove*
vai-hee	devar	yahweh/ahdōnai	el yōna

a-second-time	*to-say*
sheineet	lei-mōr

2   Arise, go unto Nineveh, that great city, and preach unto it the preaching that I bid thee.

get-up	*walk*	*to Nineveh the-city*	*the-big [one]*	*and-call/cry*
kūm	leik	el neenevei ha-eer	hahg-gedōla	vik-ra

to-it	*(direct object marker)*	*the-cry/call*	*that*	*I [am]*
eileh-ha	et	hahk-keree-a	ahsher	ahnōkee

saying	*to-you*
dōbeir	eileh-ka

3   So Jonah arose, and went unto Nineveh, according to the word of the Lord. Now Nineveh was an exceeding great city of three days' journey.

and-got-up dove and-he-walked   to nineveh according-to-[the]-word
vai-yakom yōna vai-yeilek   el neeneveh kid-var

[of] yahweh/[the] lord and-nineveh was   [a] city big
yahweh/ahdōnai veh-neenevei ha-yeta   eer gedōla

to-god(s)   [a] journey   [of] three   days [across]
lei-lōheem   mahahlahk   shelōshet yahmeem

4   And Jonah began to enter into the city a day's journey, and
he cried, and said, Yet forty days, and Nineveh shall be overthrown.

and-began dove to-go into-the-city [a] journey [of] day   one
vai-yachel yōna la-bō ba-eer   mahahlahk yōm   echahd

and-he-cried-out and-he-said   still forty   day[s] and-nineveh
vai-yikra   vai-yōmar   ōd   arba-eem   yōm   veh-neenevei

will-be-overthrown
nepaket

5   So the people of Nineveh believed God, and proclaimed a
fast, and put on sackcloth, from the greatest of them even to the
least of them.

and-believed   [the] men/people [of]   nineveh   in-god(s)
vai-ya-ahmeenū   ahnshei   neenevei   bei-lōheem

and-cried-out [a] fast   and-dressed-in   sacks
vai-yikreh-ū   tsōm   vai-yilbeshū   sahkkeem

from-great-[people]-of-them   and-to   small-[people]-of-them
mig-gedō-lahm   veh-ahd   ketahn-nahm

6   For word came unto the king of Nineveh, and he arose from
his throne, and he laid his robe from him, and covered him with
sackcloth, and sat in ashes.

and-reached   the-word   to [the] king   [of] nineveh   and-he-rose
vai-yigga   hahd-dahbar el   melek   neenevei vai-yahkom

from-throne-his   and-caused-to-pass   his-robe   from-him
mik-kis-ō   vai-ya-ahver   ahddar-tō mei-a-lav

and-covered [himself with a]   sack   and-sat   in   the-ashes/dust/dirt
vai-kahs   sahk vai-yeishev ahl   ha-eifer

7   And he caused it to be proclaimed and published through
Nineveh by the decree of the king and his nobles, saying, Let neither
man nor beast, herd nor flock, taste any thing: let them not feed,
nor drink water:

and-he-caused-to-be-called-out   and-he-said   in-nineveh
vai-yahzeik   vai-yōmer   beh-neenevei

from-[a]-decree [of]   the-king   and-grandees-his to-say
mit-ta-ahm   hahm-melek   ū-gedō-lahv   lei-mōr

the-man   and-the-animal   the-herd   and-the-flock
ha-ahdahm   veh-hahb-beheima hahb-bahkar veh-hats-tsōn

not let-them/they-shall-taste anything   not   let-them/they-will-feed
ahl yitahmū   meh-ūma   ahl   yirū

and-water not let-them/they-will-drink
ū-mahyim ahl yishtū

8   But let man and beast be covered with sackcloth, and cry
mightily unto God: yea, let them turn every one from his evil way,
and from the violence that is in their hands.

and-let-them/they-will-cover-themselves [with] sacks
veh-yitkahssū   sahkkeem

the-human-being and-the-animal   and-let-them/they-will-call/cry-out
ha-ahdahm   veh-hab-beheima veh-yikreh-ū

to god(s)   with-strength and-let/will-turn [each] man from-way-his [of]
el elōheem beh-chahzeka veh-yashūvū   eesh mid-dar-kō

the-evil and-from   the-crime/violence   that [is] in-hands-their
ha-ra-a ū-min   heh-chahmahs   ahsher beh-kahppei-hem

9   Who can tell if God will turn and repent, and turn away from
his fierce anger, that we perish not?

who   knows   will-turn   and-will-repent   the-god(s)
mee yōdei-a ya-shūv   veh-nichahm   ha-elōheem

and-will-turn from-the-blaze/anger [of] nose-his and-not
veh-shahv   mei-charōn   ahppō veh-lō

we-will-perish
nōveid

10   And God saw their works, that they turned from their evil
way; and God repented of the evil, that he had said that he would
do unto them; and he did it not.

and-saw the-god(s)   (direct object marker)   things-done-their
vai-yar ha-elōheem   et   ma-ahsei-hem

that they-turned from-way-their [of] the-evil and-repented
kee shahvū   mid-dar-kahm   ha-ra-a vai-yinnahchem

the-god(s)   to [= of] the-evil that   he-[had]-said to-do
ha-elōheem   ahl   ha-ra-a ahsher   dibber   la-ahsōt

to-them   and-not   did [it]
la-hem   veh-lō   ahsa

Paul on Circumcision (Galatians 5:1–12)

1   Stand fast therefore in the liberty wherewith Christ hath made us free, and be not entangled again with the yoke of bondage.

for-the   freedom   us   [the] anointed [one] set-free
tei   eleutheria   heimahs   christos   eileutherōsen

stand-fast   therefore   also   not   again   in-a-yoke   of-slavery
steiketeh   ūn   kai   mei   pahlin   zugō   dūleiahs

be-held-in/be-subject-to
enechestheh

2   Behold, I Paul say unto you, that if ye be circumcised, Christ shall profit you nothing.

look   I   Paul   say   to-you   that   if   you-get-circumcised
ideh   egō   paulos   legō   hūmin   hŏti   eh-ahn   peritemneistheh

[the] anointed [one] you   in-no-way   will-benefit
christos   hūmahs   ūden   ōfeleisei

3   For I testify again to every man that is circumcised, that he is a debtor to do the whole law.

I-bear-witness   on-the-other-hand   again   to-every   human-being
marturomai   deh   pahlin   pahnti   ahnthrōpō

having-been-circumcised   that owing   he-is [as to] the-whole-of
peritemnomenō   hŏti ŏfeileteis estin   holon

the law   *to do [it]*
tŏn nomon   poieisai

4   Christ is become of no effect unto you, whosoever of you are justified by the law; ye are fallen from grace.

you-have-been-nullified   *from [the] anointed [one] whoever in law*
kateirgeitheiteh   ahpŏ   christū   hoitines en nomō

are-righteous/are-just *of-the* *free-gift* *you-have-fallen-out-of*
dikaiūstheh   teis   charitos   eksepesahteh

5   For we through the Spirit wait for the hope of righteousness by faith.

we   *for* *by-[the]-spirit* *out-of* *faith/belief* *hope*
heimeis gar pneumahti ek   pisteōs   elpida

of-righteousness/justice *we-welcome*
dikaiosuneis   ahpekdechometha

6   For in Jesus Christ neither circumcision availeth any thing, nor uncircumcision; but faith which worketh by love.

in for [the] anointed *Jesus neither circumcision* *at-all has-power*
en gar   christō   yeisū ūteh peritomei   ti   ischuei

neither [a] foreskin *but* *faith/belief through love*
ūteh   ahkrobustia ahlla pistis   di'ahgahpeis

put-to-work
energūmenei

7   Ye did run well; who did hinder you that ye should not obey the truth?

you-were-running   beautifully who you   cut-off   from-the
etrecheteh   kahlōs   tis hūmahs   enekopsen tei

truth   that-not to-be-persuaded/to-believe
ahleitheia   mei   peithesthai

8   This persuasion cometh not of him that calleth you.

the persuasion   not   out-of   the [one]   calling   you
hei peismonei   ūk   ek   tū   kahlūntos hūmahs

9   A little leaven leaveneth the whole lump.

small   yeast   all   the   lump   leavens
mikra   zūmei   holon   tŏ   furahma   zūmoi

10   I have confidence in you through the Lord, that ye will be
none otherwise minded: but he that troubleth you shall bear his
judgment, whosoever he be.

I   have-come-to-believe into   you   in [the] lord   that nothing
egō   pepoitha   eis   hūmahs en   kūriō   hŏti ūden

other you-think   he   on-the-other-hand   agitating   you
ahllŏ froneiseteh hŏ   deh   tarahssōn   hūmahs

will-carry the   sentence   whoever (conditional particle) he-is
bahstahsei tŏ   krima   hostis   eh-ahn   ei

11   And I, brethren, if I yet preach circumcision, why do I yet
suffer persecution? then is the offence of the cross ceased.

I   on-the-other-hand   siblings   if circumcision   still I-preach
egō   deh   ahdelfoi   ei peritomein   eti   keirussō

why	*still*	*I-am-persecuted*	*therefore*	*has-been-removed*	*the*
ti	eti	diōkomai	ara	kahteirgeitai	tŏ

obstacle	*to-the*	*cross*
skahndahlon	tū	staurū

12　I would they were even cut off which trouble you.

would-that	*also*	*be-castrated*	*the [ones]*	*stirring-up*	*you-all*
ŏfelon	kai	ahpokopsontai	hoi	ahnastahtūntes	hūmahs

A Selected Bibliography

ORIGINAL-LANGUAGE BIBLES

Biblia Hebraica Stuttgartensa. 5th ed. Edited by K. Elliger, W. Rudolph, et al. Stuttgart: German Bible Society, 1997.

Nestle-Aland Novum Testamentum Greace. 27th ed. Edited by Barbara and Kurt Aland et al. Stuttgart: German Bible Society, 2001.

BIBLES IN TRANSLATION

Biblia Vulgata. 13th ed. Edited by Alberto Colunga and Laurentio Turrado. Madrid: Biblioteca de Autores Cristianos, 2011.

The Catholic Study Bible. Edited by Donald Senior et al. New York: Oxford University Press, 1990.

The HarperCollins Study Bible: New Revised Standard Version. Edited by Wayne A. Meeks et al. New York: HarperCollins, 1993.

Holy Bible: Revised Standard Version. New York: Thomas Nelson & Sons, 1946 and 1952.

The Jewish Study Bible. Edited by Adele Berlin, Marc Sivi Brettler, and Michael Fishbane. New York: Oxford University Press, 2004.

A Literary Bible. Translated by David Rosenberg. Berkeley, CA: Counterpoint, 2010.

The New Oxford Annotated Bible: New Revised Standard Version with the Apocrypha. 3rd ed. Edited by Michael D. Coogan et al. New York: Oxford University Press, 2001.

Novum Testamentum Latine. 6th ed. Edited by Kurt Aland and Barbara Aland. Stuttgart: Deutsche Bibelgesellschaft, 2008.

The Oxford Self-Pronouncing Bible: The Holy Bible, Authorized King James Version. London: Oxford University Press, 1897.

Septuaginta. 2nd ed. Edited by Alfred Rahlfs and Robert Reinhart. Stuttgart: German Bible Society, 2006.

Torah with Targum Onkelos and Rashi's Commentary: The Book of Genesis (Hebrew/English). Edited by A. M. Silbermann and M. Rosenbaum. Thousand Oaks, CA: BN Publishing, 2007.

LEXICONS, CONCORDANCES, AND OTHER BASIC REFERENCE WORKS

The American Heritage Dictionary of the English Language. 10th ed. Edited by William Morris. Boston: Houghton Mifflin, 1981.

Analytical Concordance of the Green New Testament. 2 vols. Edited by Philip S. Clapp, Barbara Friberg, and Timothy Friberg. Grand Rapids, MI: Baker Book House, 1991.

The Brown-Driver-Briggs Hebrew and English Lexicon. 9th ed. Edited by Francis Brown, S. R. Driver, and Charles A Briggs. Peabody, MA: Hendrickson, 2005.

The Compact Edition of the Oxford English Dictionary: Complete Text Reproduced Micrographically. 2 vols. Oxford: Oxford University Press, 1971.

A Concise Greek-English Dictionary of the New Testament. Edited by Barclay M. Newman, Jr. London: United Bible Societies, 1971.

Davidson, A. B. *An Introductory Hebrew Grammar with Progressive Exercises in Reading and Writing [1896].* 13th ed. Edinburgh: T. & T. Clark, 1896.

Durant, Will. *The Story of Civilization.* Part 1, *Our Oriental Heritage.* New York: Simon and Schuster, 1954.

Gesenius' Hebrew Grammar, as Edited and Enlarged by the Late E. Kautzsch. 2nd English ed. revised in accordance with the 28th German ed. (1909) by A. E. Cowley. New York: Oxford University Press, 1910.

A Greek-English Lexicon, with a Revised Supplement. 10th ed. Edited by Henry George Liddell, Robert Scott, et al. Oxford: Clarendon Press, 1996.

The HarperCollins Bible Commentary. 2nd ed. Edited by James L. Mays et al. San Francisco: HarperSanFrancisco, 1988.

The Hebrew-English Concordance to the Old Testament, with the New International Version. Edited by John R. Kohlenberger III and James A. Swanson. Grand Rapids, MI: Zondervan, 1998.

Koehler, Ludwig, and Walter Baumgartner. *The Hebrew and Aramaic Lexicon of the Old Testament.* 2 vols. Revised by Walter Baumgartner, Johann Jakob Stamm, et al., and translated under the supervision of M. E. J. Richardson. Leiden: Brill, 2001.

A Latin Dictionary, Founded on Andrews' Edition of Freund's Latin Dictionary. Revised, enlarged, and in great part rewritten by Charlton T. Lewis and Charles Short. 2nd ed. Oxford: Clarendon Press, 1958.

The Oxford Classical Dictionary. 2nd ed. Edited by N. G. L. Hammond and H. H. Scullard. Oxford: Clarendon Press, 1970.

Oxford Latin Dictionary. Edited by P. G. W. Glare. Oxford: Clarendon Press, 1982.

Roget's International Thesaurus. 3rd ed. Edited by C. O. Sylvester Mawson. New York: Thomas Y. Crowell, 1962.

Seow, C. L. *A Grammar for Biblical Hebrew.* Rev. ed. Nashville: Abingdon Press, 1995.

Smyth, Herbert Weir. *Greek Grammar.* Revised by Gordon M. Messing. Cambridge, MA: Harvard University Press, 1956.

Young's Analytical Concordance to the Bible. 22nd American ed. Edited by Robert Young; revised by William B. Stevenson and William F. Albright. New York: Funk and Wagnalls, 1970.

SECONDARY LITERATURE AND OTHER WORKS

Albright, W. F., and C. S. Mann. *The Anchor Bible*. Vol. 26, *Matthew: Introduction, Translation, and Notes*. Garden City, NY: Doubleday, 1971.

Armstrong, Karen. *The Bible: A Biography*. New York: Grove Press, 2007.

Auerbach, Erich. *Mimesis: The Representation of Reality in Western Literature*. Translated by Willard R. Trask. Princeton, NJ: Princeton University Press, 1953.

Bainton, Roland H. *Here I Stand: A Life of Martin Luther*. New York: Meridian, 1995.

Barton, John, ed. *The Cambridge Companion to Biblical Interpretation*. Cambridge: Cambridge University Press, 1998.

Bellos, David. *Is That a Fish in Your Ear? Translation and the Meaning of Everything*. New York: Faber and Faber, 2011.

Brown, Raymond E. *The Anchor Yale Bible*. Vols. 29 and 29A, *The Gospel According to John. A New Translation with Introduction and Commentary*. New Haven, CT: Yale University Press (as assignee from Doubleday), 1966.

Cassuto, U. *A Commentary on the Book of Exodus*. First English ed. Jerusalem: Magnes Press, 1967.

Coogan, Michael. *The Ten Commandments: A Short History of an Ancient Text*. New Haven, CT: Yale University Press, 2014.

Dahood, Mitchell. *The Anchor Bible*. Vol. 16, *Psalms I: 1–50: A New Translation with Introduction and Commentary*. New York: Doubleday, 1965.

Daniell, David. *The Bible in English: Its History and Influence*. New Haven, CT: Yale University Press, 2003.

Fitzmyer, Joseph A. *The Anchor Bible*. Vols. 28 and 28A, *The Gospel According to Luke: Introduction, Translation, and Notes*. Garden City, NY: Doubleday, 1981.

———. *The Anchor Yale Bible*. Vol. 32, *First Corinthians: A New Translation with Introduction and Commentary*. New Haven, CT: Yale University Press (as assigned from Doubleday), 2008.

Ford, J. Massyngberde. *The Anchor Bible*. Vol. 38, *Revelation: Introduction, Translation, and Commentary*. Garden City, NY: Doubleday, 1975.

Foxe, John. *Foxe's Book of Martyrs*. Edited by W. Grinton Berry. Grand Rapids, MI: Revell, 1998.

Fussell, Paul. *Poetic Meter and Poetic Form*. Rev. ed. New York: McGraw-Hill, 1979.

Gaster, Theodor H. *The Dead Sea Scriptures in English Translation with Introduction and Notes*. Garden City, NY: Doubleday Anchor Books, 1956.

Greenberg, Moshe. *The Anchor Bible*. Vol. 22A, *Ezekiel 21–37: A New Translation with Introduction and Commentary*. New York: Doubleday, 1997.

Hecht, Jennifer Michael. *Doubt: A History: The Great Doubters and Their Legacy of Innovation, from Socrates to Thomas Jefferson and Emily Dickinson*. New York: HarperOne, 2003.

Hillers, Delbert R. *The Anchor Bible*. Vol. 7A, *Lamentations: A New Translation with Introduction and Commentary*. 2nd rev. ed. New York: Doubleday, 1992.

Jacobs, Alan. *The Book of Common Prayer: A Biography*. Princeton, NJ: Princeton University Press, 2013.

Kittel, Bonnie Pedrotti, et al. *Biblical Hebrew: Text and Workbook*. 2nd ed. Fully revised by Victoria Hoffer. Hew Haven, CT: Yale University Press, 2005.

Koester, Craig R. *The Anchor Yale Bible*. Vol. 38A, *Revelation: A New Translation with Introduction and Commentary*. New Haven, CT: Yale University Press, 2014.

Kugel, James L. *The Idea of Biblical Poetry: Parallelism and Its History.* Baltimore: Johns Hopkins University Press, 1981.

Lamb, Charles. "The Old Familiar Faces." In *The New Oxford Book of English Verse: 1250–1950,* page 554. New York and Oxford: Oxford University Press, 1972.

Mann, C. S. *The Anchor Bible.* Vol. 27, *Mark: A New Translation with Introduction and Commentary.* Garden City, NY: Doubleday, 1986.

McCarter, P. Kyle, Jr. *The Anchor Bible.* Vol. 9, *II Samuel: A New Translation with Introduction, Notes, and Commentary.* Garden City, NY: Doubleday, 1984.

Miller, J. Maxwell, and John H. Hayes. *A History of Ancient Israel and Judah.* 2nd ed. Louisville, KY: Westminster John Knox Press, 2006.

Miller, John W. *The Origins of the Bible: Rethinking Canon History.* New York: Paulist Press, 1994.

Moran, William L. "The Ancient Near-Eastern Background of the Love of God in Deuteronomy." *Catholic Biblical Quarterly* 25 (1963): 77–87.

Orr, William F., and James Arthur Walther. *The Anchor Bible.* Vol. 32, *I Corinthians: A New Translation; Introduction with a Study of Paul, Notes, and Commentary.* Garden City, NY: Doubleday, 1976.

Pelikan, Jaroslav. *Whose Bible Is It?: A Short History of the Scriptures.* New York: Viking, 2005.

Reynolds, L. D., and N. G. Wilson. *Scribes and Scholars: A Guide to the Transmission of Greek and Latin Literature.* 2nd ed. Oxford: Clarendon Press, 1974.

Rogerson, John, ed. *The Oxford Illustrated History of the Bible.* Oxford: Oxford University Press, 2001.

Ruden, Sarah. *Paul Among the People: The Apostle Reinterpreted and Reimaged in His Own Time.* New York: Pantheon Books, 2010.

Sasson, Jack M. *The Anchor Yale Bible.* Vol. 24B, *Jonah: A New Translation with Introduction, Commentary, and Interpretations.* 2nd ed. New Haven, CT: Yale University Press, 2010.

Satlow, Michael L. *How the Bible Became Holy.* New Haven, CT: Yale University Press, 2014.

Scott, William R. *A Simplified Guide to BHS: Critical Apparatus, Masora, Accents, Unusual Letters & Other Markings.* 4th ed. North Richland Hills, TX: Bibal Press, 2007.

Seow, C. L. *The Anchor Bible.* Vol. 18C, *Ecclesiastes: A New Translation with Introduction and Commentary.* New York: Doubleday, 1997.

Smalley, Stephen S. *The Revelation to John: A Commentary on the Greek Text of the Apocalypse.* Downers Grove, IL: InterVarsity, 2005.

Speiser, E. A. *The Anchor Bible.* Vol. 1, *Genesis: Introduction, Translation, and Notes.* 3rd ed. Garden City, NY: Doubleday, 1982.

Vickers, Brian. *In Defence of Rhetoric.* Oxford: Oxford University Press, 1988.

Weinfeld, Moshe. *The Anchor Bible.* Vol. 5, *Deuteronomy I–II: A New Translation with Introduction and Commentary.* New York: Doubleday, 1991.

Wilson, Edmund. *Israel and the Dead Sea Scrolls.* Wakefield, RI: Moyer Bell, 1978.

Wray, T. J. *What the Bible Really Tells Us: The Essential Guide to Biblical Literacy.* Lanham, MD: Rowman & Littlefield, 2011.

Subject Index

Index of Passages Cited and Translated

A Note on the Type

This book was set in Adobe Garamond. Designed for the Adobe Corporation by Robert Slimbach, the fonts are based on types first cut by Claude Garamond (ca. 1480–1561). Garamond was a pupil of Geoffroy Tory and is believed to have followed the Venetian models, although he introduced a number of important differences, and it is to him that we owe the letter we now know as "old style." He gave to his letters a certain elegance and feeling of movement that won their creator an immediate reputation and the patronage of Francis I of France.

Composed by North Market Street Graphics,
Lancaster, Pennsylvania

Printed and bound by Berryville Graphics,
Berryville, Virginia

Designed by M. Kristen Bearse